Successful ICT Projects

in

Access

2nd Edition

P.M.Heathcote, B.Sc.(Hons), M.Sc.

Published by
Payne-Gallway Publishers
76-78 Christchurch Street
Ipswich IP4 2DE
Tel 01473 251097
Fax 01473 232758
E-mail info@payne-gallway.co.uk

2000

Acknowledgements

I am indebted once again to Sue Clark for her help. Her perceptive comments and painstaking work in testing the exercises combined with her amazing speed and ability to meet deadlines are quite invaluable. Thank you, Sue! And as usual, without Oliver to proofread, typeset and deal with mystical aspects like ozalids and acrobats, the book would probably never see the light of day.

Cover picture © "Crescendo" reproduced with kind permission from Neil Canning
Cover photography © Mike Kwasniak, 160 Sidegate Lane, Ipswich
Cover design by Tony Burton

First edition 1999. Reprinted 1999
Second edition 2000
A catalogue entry for this book is available from the British Library.

ISBN 1 903112 27 3
Copyright © P.M.Heathcote 2000

Printed in Great Britain by
W M Print Ltd, Walsall, West Midlands

Preface

Projects in Access

Access is one of the most popular and powerful database packages for standalone and networked PCs, in use all over the world in hundreds of thousands of different organisations. It is a bonus for any student to complete a course which includes an in-depth study of Access as part of the syllabus, for the chances are that the knowledge and skills gained will come in useful whatever further course of study or career is pursued.

Part 1 of the book covers most of the basic and advanced features of Access without going into any depth in Visual Basic for Applications. This is introduced near the end of Part 1 so that students who wish to pursue programming in more detail can get a flavour of the language and then find out more from a specialised text.

Part 2 gives advice on choosing a suitable project, completing the various stages of project work and writing up the project report.

The intended audience

The book was written primarily for A Level Information Technology students and contains in Appendix B the AQA mark scheme for both Minor and Major Projects. It will also be suitable for students on many other courses at different levels since the mark scheme, with minor variations, is one which applies to projects on many other courses including A Level Computing, Vocational A Level IT courses and BTEC Computing.

Version of Access

This second edition of the book is primarily for Access 2000 users. However, instructions are given throughout the book to assist Access 97 and Access 7 users where differences arise, making the book suitable for users of any of these versions.

The sample project

A sample project is included to show students how a complete project report may be laid out. No two projects will be laid out in exactly the same way, and this is intended only as a starting point from which students can diverge. Every Examination Board places emphasis on different aspects of project work, and to get the best possible results close attention should be paid to the relevant and current mark scheme.

Contents

Part 1
Database Design and Implementation   1

Part 2
Tackling the Project   143

Appendix A
Sample Project

Appendix B
AQA Project Mark Scheme

Index

Table of Contents

PART 1

DATABASE DESIGN AND IMPLEMENTATION   1

Chapter 1 – Designing a Database   2

Introduction	2
Entity-relationship diagrams	2
Attributes and key fields	3
Normalisation	3
A sample database	6
Identifying the entities, attributes and relationships	6
Table design	7
Elements of an Access database	8
Naming conventions	8
Designing the Input and Output	9

Chapter 2 – Creating Tables and Relationships   10

Loading Access	10
Creating a new database	10
The Database window	11
Creating a new table	12
Defining the primary key	13
Entering other fields (attributes)	13
Saving the table structure	14
Editing a table structure	15
Inserting a field	15
Deleting a field	15
Moving a field	15
Changing or removing a key field	15
Entering data in Datasheet view	16
Creating the NEWSPAPER table	18
Creating the DELIVERY table	18
Using the Lookup wizard	19
Defining relationships	21
Entering data in Datasheet view	25
Customising a table view	26

Chapter 3 – Creating Data Entry Forms   27

Introduction	27
Creating a columnar AutoForm	27
Changing the appearance of the form	28
Adding a form heading and arranging fields	28
Creating a tabular AutoForm	30
Arranging and sizing fields	30
Changing a form's background	31
Changing the sort order of records	32
Creating a form with a subform	32
Adjusting the size of the form and subform	35
Using the form to enter and edit data	36
Deleting a field from the subform	36
Finding a record	36
Deleting a record	37

Chapter 4 – Queries   38

Understanding queries	38
Types of query	38
Setting special criteria	41
AND and OR queries	43
Allowing the end-user to enter criteria	43
Saving a query with a different name	44
Using the Simple Query Wizard	46
Creating calculated fields with a query	47
Moving columns	48
Changing a column caption	48
Creating a form from a query	49

Chapter 5 – Advanced Queries   51

Introduction	51
Creating a totals query	51
Creating an update query	54
Using queries to process customer payments	56
Summary query	57
Creating and running a Make-Table query	58
Updating one table from another	59
Making a copy of a table structure	61
Creating and running an Append query	63
Creating and running a Delete query	64

Chapter 6 – Reports and Charts   65

Introduction	65
Creating a columnar AutoReport	65
Creating a tabular AutoReport	67
Editing the report format	67
Adding a new field to the report	68
Formatting the report	69
Basing a report on a query	74

Customising the report 75
Sorting and grouping the report 76
Inserting a page break between rounds 77

Chapter 7 – Macros and Command Buttons 81

Macros 81
Creating a macro group 82
Running a macro which is part of a group 84
Command buttons 86
Defining a button's event property 90
Setting the properties of the form 91
Using conditions in a macro 91
Dialogue boxes 92
Creating an unbound form 92
Creating the macros to open and use the
  dialogue box 94
Attaching the macros to command buttons 95
Using a field from a dialogue box as
  query criteria 96
Inserting a field from a dialogue box in a
  report 97
List of all macro actions in Access 98

Chapter 8 – Advanced Form Design 99

Introduction 99
Selecting objects 99
Moving objects 100
Aligning and spacing objects evenly 100
Resizing an area of the form 100
Changing a heading or label style 101
Rearranging and resizing fields 101
Inserting an option group 102
Changing the tab order 103
Using the Properties sheet to customise
  controls 103
Changing a form's record source 104
Combo boxes and list boxes 105
Using a combo box to find a record 105
Inserting a picture on a form 107
Adding a box to the form 108
Keeping the Find Newspaper box
  synchronised 108
Creating a form from a query 110
Design considerations 111
Using a combo box to look up a record
  from another table 111

Chapter 9 – Rounding off an Application 113

Introduction 113
The menu structure for the Newsagents
  database 113

Creating a switchboard 114
Creating the submenus 115
Viewing the main switchboard 116
Creating the main menu (switchboard) 117
Testing the switchboard 118
Editing a switchboard item 118
Customising a switchboard form 118
Setting Startup options 120
Security 120

Chapter 10 – Linking with Word and Excel 122

Mail merging using data held in Access 122
Importing data from Excel 125
Importing records into Access 126
Appending imported records to an
  existing table 129
Analysing data in Excel 129
Exporting data 130

Chapter 11 – An Introduction to Visual Basic for Applications 131

Introduction 131
Visual Basic Modules 131
A stock control application 132
Planning a Visual Basic procedure 136
A VBA procedure to find a record 137
Referring to forms, subforms, reports and
  subreports 138
A second VBA procedure 139
Selection statements in VBA 140
Debugging code 141

PART 2

TACKLING THE PROJECT 143

Chapter 12 – Project Ideas 144

Introduction 144
Finding a real user 144
Input-Process-Output 144
Using a relational database 145
Using advanced features of Access 145
Booking systems 145
Order entry systems 146
Stock control systems 146

League tables 147
General information systems 147
Inappropriate projects 147

Chapter 13 – The Systems Life Cycle 148

Introduction 148
Problem definition 148
Sample project idea 149
Analysis 149
Design 156
Development 161
Installation 161
Evaluation 161

Chapter 14 – Writing the Project Report 162

Introduction 162
The mark scheme 162
Creating an outline for your project 162
Reordering topics 164
Adding numbers to the headings 164
Turning the outline into a document 165
Adding a header and footer 165
Inserting a Table of Contents 167
Analysis 168
Design 168
Implementation 168
Testing 168
Evaluation 169
User documentation 169
Technical documentation 169
Handing it in 169

APPENDIX A

Sample Project

APPENDIX B

AQA Project Mark Scheme

INDEX

Part 1

Database design and Implementation

In this section:

Chapter 1 -   *Designing a Database*
Chapter 2 -   *Creating Tables and Relationships*
Chapter 3 -   *Creating Data Entry Forms*
Chapter 4 -   *Queries*
Chapter 5 -   *Advanced Queries*
Chapter 6 -   *Reports and Charts*
Chapter 7 -   *Macros and Command Buttons*
Chapter 8 -   *Advanced Form Design*
Chapter 9 -   *Rounding off an Application*
Chapter 10 -   *Linking with Word and Excel*
Chapter 11 -   *An Introduction to Visual Basic for Applications*

Chapter 1 – Designing a Database

Introduction

If you are setting out to do a project using MS Access, then you need to have covered some of the theory of database design. In this chapter you will briefly review some of the terminology used and look at how to approach the design of a database once you have selected a suitable topic or problem for your project.

A database is basically a collection of data. There are many different types of database, but the two that you are most likely to come across in this course are *flat file* databases and *relational* databases.

A *flat file* database consists of one or more unrelated tables. A *table* in a database is a collection of records which can be viewed in rows and columns. Thus for example you could keep a flat file database of all members of a Club:

Club Member

Member ID	Surname	First Name	Member Type	Date Joined	Subs Paid
123	Bell	Sarah	Junior	12/01/97	Y
124	Naylor	Paul	Senior	18/01/99	Y
125	Townsend	Roxanne	Senior	16/04/98	N
etc					

Club Member is the *entity* about which data is being held.

Member ID, **Surname**, **First Name**, **Member Type**, **Date Joined** and **Subs Paid** are *attributes* of this entity.

Member ID acts as the *primary key*; it is the attribute which uniquely identifies a row of the table.

A flat file database can be quite useful in a rather limited way; for example, you can use it to search for all Junior Members, or all members who have not yet paid their annual subscription, and then merge this subset of members with a letter to remind them to pay up (a *mail-merge*).

However, a flat file database is not suitable for an Advanced Level project as it does not offer sufficient scope to use the advanced features of Access. Access is a *relational* database package, meaning that you can construct a database consisting of several tables which are related to each other by means of common fields.

Entity-relationship diagrams

There are three different possible *degrees of relationship* between two entities. These are:

One-to-one   e.g. Husband and wife. A husband can have one wife, and a wife can have one husband.

One-to-many   e.g. Football team and player. A team has many players, but a player belongs to only one team.

Many-to-many   e.g. Product and component. A product has many components, and the same component can be used in many different products.

These relationships can be shown in an *entity-relationship (E-R) diagram* as follows:

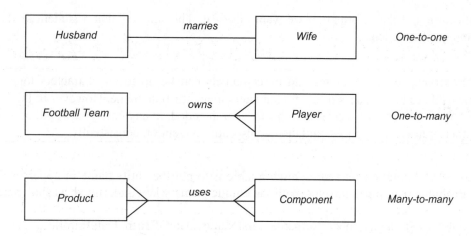

Figure 1.1: Different degrees of relationship

Attributes and key fields

Each entity will have attributes associated with it. An *attribute* is a property or characteristic, for example the entity Product will have attributes such as Product ID, Description, Cost Price. Sometimes it is hard to separate the entities and the attributes – Component, for example, is an entity in the above diagram but each component is also an attribute of a particular product.

Each entity in a database must have one or more attributes called a *primary key* which uniquely identifies it – for example Product ID would be an obvious primary key of Product.

Normalisation

Normalisation is a process used to design a database in the most efficient way, and you need to make sure you understand the process before you start designing your database. Basically, there are three stages or rules to be applied known as First, Second and Third Normal Form. Once you are familiar with these rules the whole process of normalisation seems very much like just using a bit of common sense. We'll look briefly at the three stages of normalisation.

In designing a database to hold information about students and subjects, for example, you might start by identifying the two entities STUDENT and SUBJECT. These entities are joined in a many-to-many relationship, since a student may study several subjects, and the same subject may be studied by several students. You can then draw an entity-relationship diagram as shown below:

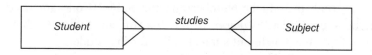

Figure 1.2: Initial stage in database design

First Normal Form

A database in *first normal form* must not contain repeating attributes.

The STUDENT entity will probably have attributes StudentNumber, Surname, FirstName, DateOfBirth, DateEnrolled, and possibly many other attributes as well, depending on the objectives of the database application and the information we want out of it. The subjects that a student studies, for example, are attributes of a student.

> **NOTE:** Names of attributes and other objects can be up to 64 characters long in Access, and it is permissible to have spaces or other characters in an attribute name. However in this book attribute names will be written without spaces, and this is recommended. In any case you would be well advised to decide whether or not to use spaces, and then apply your convention consistently.

The standard notation for representing a table is to put the entity name in uppercase letters, followed by the attributes within parentheses, with the unique primary key underlined, as shown below:

STUDENT (StudentNumber, Surname, FirstName, DateOfBirth, DateEnrolled)

What we must NOT do is to put the subjects studied by a particular student in the same table, because a student may study more than one subject. This is what is meant by a *repeating attribute*. In other words, do NOT design the table like this:

STUDENT (StudentNumber, Surname, FirstName, DateOfBirth, DateEnrolled, Subject1, Subject2, Subject3)

You can probably see the reasons for not designing a table this way. For one thing, what would happen if a student studies more than 3 subjects? For another, it would be very difficult to pick out all students doing a particular subject, because you wouldn't know which column to look in.

The STUDENT table can be left as it was originally. **Subject** is an entity and gets a table of its own. After further investigation of the problem, the designer may decide that attributes of Subject which need to be recorded include the subject code (a unique ID), the subject name, hours per week and the ID and name of the tutor in charge of that particular subject.

SUBJECT (SubjectCode, SubjectName, HrsPerWeek, TutorID, TutorName)
(but we'll be modifying this shortly, so if you've spotted a weakness, don't worry!)

Next, we need to introduce a new table to show the subjects that each student is studying.

STUDENT_SUBJECT (StudentNumber, SubjectCode)

Notice that in this table, both the StudentNumber and the SubjectCode are needed to form a unique primary key. This can be referred to as a *composite key*. If a student studies 3 subjects, there will be three records in the table specifying the 3 different subject codes for that student.

Second Normal Form

A table is in *second normal form* if it is in first normal form and no column that is not part of a primary key is dependent on only a portion of the primary key.

A bit of a mouthful, but it all boils down to common sense. What it's saying is, don't include attributes in tables that aren't needed in that table. For example, suppose we had designed the last table as

STUDENT_SUBJECT (StudentNumber, Surname, FirstName, SubjectCode, SubjectName)

Surname and FirstName are not part of the primary key, and they depend only on StudentNumber. Given a particular StudentNumber, you can look up the STUDENT table to find out the corresponding Surname and FirstName, so they are not needed in the STUDENT_SUBJECT table. The same logic applies to SubjectName.

Third Normal Form

A table is in *third normal form* if it contains no 'non-key dependencies'.

Look again at the SUBJECT table. We have specified two attributes TutorID and TutorName in this table. However, TutorID is enough to identify the subject tutor, and TutorName depends on TutorID, not on SubjectCode. Therefore it should not be in this table. We have in fact identified another entity, TUTOR.

The designer would need to find out more about tutors. Is a tutor responsible for a student or a subject? Can a tutor be responsible for more than one student or subject? Can a student or subject have more than one tutor?

We will assume that it has been established that each subject is under the administration of just one tutor who acts as subject leader, but that a single tutor may be responsible for more than one subject. For example Mrs Bell may be responsible for both Computing and Information Technology. Of course, this may not be true in some schools – the correct relationship would have to be established when the problem was being analysed.

The entity-relationship diagram may be drawn as follows:

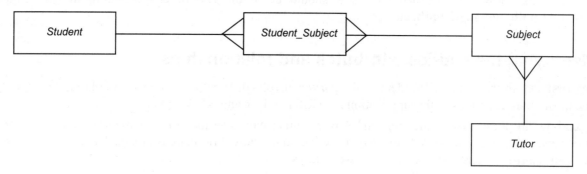

Figure 1.3: E-R diagram for the Student database application

The four 'normalised' tables that we need for this application are, therefore
STUDENT (<u>StudentNumber</u>, Surname, FirstName, DateOfBirth, DateEnrolled)
SUBJECT (<u>SubjectCode</u>, SubjectName, HrsPerWeek, TutorID)
STUDENT_SUBJECT (<u>StudentNumber</u>, <u>SubjectCode</u>)
TUTOR (<u>TutorID</u>, TutorName)

Many-to-many relationships cannot be directly implemented in a normalised database. An extra table always has to be introduced to link the two original entities. The database holding information about students and subjects needed the extra *link* table called STUDENT_SUBJECT. Notice carefully which way round the 'crowsfeet' point. It will always be the same as that shown below when you introduce a link table.

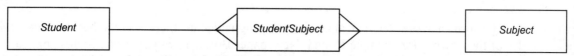

Figure 1.4: Using a 'link' table to join two entities in a many-to-many relationship

A sample database

Most of Part 1 will use as an example of Access techniques, a simple system to help a newsagent keep track of newspaper deliveries and customer accounts. Details will be held on customers and newspapers, and which newspapers the customers have delivered to them each day.

The objectives of the system are to be able to:

- Add, edit and delete details of customers, newspapers and deliveries;

- Print a 'round sheet' showing which newspapers are to be delivered to each customer on a given round each day;

- Print a summary report showing the total number of each newspaper required for each round;

- Calculate each customer's weekly bill and add it to their outstanding balance;

- Print each customer's weekly invoice;

- Update the customer's record when payment is received.

In Part 1, this case study is simply a vehicle for learning Access, so many other tasks will be tackled along the way and some parts of this system will not be implemented. However, you can see the complete system implemented in the sample project in Appendix A, and you can download the Access 97 database **newsproject.mdb** from the web site www.payne-gallway.co.uk

You can also download the database as it should be at the end of chapters 2-10 in files called **newsagt2.mdb**, **newsagt3.mdb**, etc.

Identifying the entities, attributes and relationships

The first step in the design is to identify the *entities* involved. What or who are we holding data about? The most obvious entities in this application are CUSTOMER and NEWSPAPER.

Next, how are these two entities related? Any customer can have many newspapers delivered, and the same newspaper (e.g. the Daily Mail) may be delivered to many different customers. Therefore, there is a many-to-many relationship between these two entities.

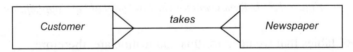

Figure 1.5: Relationship between customers and newspapers

As we saw above, a many-to-many relationship cannot be directly implemented and we will need a 'link' table to specify which newspapers each customer wants delivered. The third table could be named DELIVERY, and the new E-R diagram will be as follows:

Figure 1.6: E-R diagram for the Newspaper application

If you were to perform a more detailed analysis, you might decide there were other entities which required tables of their own – for example Round, Newspaper Boy/Girl, Supplier etc. In this application, however, we will use just the three tables for the entities CUSTOMER, DELIVERY and NEWSPAPER.

Table design

The next stage in design is to decide what data we are going to hold in each table, what format the data should be in, what validations need to be performed on the data, and whether we can set any default values to minimise data entry.

Before you design the tables for your own project, you will need to be familiar with the various data types available in Access. The most common data types are:

Text	Up to 255 characters for holding a name, address, telephone number etc. (A telephone number is normally held as text because although it consists of numbers, it may contain spaces or leading zeros and is never used in calculations.)
Number	For numeric data which is to be used in calculations. Access allows different types of number field such as **byte** (for numbers between 0-255) **integer** (for whole numbers between -32,768 and 32,767), **long integer** (for larger whole numbers), **single** and **double** for numbers with decimal points, and more.
Autonumber	A unique sequential (incrementing by 1) or random number is automatically inserted when a record is added. Commonly used as a key field.
Currency	For holding currency amounts – use it to prevent rounding during calculations.
Boolean	For fields containing only Yes/No or True/False.
Date/Time	For holding dates and/or times.
Memo	For lengthy notes of up to 64,000 characters.

The tables will be defined as follows:

CUSTOMER   (Table name: **tblCustomer**)

Attribute Name	Data Type	Description/Validation
CustomerID*	AutoNumber	Key field, automatically incremented for each new customer
Surname	Text (20)	
Initial	Text (1)	
Title	Text (4)	Lookup from list – Mr, Mrs, Miss, Ms, Dr, Rev
Address1	Text (20)	1st line of address
Address2	Text (20)	2nd line of address
Round	Integer	1-3
CurrentDue	Currency	This week's amount due
PastDue	Currency	Past amount due
HolsBegin	Date	Date holiday starts
HolsEnd	Date	Date holiday ends

NEWSPAPER   Table name: **tblNewspaper**

Attribute Name	Data Type	Description/Validation
NewspaperID*	Text (4)	Key field
NewspaperName	Text (25)	
Price	Currency	
Morning/Evening	Text (1)	M or E

DELIVERY Table name: **tblDelivery**

Attribute Name	Data Type	Description/Validation
CustomerID*	Long Integer	Part of the key field – must exist on CUSTOMER table
NewspaperID*	Text (4)	Part of the key field – must exist on NEWSPAPER table
Monday	Yes/No	Y/N indicates whether paper delivered on Monday
Tuesday	Yes/No	As for Monday
Wednesday	Yes/No	"
Thursday	Yes/No	"
Friday	Yes/No	"
Saturday	Yes/No	"
Sunday	Yes/No	"

Figure 1.7: Designs for the 3 tables CUSTOMER, NEWSPAPER and DELIVERY

Elements of an Access database

The various elements that you'll be working with in Access are referred to as *objects*. These include:

Tables	for holding information;
Queries	for asking questions about your data or making changes to it;
Forms	for editing and viewing information;
Reports	for summarising and printing information;
Macros	for performing tasks automatically;
Modules	for customising your database using Visual Basic for Applications (VBA).

Naming conventions

There are various conventions for naming the objects that you use. You don't have to use a naming convention but it will certainly make your database easier to create and maintain, and will probably earn you extra marks in project work. Shown below are the Leszynski/Reddick naming conventions, which will be used in this book.

Level 1

Object	Tag	Example
Table	tbl	tblCustomer
Query	qry	qryClientName
Form	frm	frmCustomer
Report	rpt	rptSales
Macro	mcr	mcrUpdateList
Module	bas	basIsNotLoaded

Level 2

Object	Tag	Example
Table	tbl	tblCustomer
Table (lookup)	tlkp	tlkpRegion
Table (system)	zstbl	zstblUser
Query (select)	qry	qryClientName
Query (append)	qapp	qappNewPhone
Query (crosstab)	qxtb	qxtbYearSales
Query (delete)	qdel	qdelOldCases
Query (form filter)	qflt	qfltAlphaList
Query (lookup)	qlkp	qlkpSalary
Query (make table)	qmak	qmakSaleTo
Query (system)	zsqry	zsqryMacroName
Query (update)	qupd	qupdDiscount
Form	frm	frmCustomer
Form (dialogue)	fdlg	fdlgInputDate
Form (menu)	fmnu	fmnuMain
Form (message)	fmsg	fmsgCheckDate
Form (subform)	fsub	fsubInvoice
Report	rpt	rptTotals
Report (subreport)	rsub	rsubValues
Report (system)	zsrpt	zsrptMacroName
Macro	mcr	mcrUpdateList
Macro (for form)	m[formname]	m[formname]Customer
Macro (menu)	mmnu	mmnuStartForm
Macro (for report)	m[rptname]	m[rptname]Totals
Macro (system)	zsmcr	zsmcrLoadLookUp
Module	bas	basTimeScreen
Module (system)	zsbas	zsbasAPIcall

Figure 1.8: Leszynski/Reddick naming conventions

Designing the Input and Output

When you start your own project, you will be expected to design the whole system including the menu, input forms, queries, processing and reports before you start implementation. However, the purpose of Part 1 of this book is to teach you how to use Access and what its capabilities are, so the design of each part of the system will be explained as we come to implement it.

We're ready to load Access and create the tables!

Chapter 2 – Creating Tables and Relationships

Loading Access

The way that you load Access will depend on which version of Access you are using and whether you are working at home or on a school or college network. There may be an icon in the Main Window or Applications Window that you can click on, or you can click the **Access** icon in the Office Shortcut Bar at the top of the screen if this is visible. In Windows 95 or 98 you can click on **Start** in the bottom left hand corner and select **Programs**, **Microsoft Access**.

Task 2.1:   Create a new database and tables for the Newsagent application

---

Creating a new database

When you first start Access, you have the option of either opening an existing database or creating a new one. Access provides many ready-made databases for you to use, and also several wizards to help you to quickly create a database. However in this case, we will create a new database from scratch. You will see a screen similar to the one shown below.

Access icon in the Office Shortcut Bar

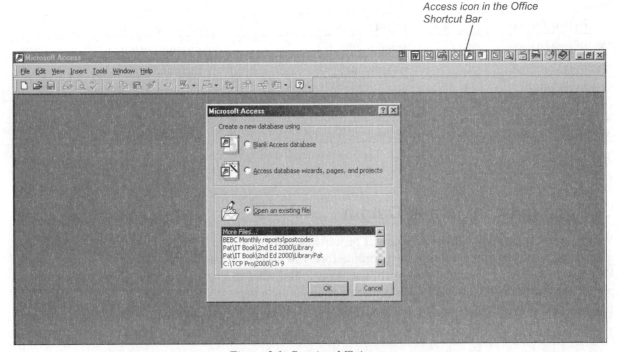

Figure 2.1: Starting MS Access

- Select the **Blank Access Database** button and press **OK**.

A window opens as shown below, asking you to select a folder and a name for your new database. It is a good idea to keep each Access database in its own folder.

- Click the **Create New Folder** button and create a new folder named *News*.

- In the **File Name** box, type the name *NewsAgt.mdb* and press the **Create** button.

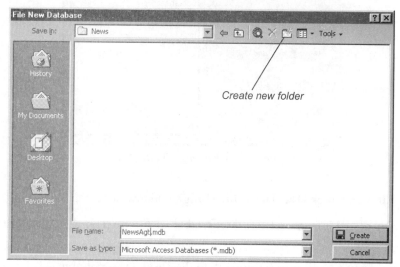

Figure 2.2: Naming a new database

The Database window

Every Access database has a database window. The window has buttons (tabs in 7 and 97) for each type of database object: Tables, Queries, Forms, Reports, etc. In addition, there are options to open an object, change its design, or create a new object. **Tables** is currently selected and since at the moment there are no existing tables to Open or Design, only the **Create** options are active.

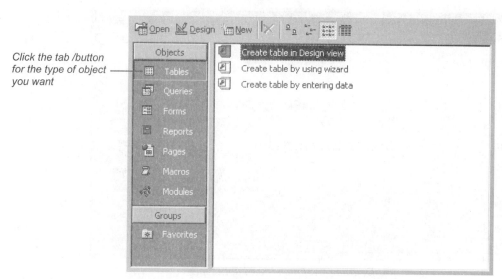

Figure 2.3: The Database window

Creating a new table

- In the Database window make sure **Create table in Design View** is selected (in Access 7 or 97, make sure the **Tables** option is selected), and press **New**.

- A new window appears as shown below.

Figure 2.4: Choosing a table view

- Select **Design View** and click **OK**. The Table Design window appears.

- Look back at the design for the CUSTOMER table in Figure 1.7. All these attributes need to be entered in the new table.

- Enter the first field name, *CustomerID*, and tab to the **Data Type** column.

- Click the Down arrow and select the field type **AutoNumber**.

- Tab to the **Description** column and type *Unique Primary key*. Notice that in the **Field Properties** list below, AutoNumber is automatically given a **Field Size** property of **Long Integer**. **New Values** has the property **Increment**, which means that this field will automatically be increased by 1 for each new customer. The **Indexed** property currently shows **Yes (Duplicates OK)**. Since this is to be a unique key field, duplicates must not be allowed: we'll correct that below.

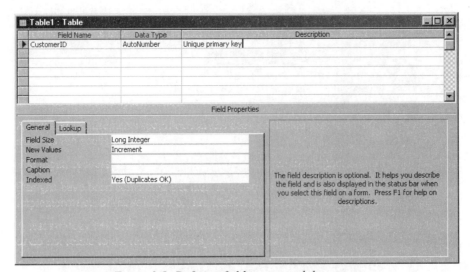

Figure 2.5: Defining field names and data types

> **NOTE:** Access 97 automatically builds an index for a table using the key field(s). You can index any other fields in order to speed up searches – for example, if you thought you were often going to search for a customer by surname, you could specify that the **Surname** field is to be indexed, with duplicates allowed (since two people may have the same surname).

Defining the primary key

- With the cursor still in the row for the **CustomerID**, press the **Primary Key** button on the toolbar. The key symbol appears in the left hand margin (termed the *row selector*) next to **CustomerID**, and the **Indexed** property automatically changes to **Yes (No Duplicates)**.

> **WARNING:** If you join a Number field to an **AutoNumber** field to relate two tables, leave the **Field Size** for the Number field set to **Long Integer**, otherwise Access will not be able to link the fields.

Entering other fields (attributes)

Now we can enter all the other fields. (The correct database terminology is *attribute*, but Microsoft Access refers to attributes as *fields*.) Don't worry if you make a few mistakes – after all the fields are entered, you will learn how to move fields around, delete them or insert new fields. You can correct any mistakes at that point, and it'll be good practice.

> **NOTE:** A field name can be up to 64 characters long, can contain letters, numbers, spaces and other characters except for full-stops, exclamation marks and brackets.

- Enter the field name *Surname* in the next row. Tab to the **Data Type** column and the default is **Text**, which is fine. You need to change the **Field Size** property in the bottom half of the screen from the default 50 characters to *20*.

- In the next row, enter the field name *Initial*, and give it a **Field Size** of *1* character.

- In the next row, enter the field name *Title* and tab to the **Data Type** column. This time, select **Lookup Wizard...** as the data type for the field.

- In the first step of the Lookup Wizard, select **I will type in the values that I want** and click **Next**.

- In the next window, enter titles as shown in the figure below, and adjust the column width. Click **Next**.

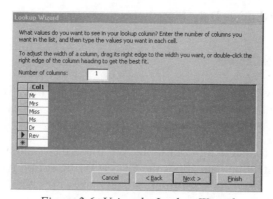

Figure 2.6: Using the Lookup Wizard

- In the next window, leave the label for the Lookup column as **Title** and click **Finish**.

- Click the **General** tab in the bottom half of the window. Set the default value to *Mr.* It's not necessary to type quotation marks around a constant unless it contains punctuation such as full stops or commas, for example "U.K." Access will automatically add quotation marks, as shown in the figure below.

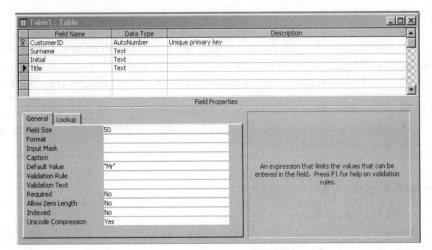

Figure 2.7: Setting a default value

- Enter **Address1** and **Address2** as **Text** fields of 20 characters.

- Enter **Round** as a **Number** field and specify **Integer** in the **Field Size** property. We are going to put a validation rule on this field, specifying that it must be in the range 1 to 3.

NOTE:	There are several types of number field. For example:
Byte	Stores numbers from 0 to 255 (no fractions).
Integer	Stores numbers from –32,768 to 32,767 (no fractions).
Long Integer	(Default) Stores numbers from –2,147,483,648 to 2,147,483,647 (no fractions).

- In the **Validation Rule** property, type *1 or 2 or 3*

- In the **Validation Text** property, type the message that will appear if the user enters an invalid character: *Must be in the range 1 – 3.*

- Enter **CurrentDue** and **PastDue** as **Currency** fields.

- Enter **HolsBegin** and **HolsEnd** as **Date/Time** fields.

Saving the table structure

- Save the table structure by pressing the **Save** button or selecting **File, Save** from the menu bar. Don't worry if you have some mistakes in the table structure – they can be corrected in a minute.

- You will be asked to enter a name for your table. We'll use the naming conventions shown in Figure 1.8. As this is a table containing data about the CUSTOMER entity, type the name *tblCustomer* and click **OK**. (Note the uppercase **C** in **Customer**, which makes the name more legible.)

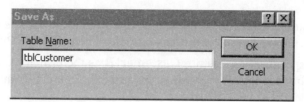

Figure 2.8: Naming and saving the table structure

- Click the Close icon (**X**) in the top right hand corner to close the window. You will be returned to the database window.

Editing a table structure

- In the Database window you will see that your new table is now listed.

> **NOTE:** If you have named the table wrongly, or made a spelling mistake, right-click the name and select **Rename**. Then type in the correct name.

- Select the table name, click the **Design View** button and you are returned to *Design View*.

Inserting a field

To insert a new row for **Address3** just above **Round**:

- Click the row selector (the left hand margin) for **Round**.
- Press the **Insert** key on the keyboard or click the **Insert Rows** button on the toolbar.
- Enter the new field name, *Address3*, data type **Text**. Accept the default length.

Deleting a field

To delete the field you have just inserted:

- Select the field by clicking in its row selector.
- Press the **Delete** key on the keyboard or click the **Delete Rows** button on the toolbar.

If you make a mistake, you can use **Edit, Undo Delete** to restore the field.

Moving a field

- Click the row selector to the left of the field's name to select the field.
- Click again and drag to where you want the field to be. You will see a line appear between fields as you drag over them to indicate where the field will be placed.

Changing or removing a key field

- To change the key field to **Surname**, click the row selector for the **Surname** field and then click the **Primary Key** button on the toolbar.
- To remove the primary key altogether, select the row that is currently the key field and click the **Primary Key** button on the toolbar.

- Sometimes a primary key is made up of more than one field (a *composite* or *compound* key). Select the first field, hold down **Ctrl** and select the second field. Then click the **Primary Key** button.

When you have finished experimenting, restore **CustomerID** as the primary key field of this table. Make any other necessary corrections to leave the fields as specified in Figure 1.7, and save the table structure.

Entering data in Datasheet view

It's time to enter some data. This can be done in Datasheet View.

- On the Toolbar, click the **Datasheet View** button.

The table now appears in Datasheet view as shown below.

Toggles between Design and Datasheet view

CustomerID	Surname	Initial	Title	Address1	Address2	Round	Currei
(AutoNumber)			Mr			0	

Figure 2.9: Datasheet view

- You can drag the right border of the header (field name) of any field to alter its width. Drag the borders so that the whole row appears on the screen:

CustomerID	Surname	Initial	Title	Address1	Address2	Round	CurrentDue	PastDue	HolsBegin	HolsEnd
(AutoNumber)			Mr			0	£0.00	£0.00		

Figure 2.10: Field widths adjusted

- Enter the following record:

Customer ID	Surname	Initial	Title	Address1	Address2	Round	CurrentDue	PastDue	HolsBegin	HolsEnd
(Auto)	Robson	C	Mr	11 Dales Rd	Broughton	1	8.50	17.00	23/04/99	30/04/99

Figure 2.11: First customer record will have ID 1, or 2 after deletion and reentry

> **NOTE:** You can press **Tab** to move to the next field, or **Shift-Tab** to move to the previous field. You can't enter anything in the **CustomerID** field – just tab to the next field and Access will automatically allocate the next number, starting with 1. If you delete the record you have just entered and enter it again, it will have **CustomerID** number 2.

- If you want your records to have the same ID numbers as the ones in the text, you must now delete the record for Robson and then reenter it. Click in the record's row selector (the left hand margin) to select the record and press the **Delete Record** button.

- Reenter the record for Robson. It will have **CustomerID** number 2. (If you add and delete other records and end up with different IDs from the ones in the screenshots it does not matter.)

The records shown below in Figure 2.14 are now to be entered. **Don't enter them** until you have read on a little bit.

You will notice that all the addresses are in the town of Broughton. Probably this should have been made a default value. However, perhaps there is a quick way of entering the same value as in the previous record. The best way to find out something you don't know is to use the extensive Help system.

- Press the **Office Assistant** button on the toolbar.

- The Office Assistant (a kinky paperclip, cat or dog) appears with a dialogue box asking you to type in your question. *(In Access 7, select **Help, Answer Wizard**.)*

- Type *How do I enter same value as in previous record?* Or, simply type *enter same value as in previous record*. Click **Search**.

- The Office Assistant scrutinises and (in Access 97) manages to interpret this request, assuming you've spelt it correctly. It comes back with another dialogue box, as shown below:

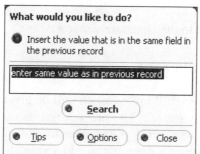

The Office Assistant in Access 2000 is worse than useless, may as well leave it asleep…

Figure 2.12: Using the Office Assistant

- Click **Insert the value that is in the same field in the previous record**. The answer comes back:

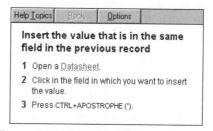

Figure 2.13: Office Assistant to the rescue

- Now enter the 5 records shown below, pressing **Ctrl-'** in the **Address2** field in each record. You can select the **Title** from a drop-down list. Note that you must finish entering a record before Access checks the validation rule on the **Round** field and shows an error message if it is not in the range 1-3.

Customer ID	Surname	Initial	Title	Address1	Address2	Round	Current Due	Past Due	HolsBegin	HolsEnd
(Auto)	Brindley	J	Mr	1 Chestnut Ave	Broughton	3	6.00	12.00		
	Nazarali	N	Mr	13 Dales Rd	Broughton	1	5.00	25.00		
	Newbourne	S	Miss	Mill Hse, Mill Lane	Broughton	2	7.50	0.00	27/04/99	30/04/99
	Carter	J	Mrs	Bridge Hse, Mill La	Broughton	2	4.20	8.40		
	Gamukama	M	Mr	23 Dales Rd	Broughton	1	3.00	6.00		

Figure 2.14: More customer records

- Click the Close icon in the top right corner of the current window. (Be careful to close just the Table window, not Access.)

- If you have changed column widths, you will be asked if you want to save the changes you made to the layout.

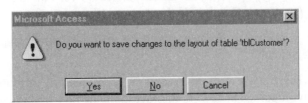

Figure 2.15: Saving changes to the Datasheet layout.

- Click **Yes**. You will be returned to the Database window.

Creating the NEWSPAPER table

Now you need to create the NEWSPAPER table, which will be given the name *tblNewspaper*. This table has just four fields as shown in Figure 1.7. The process is exactly the same as was used for creating **tblCustomer**, so no help will be given here! Remember to make **NewspaperID** the key field of type **Text**, to adjust field lengths to the given values and to add a validation rule for **Morning/Evening** (*"M" or "E"*).

- When you have created the table structure, save it as *tblNewspaper*, change to Datasheet View and enter the following records:

NewspaperID	NewspaperName	Price	Morning/Evening
GU	Guardian	.45	M
SUN	Sun	.30	M
STAR	Evening Star	.40	E
DT	Daily Telegraph	.45	M
TIM	The Times	.25	M
MERC	Mercury	.35	M
OBS	Observer	1.00	M
ST	Sunday Times	1.00	M

Figure 2.16: Newspaper records

- Switch to Design view and then back to Datasheet view. You'll notice that the records will be displayed in key field order even though they were not entered in this order.

- Close the datasheet window and return to the Database window.

Creating the DELIVERY table

The DELIVERY table links the CUSTOMER table to the NEWSPAPER table, specifying which newspapers each customer takes.

- In the Database window, make sure **Tables, Create Table in Design view** is selected and click **New**.

- In the next dialogue box select **Design View** and click **OK**. The Table Design window appears.

- Look back at the fields specified in Figure 1.7.

- Type the first field name, *CustomerID*, and tab to the **Data Type** column.

- Select the data type **Number**, and leave the **Field Size** property as **Long Integer**.

- Type the second field name *NewspaperID*, a **Text** field with a **Field Size** property of *4* characters.

- Enter all the other fields *Monday – Sunday* with data type **Yes/No**. (If you type *y* in the Data Type column Access correctly inserts **Yes/No**.)

- Select **CustomerID** and **NewspaperID** by dragging across their row selectors, and click the **Primary Key** button on the toolbar to make both these fields part of the primary key.

- Click the **Save** button or select **File, Save**, and name the table *tblDelivery*.

Using the Lookup wizard

It will make data entry easy for the user if they can look up and enter the customer name rather than the Customer ID, and the newspaper name instead of the Newspaper ID.

CustomerID will be looked up from the records on the **Customer** table. Access can do this automatically with the help of the Lookup Wizard.

- With **tblDelivery** in Design view, tab to the **Data Type** column in the **CustomerID** row. From the list of data types select **Lookup Wizard**. A dialogue box appears.

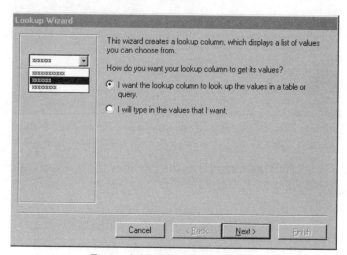

Figure 2.17: The Lookup Wizard

- Click **Next**.

- Select **tblCustomer** as the table you want to look up the values from. Click **Next**.

- In the next dialogue box, with **CustomerID** selected in the **Available Fields** box, press the single arrow to move it to the **Selected Fields** box. Repeat for the fields **Surname**, **Initial**, **Title** and **Address1**. The window should look like the one shown below.

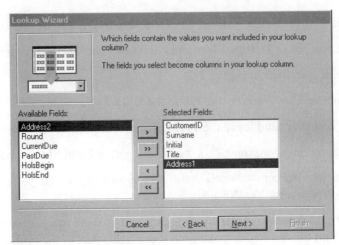

Figure 2.18: Selecting fields to include in the lookup column

- Click **Next**. In the next dialogue box accept the default **Hide key column** and adjust the column widths as shown in the figure below. Click **Next**.

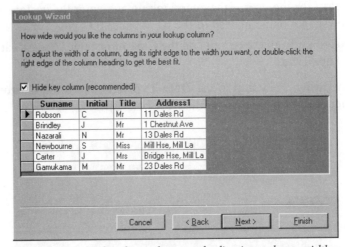

Figure 2.19: Hiding key column and adjusting column widths

- In the next dialogue box accept **CustomerID** as the label for the Lookup Column and click **Finish**. You will see a message:

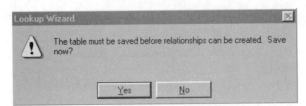

Figure 2.20: Saving the table

- Click **Yes**.
- Now tab to the **Data Type** column for **NewspaperID**. Change the data type to **Lookup Wizard**, and specify that you want to look up the values from **tblNewspaper**.

- Select the fields **NewspaperID** and **NewspaperName** in the dialogue box as shown below:

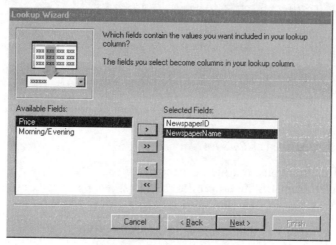

Figure 2.21: Selecting fields

- Accept the default **Hide key column** in the next dialogue box and click **Finish**.

- Click **Yes** when asked if you want to save the table, close it and return to the database window.

Task 2.2: Define relationships between tables

Defining relationships

In Chapter 1 we drew an E-R diagram representing the relationships between the three entities CUSTOMER, NEWSPAPER and DELIVERY (Figure 1.6). We can define these relationships in Access.

- Open the Relationships window using any one of three methods:
  1. Right-click anywhere in the Database window and select **Relationships**;
  2. Press the **Relationships** button on the toolbar;
  3. Select **Tools, Relationships** from the menu bar.

  The following window appears, showing that Access has already recognised that relationships exist between the three tables, which are linked by common fields.

NOTE: If the tables that you want to relate are not visible in the Relationships window, click the **Show Table** button on the toolbar, and double-click the name of each of the tables you are relating. Then close the Show Table dialogue box.

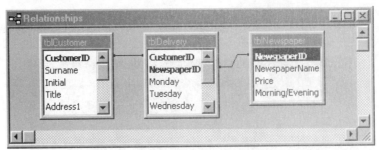

Figure 2.22: The Relationships window

The relationships need to be defined as *One-to-Many*.

- To set the degree of the relationship (one-to-many) between **tblCustomer** and **tblDelivery**, drag the key field **CustomerID** from **tblCustomer** (the ONE side of the relationship) to **CustomerID** in **tblDelivery** (the MANY side of the relationship.)

- A message appears warning you that a relationship already exists, and asking if you want to edit it. Click **Yes**.

- The Relationships window appears as shown below. Check **Enforce Referential Integrity** to select it. Leave the other boxes unchecked. Click **OK**.

  Enforcing *referential integrity* means that Access will not allow the user to enter a delivery record for a customer who has not already been entered on the **tblCustomer** table, or specify a newspaper delivery for a newspaper which is not in **tblNewspaper**.

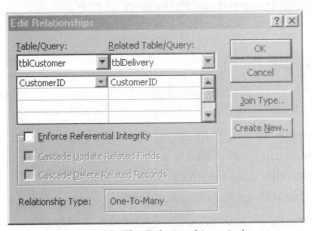

Figure 2.23: The Relationships window

> **NOTE:** **Cascade Update Related Fields** changes the values in related records when the linking value in a master record is changed.
>
> **Cascade Delete Related Records** deletes related records when the master record in a relationship is deleted. For example, if you delete customer number 2, all the corresponding delivery records will automatically be deleted.

- Next, drag **NewspaperID** from **tblNewspaper** to **NewspaperID** in **tblDelivery**. Click **Yes** in the warning message box.

- Check **Enforce Referential Integrity** to select it. Do **not** check **Cascade Update Related Fields** or **Cascade Delete Related Records.** Click **OK**.

- The relationships window now looks slightly different, showing the one-to-many relationships as shown below.

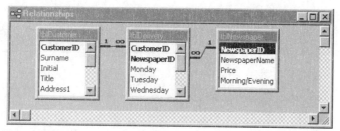

Figure 2.24: One-to-many relationships with referential integrity

> **NOTE:** To delete a relationship, right-click the line for the relationship and choose **Delete** from the shortcut menu.

- Save the relationships you have created by closing the Relationships window and choosing **Yes** when asked if you want to save.

Task 2.3: Sort the Delivery table lookup fields and enter data in Datasheet view

We have already used Datasheet view to enter data for customers and newspapers. Now we'll enter some data for deliveries.

- In the Database window make sure **Tables** is selected.

- Double-click **tblDelivery**. (You could also highlight the table's name and click **Open**, or right-click the table name and select **Open**.) The table opens in Datasheet view.

- Adjust the column widths by dragging so that all the columns are visible on the screen.

- As soon as you click in the first column for **CustomerID** the arrow appears, and you can click it to display and select a customer from the list.

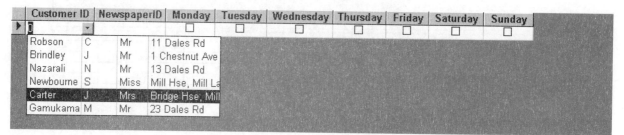

Figure 2.25: Entering data in Datasheet View

Notice that the customers appear in the order that they were originally entered (i.e. in Autonumber key field order), which would be inconvenient if the list was very long. Before we enter any data, we'll sort the list so that it appears in alphabetical order.

- Click the **Design View** button. (If you get an error message **Index or primary key can't contain a Null value**, click **OK** and then press **Esc** to delete any fields you have entered.)

23

- With the cursor in the **CustomerID** field, click the **Lookup** tab in the bottom half of the screen. The Lookup properties will appear as shown below.

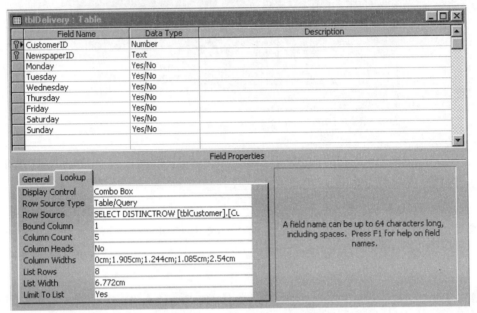

Figure 2.26: Lookup properties of CustomerID

- Click in the **Row Source** property. The **Build** button appears (**...**).

- Click this button and the Query Builder window appears. Queries are covered in Chapter 4, but for now, all we want to do is sort the **CustomerID** combo box on **Surname**.

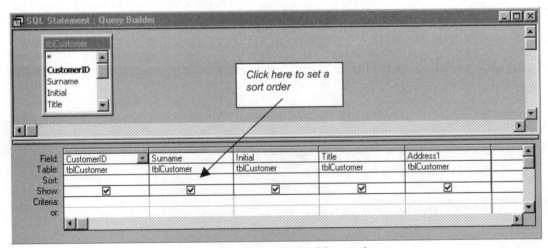

Figure 2.27: The Query Builder window

- In the **Surname** column, click in the **Sort** row and select **Ascending**.

- Click the Close icon in the top right hand corner of the window (**X**) and click **Yes** when asked if you wish to save the changes.

- You are returned to the Table design view. Move the cursor down to the **NewspaperID** field and set the sort order in ascending sequence of **NewspaperName** in exactly the same way.

- Click the **Datasheet View** button on the toolbar. You will be asked if you want to save the table. Click **Yes**.

- Now test out the combo boxes for **CustomerID** and **NewspaperID**. The entries should appear in alphabetical order.

Entering data in Datasheet view

- Enter the records in the Delivery table **tblDelivery** as shown in Figure 2.28. Note that you can either select a customer from the list, or type a name in. If the name is in the list, it will be accepted; if it is not in the list an error message will be displayed and you will have to enter another name. You can toggle check boxes on or off using either the mouse or the **Spacebar**.

> **NOTE:** Before you leave a field or record, you can undo your last changes with the **Esc** key.
>
> Press **Esc** to undo changes to a field, or **Esc** twice to undo changes to both the field and the record.

Customer	Newspaper	Delivery days
Carter	Daily Telegraph	Mon-Sat
Carter	Sunday Times	Sun
Brindley	Guardian	Mon-Sat
Brindley	Observer	Sun
Gamukama	Sun	Mon-Sat
Gamukama	Evening Star	Mon-Sat
Robson	Mercury	Mon, Wed, Fri
Robson	Sunday Times	Sun
Newbourne	Guardian	Mon-Sat
Newbourne	Mercury	Mon-Sat

*Figure 2.28: Test data for **tblDelivery***

Your table should now appear as in Figure 2.29. (Access adds a blank record at the end with ID **0**.)

Customer ID	NewspaperID	Monday	Tuesday	Wednesday	Thursday	Friday	Saturday	Sunday
Carter	Daily Telegraph	☑	☑	☑	☑	☑	☑	☐
Carter	Sunday Times	☐	☐	☐	☐	☐	☐	☑
Brindley	Guardian	☑	☑	☑	☑	☑	☑	☐
Brindley	Observer	☐	☐	☐	☐	☐	☐	☑
Gamukama	Sun	☑	☑	☑	☑	☑	☑	☐
Gamukama	Evening Star	☑	☑	☑	☑	☑	☑	☐
Robson	Mercury	☑	☐	☑	☐	☑	☐	☐
Robson	Sunday Times	☐	☐	☐	☐	☐	☐	☑
Newbourne	Guardian	☑	☑	☑	☑	☑	☑	☐
Newbourne	Mercury	☑	☑	☑	☑	☑	☑	☐

Figure 2.29: Data entered in the table in Datasheet view

Customising a table view

When you open a table in Datasheet view you can customise its appearance in many different ways. You have already seen that you can change the column widths. You can also:

- change the row height to show more or fewer records in the window;
- move columns around;
- freeze columns so they are always in view, even when you scroll through other columns;
- hide columns from view.

To change the row height:

- Point to one of the lines between the rows in the row selector column (left hand margin) and drag the row divider up or down until the rows are the required size.

To move columns, e.g. to position **Sunday** before **Monday**:

- Click in the column header of the **Sunday** column, and release the mouse button.

- Click and hold in the column header, and drag to between the columns **NewspaperID** and **Monday**.

- Release the mouse button.

- Now put the column back to its original position!

To freeze columns, e.g. **CustomerID** and **NewspaperID**:

- Select the columns you want to freeze by clicking in the **CustomerID** column header and dragging across **NewspaperID**.

- Select **Format, Freeze Columns** from the menu bar.

- To see the effect of this, widen several columns so that not all columns are visible on screen. Then scroll to the last column. The first two columns will remain on the screen.

- To unfreeze the columns, select **Format, Unfreeze All Columns**.

To hide columns, e.g. Monday to Saturday:

- Select the columns you want to hide.

- Select **Format, Hide Columns** from the menu bar.

- To bring the columns back into view, select **Format, Unhide Columns**.

- Click the check box of all columns you want to unhide.

When you have finished experimenting, click the **Close** icon and answer **Yes** when asked if you wish to save the table layout.

We have now created the foundation of the database, by defining the structure of the tables and defining relationships between them. In the next chapter, we'll be looking at ways of making it easy for the user to input data.

Chapter 3 – Creating Data Entry Forms

Introduction

Once you've created tables for all the entities in your database and created relationships between them, you can turn your attention to how the user will enter data. There are two ways of entering data into an Access database, known respectively as *Datasheet View* and *Form View*. Datasheet view is useful for entering test data as you are developing your database, but for a more customised system you will almost certainly want to design special screen 'forms' to make data entry and editing easier for the end-user.

- Open the **NewsAgt** database created in the last chapter. If you have not got this to hand, you will need to download **NewsAgt2.mdb** from the web site www.payne-gallway.co.uk

Task 3.1: Create a data entry form for Newspapers

Creating a columnar AutoForm

Access makes it very easy to create a basic form for data entry. There are three types of AutoForm:

- Columnar
- Tabular
- Datasheet.

We'll start by creating a columnar form to enter details of newspapers.

- In the Database window, click the **Forms** tab and click **New**. The New Form window opens.

- In the window, select **AutoForm: Columnar**, and select **tblNewspaper** as the table or query where the object's data comes from, as shown in the figure below.

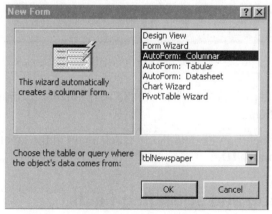

Figure 3.1: Creating a columnar AutoForm

- Click **OK**. The AutoForm Wizard creates a form for data entry, as shown below.

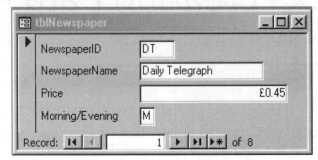

Figure 3.2: A columnar AutoForm

Changing the appearance of the form

We will just make some minor changes to this form, altering the size of the **Price** field and inserting a space in the **NewspaperName** label. By default, the field names are used as labels when the form is created, but you can change them without affecting the field names in the underlying table.

- Click the **Design View** icon on the toolbar.

TIP: If the Form Design toolbar is not visible, select **Toolbars**, **Form Design** from the **View** menu.

- The form appears in Design view. Increase the size of the window so that all the fields are visible as shown below.

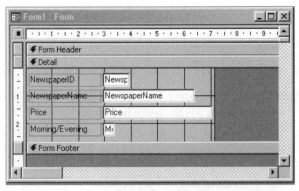

Figure 3.3: The form in Design view

- Click in the **Price** data field (not the label). Make the field smaller by dragging the middle handle on the right hand side of the field.

- Click the **NewspaperID** label (not the data field). Click again in the label name and insert a space so that the label reads **Newspaper ID**.

Adding a form heading and arranging fields

- Press the **View** button again to return to Form View. The form still looks very small and cramped. It needs more space and a heading at the top. Return to Design view.

- Enlarge the window, and drag the top edge of the **Form Footer** down to enlarge the **Detail** section of the form. Drag the right hand edge of the form further over to the right to fill the window.

- Select all the fields and labels in the **Detail** section by dragging the mouse pointer so that a box surrounds them all. Every field should appear with a handle.

- When you move the mouse over any of the fields the pointer changes to a hand. Drag the fields down and to the right to leave space at the top for a heading.

- The toolbox as shown below should be visible on the screen. If it is not, click the Toolbox icon on the toolbar.

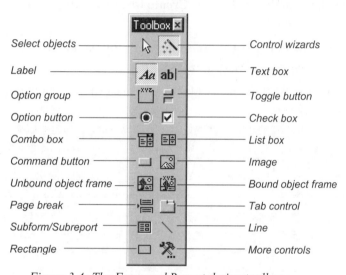

Figure 3.4: The Form and Report design toolbox

- Click the **Label** tool on this toolbox and drag out an area in the upper centre of the **Detail** section of the form. Type the heading *Newspapers*.

- Click on the outside border of this box and make the text **bold, 14 point** and **centred** using tools on the Formatting toolbar.

- Press the **View** button on the toolbar to return to Form view. Your form should look something like the one below, though it may have a different background. We'll be looking at how to change the background style later in this chapter.

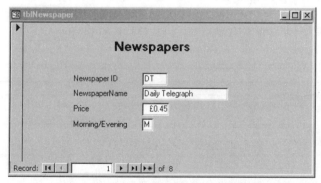

Figure 3.5: The edited Newspaper form

- Press the **Save** icon and save the form as *frmNewspaper*. Close the form.

Task 3.2: Create data entry forms for entering customers and newspaper deliveries

Creating a tabular AutoForm

We'll look next at the second type of AutoForm.

- In the Database window, make sure **Forms, Create form by using wizard** is selected and click **New**. The New Form window appears.

- In the window, select **AutoForm: Tabular** and select **tblCustomer** as the table or query where the object's data comes from.

- Click **OK**. The AutoForm wizard creates a tabular form as shown below.

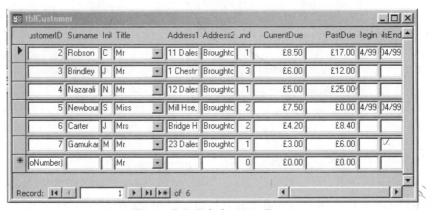

Figure 3.6: Tabular AutoForm

- Maximise the window, and then click the **View** button to go to Design view. The form needs to be enlarged and the fields spread out so the headings and data are visible.

Arranging and sizing fields

- In the Form Header, click the label **HolsEnd**, and hold down the **Shift** key while you select the **HolsEnd** data field underneath. Drag the right hand handle to enlarge the fields till the whole title is visible. Then drag both fields to the right hand edge of the window.

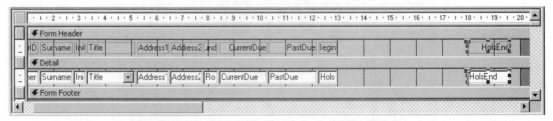

Figure 3.7: Adjusting and positioning column headers together with the corresponding fields

- Repeat for all the other fields.

- Double-click the heading **CustomerID** and shorten it to **Cust ID**.

- The headings should now all be visible and the form in Form view should look something like the one below.

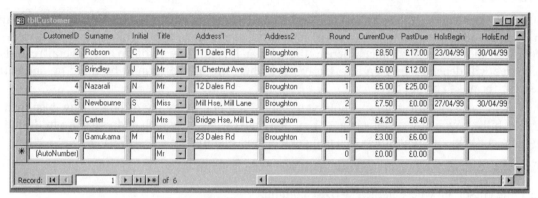

Figure 3.8: The tabular form in Form view

Changing a form's background

You can change the form's background style using AutoFormat.

- Change back to Design view.

- In the **Object** drop-down list at the left-hand end of the Formatting toolbar, select **Form**.

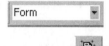

- Press the **AutoFormat** button on the Form Design toolbar.

- The AutoFormat window appears a shown below. Select a background and click **OK**.

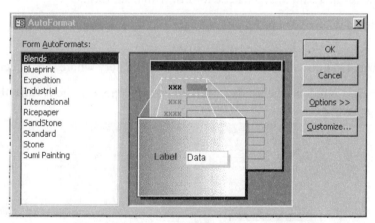

Figure 3.9: Selecting a new background style

- Save the form, naming it *frmCustomer*.

> **WARNING:** Some backgrounds may look attractive on the screen but use more toner and take longer to print than a plain or standard background. Remember that you may need to print out forms as evidence of implementation in your project work.

Changing the sort order of records

One of the choices you will have to make as a system designer is what type of form to use – columnar, tabular or some other kind of form. You will probably have noticed that a columnar form displays only one record on the screen at a time, whereas the tabular layout allows you to see several records. The design choice will depend partly on how many fields there are on the form to be filled in, and partly on what use the form is to be put to.

A columnar layout is useful if for example you wanted a quick overview of how many customers have outstanding bills, how many customers are on holiday next week, or which addresses are in Round 1. By sorting the records in different orders you can get a clearer picture.

- Make sure you are looking at the **frmCustomer** form in Form view.

- Place the cursor anywhere in the **PastDue** column.

- Press the **Sort Descending** button. The records will be sorted in descending order of **PastDue** amounts.

- Now place the cursor in the **Round** field. Press the **Sort Ascending** button. This time the records will be sorted with all the Round 1 records at the beginning.

- Sort the records back in their original sequence of **CustomerID**, and close the form to return to the Database window.

Creating a form with a subform

It would be useful to be able to see all the details about each customer and which newspapers they have delivered, on the same form. To do this, we need a form with a subform.

- In the Database window, make sure **Forms, Create form by using wizard** is selected and then click **New**.

- Select **Form Wizard**. Choose **tblCustomer** as the table or query where the object's data comes from.

- Click **OK**. In the next window, the fields in **tblCustomer** appear in the **Available Fields** list box, as shown below.

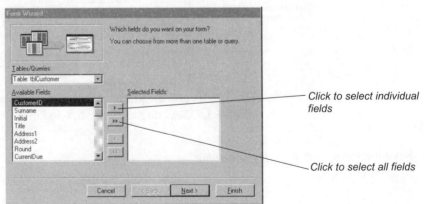

Figure 3.10: The Form Wizard dialogue box

- You can select fields one by one that you want to appear on your form by selecting each one and clicking the single arrow between the **Available Fields** and the **Selected Fields** list boxes. In this particular case we want all the fields, so click the double arrow between the list boxes. All the fields move into the **Selected Fields** list box.

  We now want to select the fields to put on the subform. They will come from the **Delivery** table.

- Click the **Tables/Queries** down arrow and select **Table: tblDelivery**.

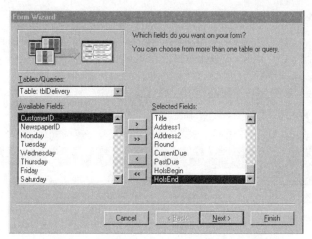

Figure 3.11: Selecting fields for the subform

- Click the double arrow between the list boxes. All the fields move into the **Selected Fields** list box.

- Click **Next**.

- The next Form Wizard dialogue box asks "How do you want to view your data?"

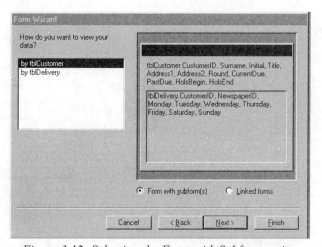

Figure 3.12: Selecting the Form with Subform option

- Select the **tblCustomer** option, make sure **Form with Subform(s)** is checked and click **Next**.

- The next dialogue box asks "What layout would you like for your subform?" Select **Datasheet**, and then click **Next**.

- Select the **Standard** style for the form and then click **Next**.

- In the next dialogue box give the main form the title *frmCustomerMain* and the subform the title *fsubDelivery*.

- Make sure the **Open the Form to View or Enter Information** option is selected and click **Finish**.

  The form and subform open in Form View, and should appear as shown below:

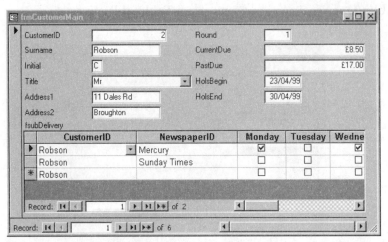

Figure 3.13: Form with subform

WARNING: Access 97 has a very strange quirk. Sometimes the subform will be displayed as shown in Figure 3.14, with the customer ID and newspaper ID appearing in the first two fields, and Yes/No fields instead of check boxes. This seems to depend partly on the names you choose for your main and subforms. Do not, for example, leave a space in the form name, e.g. *frmCustomer Main*.

If you get a similar situation in your project work, try accepting the default Access names for the form and subform, and then rename the forms in the database window.

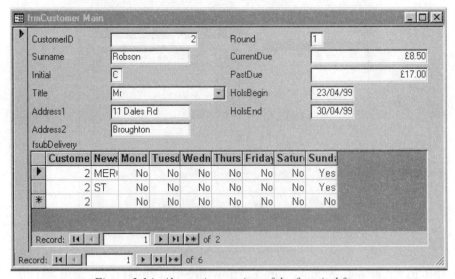

Figure 3.14: Alternative version of the form/subform

Adjusting the size of the form and subform

We need to be able to see the whole subform on the screen. We'll work with the first version as shown in Figure 3.13.

- Make the form window bigger by dragging the corner of the window.

- Click the **Design View** button on the toolbar.

- Drag the edge of the form so that it fills the window.

- Click the subform and drag its right hand edge so that it almost touches the right hand of the window. At this stage your window should look like the figure below. (In Access 7 and 97, the subform will appear blank.)

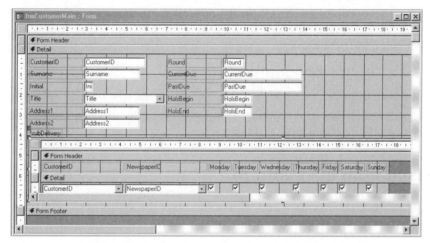

Figure 3.15: The form and subform in Design view

- Return to Form view and drag each of the boundaries between the column headers in the subform so that all the headings are visible, as shown below.

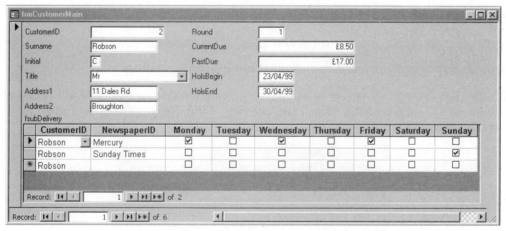

Figure 3.16: The adjusted column widths of the subform

Using the form to enter and edit data

We'll start by adding a new record for a new customer *Mrs S. Murphy* of *15 Elgar Crescent, Broughton Round 1*.

- To add a new customer record, your cursor must be in the main form, not the subform. Click the **New Record** button on the toolbar or on the record selector at the bottom of the form. A new blank record appears.

- Tab out of the AutoNumber field and enter the customer details as given above.

- Mrs Murphy will take the *Guardian* and the *Evening Star* every day except Sunday. Tab into the **NewspaperID** field and select **Guardian**.

- Tab to the **Monday** field, and click to select. Repeat for fields **Tuesday** to **Saturday**.

- On the next line, try entering *EVG STAR* for the newspaper name. As soon as you try to tab out of the last field in the row, an error message appears. Access will not allow you to enter a record for a newspaper that is not in **tblNewspaper**. That is what is meant by *'maintaining referential integrity'*.

- Click **OK** to accept the error message advice.

- Select **Evening Star** from the list of newspapers and check the **Monday** to **Saturday** fields.

The **CustomerID** will not appear in the subform until you close the form and reopen it. It is superfluous in the subform, and could be deleted. We'll do that now.

Deleting a field from the subform

- Return to Design view. (In Access 7 and 97, double-click the subform to select and display it. If you have any difficulty with this, click away from it and then try double-clicking it again.)

- Select the heading **CustomerID**, and keep the **Shift** key down while you select the field **CustomerID**. Press the **Delete** key.

- In Access 7 or 97, close the subform and reply **Yes** when asked if you want to save the changes.

- Switch to Form View to view the changes, adjust the subform width if necessary and save the form.

Finding a record

Suppose we now want to find and delete the record for Mr Gamukama.

- Click in the **Surname** field, and then click the **Find** icon on the toolbar.

- A dialogue box appears for you to enter the name you are trying to find. It is not necessary to enter the whole name – try entering *Gam** and pressing **Find Next**. (The * is known as a *wildcard* character and represents any number of letters.)

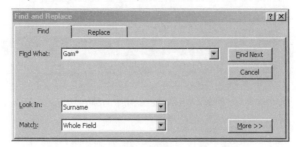

Figure 3.17: Finding a record

- The record appears on screen.

- Press **Close** to close the dialogue box.

Deleting a record

- With the record for Gamukama on screen, put the pointer somewhere in the main form and press the **Delete Record** button on the toolbar.

- An error message appears:

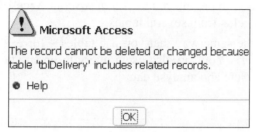

*Figure 3.18: Deleting this customer would leave 'orphan' records in **tblDelivery***

- You cannot delete this customer record as this would leave unrelated records on **tblDelivery**.

NOTE: If you had checked **Cascade Delete Related Records** when you defined the One-to-Many relationship between **tblCustomer** and **tblDelivery** (Figure 2.23) the related records would be automatically deleted when you deleted the Customer record. Because this was not checked, you must first manually delete all related records.

- Put the cursor in the first row of the subform and press the **Delete Record** button. You will be asked if you are sure you want to delete the record. Press **Yes**.

- Delete the second Delivery record for this customer.

- Now delete the Customer record.

In Chapter 8 we'll look at ways of improving the appearance of forms and giving them extra functionality.

NOTE: We have not yet covered *queries*, and in this chapter the forms have been based on *tables*. You can also base forms on queries, and it is a good idea to do so as it provides greater flexibility during development. Bear this in mind when you design your own forms.

Chapter 4 – Queries

Understanding queries

Queries are one of the most important tools in a database for converting raw data into useful information. A query can be thought of as a request to find all records satisfying certain criteria so that they can be displayed in a form or record. The terminology used here is rather confusing, since the word *query* in Access refers not only to the question ("Find all the customers on Route 1"), but also to the resulting *object*, a set of records. (This used to be referred to as a *dynaset* in Access 2). Queries may be made up of records that were created from fields from several tables.

You can use queries in much the same way that you use tables – for example, a form or report may be based on either a *table* or a *query*. You can also use a query to update tables, to perform global 'search and replace' tasks, to append, delete and analyse data.

Types of query

There are six different types of query in Access, each used for different purposes. They are:

- Select query;
- Crosstab query;
- Make-table query;
- Update query;
- Append query;
- Delete query.

We will start with the simplest, the **Select query**.

Task 4.1: Create a query involving only one table

The simplest use of a query is to show selected fields and records from one table. We'll create a query that displays the names, addresses and holiday dates of all customers on Round 1.

- In the database window click **Queries**, select **Create Query in Design View** (not in Access 7 or 97) and then click **New**. The following window appears:

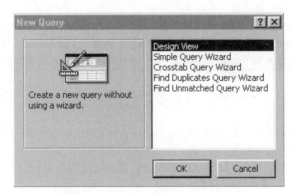

Figure 4.1: Creating a new query

- Double-click **Design View** to open the Show Table dialogue box:

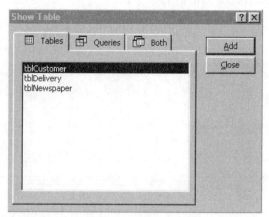

Figure 4.2: The Show Table dialogue box

- With **tblCustomer** selected, click **Add**, and then **Close**. A query window appears as shown below:

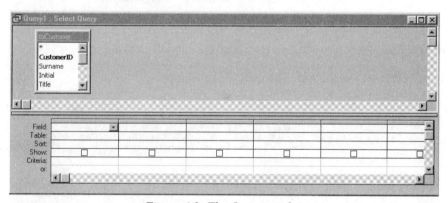

Figure 4.3: The Query window

Selecting fields

The next step is to select the fields that you want to see in the query. We'll select **Surname**, **Initial**, **Address1**, **HolsBegin** and **HolsEnd**. The fields can be placed on the query grid in a number of different ways:

- Double-click the field name;
- Drag the field name from the table onto the top line of the query grid;
- Click the Down arrow in the Field cell in the query grid to display a list of field names from which you can select.

- Double-click **Surname, Initial**, **Address1**, **Round**, **HolsBegin** and **HolsEnd** in turn to place them in the query grid.

NOTE: If you place a wrong field by mistake, move the cursor over the top margin of the column (the column selector) until it changes to a downward pointing arrow, click to select the column and press the **Delete** key to delete it. You can move a column by dragging the column selector once the column is selected.

Setting the criteria

We only want to see the customers for Round 1.

- In the Criteria row, type *1* in the column for **Round**. The query grid now appears as shown:

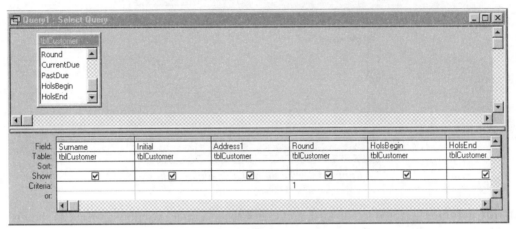

Figure 4.4: Selecting fields and setting criteria

Running the query

- Click the **Run** button on the toolbar. The query results appear:

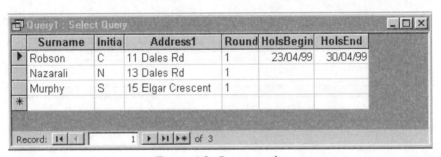

Figure 4.5: Query results

Sorting records and hiding fields

You can control certain aspects of the query result table, such as the sort order and which fields you want to see. For example you may want the results displayed in alphabetical order of surname, and you may not want the Round field displayed since you know all these customers are on Round 1.

- Click the **Design View** tool to return to Design view.

- In the **Surname** column, click in the **Sort** row and select **Ascending** from the drop-down list.

- In the **Round** column, click the check box in the **Show** row to deselect it.

- Run the query again. You can adjust the column widths of the resultant query so that the results appear as follows:

	Surname	Initial	Address1	HolsBegin	HolsEnd
▶	Murphy	S	15 Elgar Crescent		
	Nazarali	N	13 Dales Rd		
	Robson	C	11 Dales Rd	23/04/99	30/04/99
✳					

*Figure 4.6: Query results after sorting on **Surname** and hiding **Round** field*

- Save the query, naming it *qryRound1*.

Setting special criteria

If you want to look for all records with a constant value in a particular column, you simply type the value in the appropriate column, as you did when searching for all customers on Round 1. You can also:

- Look for all records with a blank in a particular field;
- Look for records that satisfy a range of values;
- Use expressions involving Visual Basic functions such as **Date()**.

Looking for blanks

Suppose you want to look for all customers who have entries in the **HolsBegin** field.

- Return to Design view.

- Delete the criteria from the **Round** field so that we have a few more records to choose from, and check its Show box to select it.

- In the criteria for **HolsBegin**, type *Is not null* as shown below:

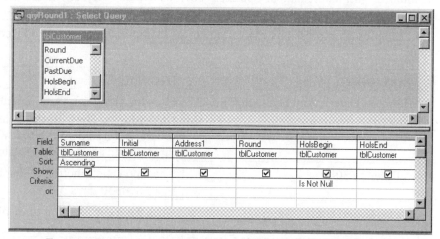

*Figure 4.7: Searching for records with a non-blank **HolsBegin** field*

- Run the query. This time you should see only the records for Newbourne and Robson.

Looking for a range of values

Now supposing you want to find all customers whose holidays begin on or after April 27th.

- Return to Design view.

- Delete the criteria **Is Not Null** in the **HolsBegin** field and type *>=27/04/99* instead.

- Run the query, and this time you should see only the record for Newbourne.

You can include the words 'and' and 'or' in your query criteria. For example if you want to find all customers whose **PastDue** amount is between £10 and £20 inclusive, you could add the **PastDue** field to the list of selected fields by dragging it onto the query grid, and type *>=10 and <=20* as the criteria in the **PastDue** field, as shown below. (You can also type *Between 10 and 20* for the criteria. This is a more convenient format, especially for dates.)

Field:	Surname	Initial	Address1	Round	HolsBegin	HolsEnd	PastDue	
Table:	tblCustomer	tblCustomer	tblCustomer	tblCustomer	tblCustomer	tblCustomer	tblCustomer	
Sort:	Ascending							
Show:	☑	☑	☑	☑	☑	☑	☑	
Criteria:							>=10 And <=20	
or:								

Figure 4.8: Looking for a range of values in a field

Using wildcards

Suppose you wanted to find all the customers living in Dales Road.

- Type **Dales** in the criteria for **Address1**. (* is known as a *wildcard* character. You can look up other wildcard characters in the Access Help system.)

- If you want to check the result of this query, first delete any other criteria you may have set. The records for Nazarali and Robson should be displayed.

Using a function to find records

Date functions combined with mathematical operators such as + and - are sometimes useful to find, for example, all dates more than 30 days ago.

The following are examples of expressions that calculate or manipulate dates, reproduced from the MS Access Help system.

Field	Expression	Description
RequiredDate	Between Date( ) And DateAdd("m", 3, Date( ))	Uses the Between...And operator and the DateAdd and Date functions to display orders required between today's date and three months from today's date.
OrderDate	< Date( ) - 30	Uses the Date function to display orders more than 30 days old.
OrderDate	Year([OrderDate]) = 1996	Uses the Year function to display orders with order dates in 1996.
OrderDate	DatePart("q", [OrderDate]) = 4	Uses the DatePart function to display orders for the fourth calendar quarter.
OrderDate	DateSerial(Year([OrderDate]), Month([OrderDate])+1, 1)-1	Uses the DateSerial, Year, and Month functions to display orders for the last day of each month.
OrderDate	Year([OrderDate]) = Year(Now()) And Month([OrderDate]) = Month(Now())	Uses the Year and Month functions and the And operator to display orders for the current year and month.

Table 4.1: Date functions used in criteria

AND and OR queries

Select queries can include multiple criteria to find records. If you need to use more than one criterion in the same field, you can separate the criteria with the word *and*. If the criteria are in different fields, enter each one in the appropriate column.

To use an OR query, put the criteria on different rows. The query below finds all customers who live in Dales Road or Elgar Crescent. The criteria are entered on two separate rows as *Like "*Dales*", Like "*Elgar*"*. Note that the use of the wildcard * allows you to find all records containing the word **Dales** or **Elgar**.

Field:	Surname	Initial	Address1	Round	HolsBegin	HolsEnd	PastDue	
Table:	tblCustomer	tblCustomer	tblCustomer	tblCustomer	tblCustomer	tblCustomer	tblCustomer	
Sort:	Ascending							
Show:	☑	☑	☑	☑	☑	☑	☑	
Criteria:			Like "*Dales*"					
or:			Like "*Elgar*"					

Figure 4.9: Using OR in query criteria

The two parts of the OR do not necessarily have to be in the same column – you could, for example, look for all customers who either live in Dales Road OR are on Round 1, by putting the criteria on different rows in the appropriate columns.

Allowing the end-user to enter criteria

It is often useful when you are developing a customised application to be able to save a query but let the user type in the criteria when the query is run. For example, you could allow the user to specify the Round number in the original query instead of having the query always find customers in Round 1.

There are two ways of doing this.

Method 1: Use a form to enter query criteria

Open a dialogue box (see Task 7.8 in chapter 7) and ask the user to specify criteria. Suppose for example you create a dialogue box named **fdlgEnterRound** which asks the user to enter the Round number in a text box named **RoundNumber**. In the query, you would enter *Forms![fdlgEnterRound].[RoundNumber]* in the Criteria row of the Round column.

(The Help system explains this further, with examples. Type *Entering Criteria* and then select **Use a form to enter report criteria**. (In Access 97, type *Dialog* and then select **Using to prompt for criteria**.)

Method 2: Enter a prompt to the user in the Criteria row of the query.

The prompt must be enclosed in square brackets. This method is quicker to implement but does not give you the flexibility of using a dialogue box, in which you can use list boxes or option groups to limit the user's entries and thus eliminate the possibility of an invalid entry (e.g. a non-existent Round 4).

You can try this method now, as shown below:

- In Design view, delete any existing criteria and in the **Criteria** row of the **Round** column type *[Please enter Round number:]*. Make sure **Show** is selected in this column.

- Press the **Run** button to run the query. The message you typed is displayed asking the user to enter the Round number:

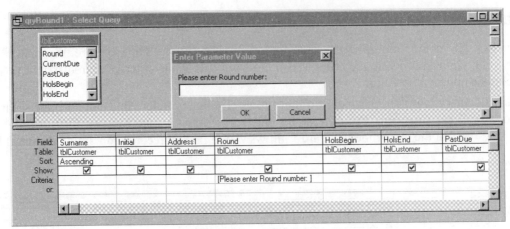

Figure 4.10: Allowing the user to specify criteria

- Enter *1* and press **OK**. The query finds all customers on Round 1.

Saving a query with a different name

- From the menu select **File, Save As/Export** to leave the original **Round1** query unchanged. Save the new query as *qryRound*.

- Close the query to return to the database window.

Task 4.2: Query linked tables and create a form from a query

Queries can be used to bring together fields from several related tables. We will use a query to display newspaper deliveries to a customer.

- Make sure **Queries, Create query in design view** is selected in the Database window and then click **New**.

- Select Design View and click **OK**.

- In the Show Table dialogue box, select and add each table in turn. (You can hold down the **Shift** key while you select the bottom table to select all three tables and add them in one operation.)

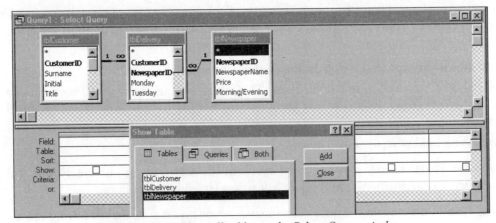

Figure 4.11: Adding all tables to the Select Query window

- Click **Close** in the Show Table dialogue box.

TblDelivery is the table that links the other two tables together. Suppose we want to display for a particular customer, their Surname, Initial and Title, and for each newspaper they have delivered, the newspaper name and whether it is a morning or evening paper. It makes no difference whether you select **CustomerID** and **NewspaperID** from **tblDelivery** or from **tblCustomer** and **tblNewspaper** respectively. (Which records appear when you run the query depends on the Join type, as described in the note below.) **Surname** and **Initial** will be selected from **tblCustomer** and **NewspaperName** and **Morning/Evening** from **tblNewspaper**.

NOTE: There are different types of Join that can be used in a query. If you double-click the line between **tblCustomer** and **tblDelivery**, you will see that the default type of Join is **Only include rows where the joined fields from both tables are equal**. This means that if you had customers on file who have no deliveries, they would not be listed when the query was run, which is probably what you want in this case and in most other cases.

- Double-click **CustomerID** in the **tblDelivery** table (not **tblCustomer**) to add it to the query grid.

- Because we used the Lookup wizard to define the field for **CustomerID** when the table structure was created in Chapter 2, the Surname rather than the ID number will automatically be displayed. Just run the query as it is now to convince yourself of this fact, and then return to the Design window.

- Double-click **Initial** and **Title** on **tblCustomer**, and **NewspaperName** and **Morning/Evening** on **tblNewspaper**.

- Run the query. Results are displayed as follows (they may be in a different order):

Customer ID	Initial	Title	NewspaperName	Morning/Evening
Carter	J	Mrs	Daily Telegraph	M
Carter	J	Mrs	Sunday Times	M
Brindley	J	Mr	Guardian	M
Brindley	J	Mr	Observer	M
Robson	C	Mr	Mercury	M
Robson	C	Mr	Sunday Times	M
Newbourne	S	Miss	Guardian	M
Newbourne	S	Miss	Mercury	M
Murphy	S	Mrs	Guardian	M
Murphy	S	Mrs	Evening Star	E

Figure 4.12: Query combining fields from different tables

Now suppose we want to display only the records for Carter. Notice that the heading at the top of the first column is **CustomerID** even though surnames are displayed. You won't be able to put the criteria "Carter" in the first column because this is an AutoNumber field, in spite of the fact that the Surname is displayed.

- Return to Design view.

- Drag **Surname** from **tblCustomer** on to the first column of the query grid. This automatically inserts a new column to the left of column 1.

- Type the criteria *Carter* in the **Surname** column.

- Uncheck the **Show** box in the **CustomerID** column, as shown below.

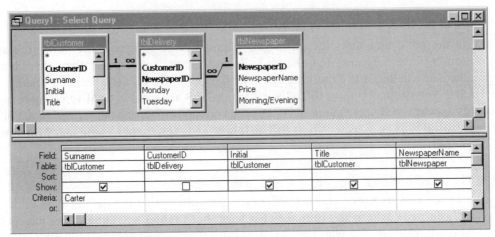

Figure 4.13: Setting the Surname criteria

- Run the query.

- Save the query as *qryDelivery* and close it to return to the Database window.

Using the Simple Query Wizard

The simple Query Wizard can be used when you do not need to enter any criteria.

- In the Database window, make sure **Queries, Create query by using wizard** is selected and click **New**.

- This time we will use the Simple Query Wizard to create the basic query, which we can then edit. Select **Simple Query Wizard** and click **OK**.

- In the next window, select **Table: tblCustomer** in the **Tables/Queries** box and click the double arrow between the list boxes to transfer all the fields from the **Available Fields** to the **Selected fields** list boxes. Click **Next**.

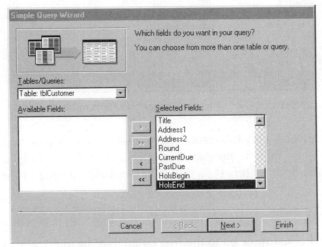

Figure 4.14: Using the Simple Query Wizard

- On the next screen, make sure **Detail (shows every field of every record)** is selected, and click **Next**.

- Name the query *qryCustomer* and click **Finish**.

- The records appear in Datasheet view. (Column widths have been adjusted in the figure below.)

	CustomerID	Surname	Initia	Title	Address1	Address2	Round	Current[	PastDue	HolsBegin	HolsEnd
▶	2	Robson	C	Mr	11 Dales Rd	Broughton	1	£8.50	£17.00	23/04/99	30/04/99
	3	Brindley	J	Mr	1 Chestnut Ave	Broughton	3	£6.00	£12.00		
	4	Nazarali	N	Mr	13 Dales Rd	Broughton	1	£5.00	£25.00		
	5	Newbourne	S	Miss	Mill Hse, Mill La	Broughton	2	£7.50	£0.00	27/04/99	03/04/99
	6	Carter	J	Mrs	Bridge Hse, Mill La	Broughton	2	£4.20	£8.40		
	8	Murphy	S	Mrs	15 Elgar Crescent	Broughton	1	£0.00	£0.00		
*	AutoNumber)			Mr				£0.00	£0.00		

Record: I◄ ◄ [1] ► ►I ►* of 6

Figure 4.15: Query results

Creating calculated fields with a query

You can add extra fields to a query to show values calculated from other fields. In the next example we will add a field to *qryCustomer* that will calculate the total amount that each customer owes by adding together the **PastDue** and the **CurrentDue** amounts.

- Return to Design View.

- Scroll along the query grid until you can see a blank column. In the top row type as shown below
  [CurrentDue] + [PastDue]

- As soon as you press **Enter** or tab out of the column, Access adds **Expr1:** as the field name to be used for your calculation. (Widen the column if necessary so that you can see the whole expression.)

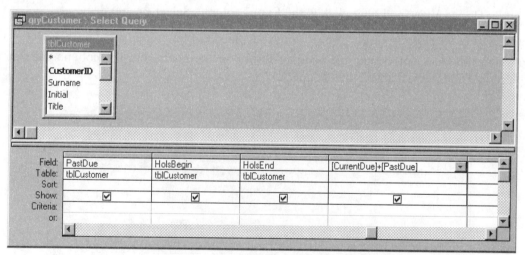

Figure 4.16: Adding a calculated field

- Click either the **Run** button or the **View** button to see the query in Datasheet view. You'll see the new column headed **Expr1** appear after **HolsEnd**. You may need to scroll along to see it.

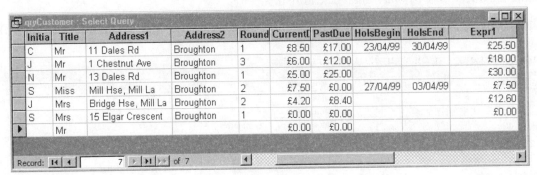

Figure 4.17: Datasheet view

Moving columns

We'll move the new column so that it appears before the **HolsBegin** field.

- Place the pointer in the top margin above the new calculated column so that it appears as a down arrow, and click to select the column.

- Now click again in the same place, and the pointer changes to an upward pointing arrow. Drag the boundary to between **PastDue** and **HolsBegin**.

Changing a column caption

You can change the caption at the head of the column in either of two ways:

- by changing the **Caption** property of the field, or
- by changing the name in the Design grid.

We'll change the caption of the **Expr1** field to **TotalDue** using the first method.

- Return to Design View, and right-click in the **Expr1** column. Select **Properties**.

- The Properties sheet is displayed. Type *TotalDue* in the **Caption** property and press **Enter**.

  (Note that this does not change the heading **Expr1** in the query, but the column caption will be changed to **TotalDue** when you run the query.)

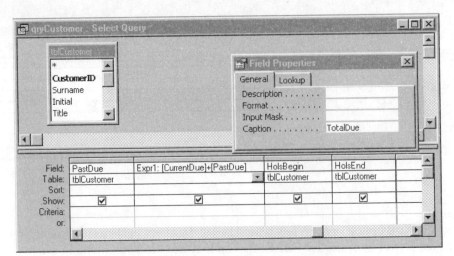

Figure 4.18: Changing the column caption

- Close the Field Properties box.

  We'll use the second method to change the caption of the **CustomerID** column to *ID*.

- In Design View, place the cursor to the left of the field name CustomerID and type *ID:* (Note: You must type the colon between **ID:CustomerID**).

- Run the query.

- Right-click the **Address2** column header and click **Hide Columns**. (Note: To restore a column, select **Format, Unhide Columns**.)

- The query appears as shown below, after adjusting column widths.

ID	Surname	Initial	Title	Address1	Round	CurrentD	PastDue	TotalDue	HolsBegin	HolsEnd
2	Robson	C	Mr	11 Dales Rd	1	£8.50	£17.00	£25.50	23/04/99	30/04/99
3	Brindley	J	Mr	1 Chestnut Ave	3	£6.00	£12.00	£18.00		
4	Nazarali	N	Mr	13 Dales Rd	1	£5.00	£25.00	£30.00		
5	Newbourne	S	Mis	Mill Hse, Mill La	2	£7.50	£0.00	£7.50	27/04/99	30/04/99
6	Carter	J	Mrs	Bridge Hse, Mill La	2	£4.20	£8.40	£12.60		
8	Murphy	S	Mrs	15 Elgar Crescent	1	£0.00	£0.00	£0.00		

Figure 4.19: Column captions have been changed and a column hidden

- Save **qryCustomer** and close the query.

You can look up more detail on renaming fields and the effects of doing this if you need to, by asking the Office Assistant. Type *How do I change the field name in a query?* and the paperclip will be pleased to instruct you. (*In Access 7, use* **Help, Answer Wizard**.)

Creating a form from a query

Queries are often used as the basis for a form. This means for example that fields from two or more separate tables can first be combined using a multi-table query, and then a form using all the fields can be created and used for data entry. The data will automatically be stored in the correct table. You can also use a query to display calculated fields, change captions, sort on a particular field etc and then create a form which reflects these operations.

For these reasons, you should consider basing *all* your forms on queries rather than on tables, as you will have much more control over what you can put on the form. You will be able to amend your forms more easily too if you later decide you need to display a calculated field.

We'll create a customer form based on the query **qryCustomer** that we have just created.

- In the Database window, click **Forms, Create form by using wizard** and click **New**.

- In the New Form dialogue box, select **AutoForm: Columnar**. Select **qryCustomer** as the **Table or query where the object's data comes from**, and click **OK**.

- The new form is automatically created and appears as shown below:

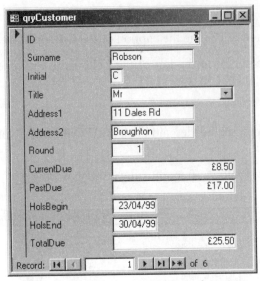

Figure 4.20: A form created from the query

Note that:

- The label for the **CustomerID** field appears as **ID** because the field was renamed in the query;

- In Access 97 the label for the **TotalDue** field remains as **Expr1** although we gave the field a new **Caption** property. You can manually edit the label.

- **TotalDue** (or **Expr1**) is based on an expression and cannot be edited.

- (Access 97 only.) In the original table **tblCustomer**, the **Title** field used the Lookup wizard to create a drop- down list. Forms based on **tblCustomer** will display the field as a drop-down list but a form based on a query will not. You could replace the existing **Title** field on this form with a drop-down list if you needed to.

- The form caption by default shows the source of the form, **qryCustomer**. You can customise this by altering the form's **Caption** property in Design view.

• Add a new record for a customer named Miss J.Patel, 3 Elgar Crescent, Broughton, Round 1, with **CurrentDue** of £5.00 and **PastDue** of £3.75. You'll notice that **TotalDue** is calculated automatically as soon as you tab out of the **PastDue** field.

• Save your form as *frmCustomerDues* and close it to return to the Database window.

In Chapter 5 we'll look at other types of query, and in Chapter 6 we'll look at more advanced form design features.

Chapter 5 – Advanced Queries

Introduction

In this chapter we'll be looking at some of the more advanced capabilities of queries and also looking at different types of query such as Update, Make-Table, Append and Delete queries. Queries are useful for performing many different types of data processing such as summarising and updating.

We'll start by creating a Totals query to find out how many of each newspaper are needed on a particular morning of the week so that the newsagent knows how many to order from the wholesaler.

Before we do, we need a few more records on our database.

- Open the Customer form **frmCustomerMain** and add the following delivery records to the subform:

Robson:	Sun (SUN)	Mon-Sat
Nazarali:	Guardian (GU), Mercury (MERC)	Mon-Sat
Carter:	Sun, Mercury	Mon-Sat
Patel:	Sun, Mercury	Mon-Sat

  Use the navigation buttons < > to show each record. You can also check boxes by pressing **Spacebar**.

- Close the form to return to the Database window.

Task 5.1: Create a Totals query to find the total number of each newspaper delivered on Monday.

Adding some new test data

You need to make sure that there is at least one customer who has holiday dates that are now in the past, one who has holiday dates in the future, and one who is currently on holiday. Then you can be sure that the query criteria are working properly.

- Open **tblCustomer** and edit the holiday dates so that:

  Robson and Newbourne have holiday dates that are in the past;

  Brindley has holiday dates in the future;

  Patel is currently on holiday.

- Close the table.

Creating a totals query

- In the Database window, click **Queries, Create query in Design view** and click **New**.

- In the next window, select **Design View** and click **OK**.

- In the Show Table window, add **tblCustomer**, **tblDelivery** and **tblNewspaper** and then click **Close**.

- Place fields and criteria onto the query grid as shown below, making sure the ID fields are from the correct table. (Where possible, fields should be taken from the Link table rather than the Parent table, i.e. take the foreign key.) The criteria are set to find all customers who have no dates recorded, whose holiday start date is in the future, or whose holiday end date is in the past. In each of these cases we only want to find Monday deliveries.

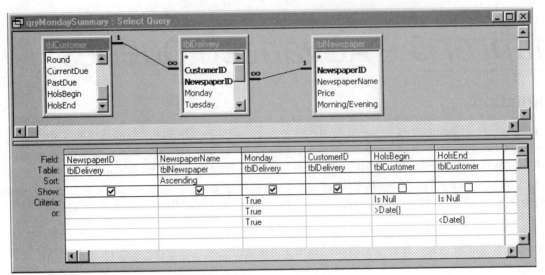

Figure 5.1: First stages of the query

- Run the query to see what you've achieved so far. It should look like the figure below.

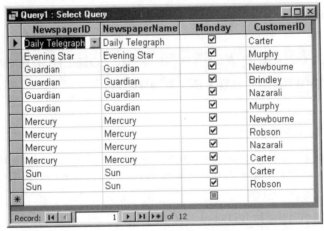

Figure 5.2: Query results

We want the query to count up the number of each newspaper and present us with a summary.

- Return to Design view. With the pointer in the first column, click the **Totals** button. A new **Total** row appears in the query grid. Σ

- From the drop-down list in the **Total** row select **Count**. **Count** now replaces **Group by** in the first column.

- Type in a new field name *Quantity* followed by a colon, as shown in the figure below.

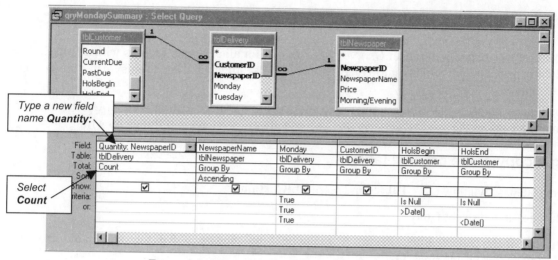

*Figure 5.3: Using the summary operator **Count** in a query*

- Run the query again. It should appear as shown below.

Quantity	NewspaperName	Monday	Customer ID
1	Daily Telegraph	☑	Carter
1	Evening Star	☑	Murphy
1	Guardian	☑	Brindley
1	Guardian	☑	Nazarali
1	Guardian	☑	Newbourne
1	Guardian	☑	Murphy
1	Mercury	☑	Robson
1	Mercury	☑	Nazarali
1	Mercury	☑	Newbourne
1	Mercury	☑	Carter
1	Sun	☑	Robson
1	Sun	☑	Carter

Figure 5.4: Query results

Note that you cannot make Access add up the number of each newspaper without first removing the fields **CustomerID**, **HolsBegin** and **HolsEnd** from the query grid. However by doing that, you would not be able to specify the necessary holiday criteria, and you will get the following results:

Quantity	NewspaperName	Monday
1	Daily Telegraph	☑
1	Evening Star	☑
4	Guardian	☑
5	Mercury	☑
3	Sun	☑

Figure 5.5: Summary query (ignoring holiday absences)

The solution is to leave the query in its current state (Figure 5.3) and use it to produce a summary report. This will be done in Chapter 6.

- Save the query as *qryMondaySummary*, and close it.

Task 5.2: Create and run an Update query

In this exercise we are going to run an *Update query* to look for all customer records with a **HolsEnd** date that is already past, and put a blank into **HolsBegin** and **HolsEnd** since these holiday dates are no longer of interest to us.

An Update query changes the values in the table, and so before experimenting with an Update query it is wise to make a copy of the original table so that you can always start again if things go wrong.

Making a copy of the original table

- In the Database window click **Tables** and select **tblCustomer**.

- Right-click it and select **Copy**.

- From the menu select **Edit, Paste**. A dialogue box appears. Give the new table the name *tblCustomerBackup* and press **OK**.

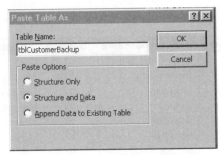

Figure 5.6: Making a copy of a table

Checking the test data

Once again you need to make sure that there is at least one customer who has holiday dates that are now in the past, one who has holiday dates in the future, and one who is currently on holiday. Then you can be sure that the Update query is working properly.

- Open **tblCustomer** and ensure that the holiday dates are such that:

    Robson and Newbourne have holiday dates that are in the past;

    Brindley has holiday dates in the future;

    Patel is currently on holiday.

- Close the table.

Creating an update query

- In the Database window click **Queries, Create query in Design view** and click **New**.

- Select **Design View** in the next dialogue box and click **OK**.

- In the Show Table dialogue box, add **tblCustomer** and click **Close**.

- Add **CustomerID**, **Surname**, **HolsBegin** and **HolsEnd** to the Query grid.

- From the menu bar select **Query**, **Update Query**. An extra row appears in the query grid, in which you will specify which fields are to be updated, and what the new values will be.

- Enter *Null* in the **Update To** row under **HolsBegin** and **HolsEnd**.

- Enter *<Date()* in the **Criteria** row under **HolsEnd**. Your screen should look like the one below:

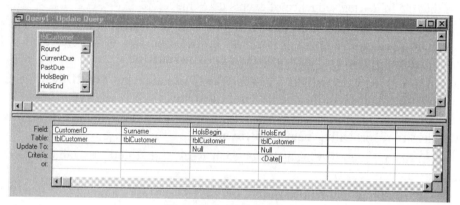

Figure 5.7: Update query

- Click the **Run** button. Access displays a warning message:

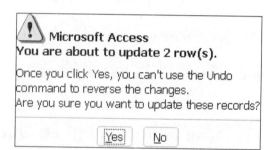

Figure 5.8: Warning message before running an Update Query

- Click **Yes**. Nothing appears to happen.

- Click the **View** button to view the query in Datasheet view. You will see the following:

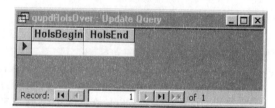

Figure 5.9: Update query in Datasheet view

This is not very informative! We need to look at the actual table **tblCustomer**.

- Save and close the query, naming it *qupdHolsOver*.

- Open the table **tblCustomer** and verify that the holiday dates for Robson and Newbourne have been deleted, then close the table.

Using queries to process customer payments

Before trying the next task, let's look at a possible system that could be used by our Newsagents for printing invoices, recording payments and updating customer records. Obviously, if you are planning to tackle a Newsagent's database for your project, you would need to find out how the Accounts are done, if financial transactions are to form part of the project.

We will assume that the following sequence of events takes place:

1. At the end of each week, the **CurrentDue** amount is calculated from this week's newspaper deliveries. (This can be done by running specially designed queries as demonstrated in Task 5.3; the queries will be named **qmakDueThisWeek** and **qupdCurrentDue**.)

2. A query is run to add the **CurrentDue** and **PastDue** to calculate the **TotalDue**. (We performed this task in the last chapter and saved the query as **qryCustomer**.)

3. Customer invoices are produced and printed from this query. (We'll look at reports in the next chapter. The invoice report will be named **rptInvoices**.)

4. Customer payments are recorded each day or each week and stored in a table named **tblPayment** (still to be created – see Task 5.4).

5. An Update query (which will be named **qupdCurrentToZero**) is run to add **CurrentDue** to **PastDue** and set the **CurrentDue** back to zero ready for the coming week.

6. An Update query (which will be called **qupdPostPayment**) is run once a week to subtract each customer's payment from their **PastDue** amount.

7. An Append query (which will be named **qappPayment**) is run to add the week's payments to an archive table.

8. A Delete query (which will be named **qdelPayment**) is run to delete all the week's payments from the **Payment** table.

We'll go through the steps outlined above to illustrate the use of the different types of query that you can perform in Access.

Task 5.3: Use summary, make-table and update queries to calculate this week's amount due

When we originally created the table **tblCustomer** to hold customer details, we cheated by entering data for **CurrentDue** and **PastDue**. In the more realistic system which we will now implement, these values will be calculated automatically and the user will not be allowed to alter the calculated values directly. In this task we will use different types of query to calculate the week's invoices. The queries to be created in this task are:

Query name	Query type	Purpose
QryDueThisWeek	Summary query	Calculate the total amount due and place in a new field named **DueThisWeek** in the resulting query object. (This query will not be used in the final system, and is simply used as a 'stepping stone' to help you to understand the more complex Make-table query created in the next step.)
QmakDueThisWeek	Make-Table query	Create a new table named **tblDueThisWeek** which includes the field **DueThisWeek** as calculated above. (This query will be created by editing the above query **qryDueThisWeek**.)
QupdCurrentDue	Update query	Update the values (currently zero) in the **CurrentDue** field of **tblCustomer** from the values in the field **DueThisWeek** in **tblDueThisWeek**.

Summary query

We will use a calculation and a summary operator **Sum** in a query to calculate this week's payment.

- From the database window start a new query, select **Design** as the query type and add **tblCustomer**, **tblDelivery** and **tblNewspaper** to the query window. (You can hold down the **Ctrl** key while you select the tables.) Close the Show Table dialogue box.

- Place **CustomerID** from **tblDelivery** and **Surname** from **tblCustomer** on the query grid.

- Place **NewspaperID** from **tblDelivery** on the query grid. (Be sure to place from the correct table.)

- In the next field type the following exactly as shown:

DueThisWeek: -([Monday]+[Tuesday]+[Wednesday]+[Thursday]+[Friday]+[Saturday]+[Sunday]) *[Price]

This works because Yes/No fields take the value -1 when True and 0 when False. So we are adding all the Monday to Sunday Boolean values, changing the sign by putting a minus sign in front of the bracket, and then multiplying the sum by the price of the newspaper.

> **NOTE:** You can zoom in on an expression by clicking in it and pressing **Shift-F2**.

- With the pointer in the column which you have named **DueThisWeek**, click the **Totals** button on the toolbar.

- Select **Sum** in the **Group By** drop-down list.

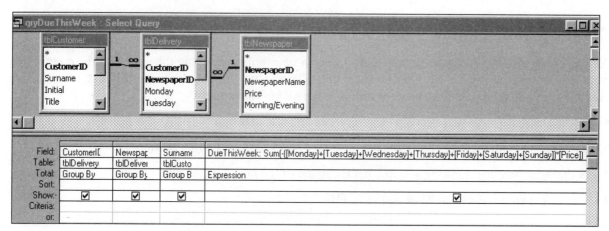

Figure 5.10: Calculating the weekly amount due

- Run the query.

Customer ID	NewspaperID	Surname	DueThisWeek
Robson	Mercury	Robson	£1.05
Robson	Sunday Times	Robson	£1.00
Robson	Sun	Robson	£1.80
Brindley	Guardian	Brindley	£2.70
Brindley	Observer	Brindley	£1.00
Nazarali	Guardian	Nazarali	£2.70
Nazarali	Mercury	Nazarali	£2.10
Newbourne	Guardian	Newbourne	£2.70
Newbourne	Mercury	Newbourne	£2.10
Carter	Daily Telegraph	Carter	£2.70
Carter	Mercury	Carter	£2.10
Carter	Sunday Times	Carter	£1.00
Carter	Sun	Carter	£1.80
Murphy	Guardian	Murphy	£2.70
Murphy	Evening Star	Murphy	£2.40
Patel	Mercury	Patel	£2.10
Patel	Sun	Patel	£1.80

Figure 5.11: Query results

You will notice that Access does not appear to have summed the amounts due for each customer, although we asked it to do so. This is because we included the **NewspaperID** field, so the sum is calculated for each separate newspaper. In order to get the totals for each customer, the field **NewspaperID** must be removed from the query grid. This is a common error when designing summary queries.

- Return to design view and delete the **NewspaperID** column by clicking in its top margin and pressing the **Delete** key.

- Run the query again. This time the results should be what you want, as shown below.

Customer ID	Surname	DueThisWeek
Robson	Robson	£3.85
Brindley	Brindley	£3.70
Nazarali	Nazarali	£4.80
Newbourne	Newbourne	£4.80
Carter	Carter	£7.60
Murphy	Murphy	£5.10
Patel	Patel	£3.90

Figure 5.12: Totals for each customer

- Save this query as *qryDueThisWeek* and close it.

Creating and running a Make-Table query

We can create a *Make-Table query* to actually create a new table containing the results of the query. This table can in turn be used in an Update query to update values in, for example, **tblCustomer**. In this example we will edit *qryDueThisWeek* to turn it into a Make-Table query.

- In the Database window select *qryDueThisWeek* and click **Design**.

- The Query window opens. From the menu select **Query**, **Make-Table Query**.

- A dialogue box opens asking you to enter the name of the new table.

- Enter the name *tblDueThisWeek* and click **OK**.

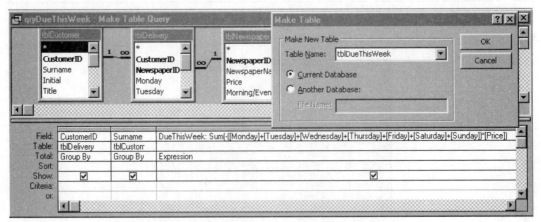

Figure 5.13: Entering a table name in the Make-Table query

- Run the query. You will see a warning message:

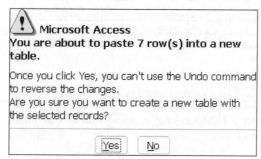

Figure 5.14: Warning message when running the Make-Table query

- Click **Yes**. Nothing appears to happen, but switch to Datasheet view and you will see the new table, which will look the same as Figure 5.12.

- From the menu select **File, Save As/Export** and save the query as *qmakDueThisWeek*.

- Close the query.

Updating one table from another

The next stage is to use the **DueThisWeek** values in the table we have just created to replace the **CurrentDue** field in **tblCustomer**.

- In the Database window make sure **Queries, Create query in Design view** is selected and click **New**. Select **Design View** in the next window.

- Add **tblCustomer** and **tblDueThisWeek** to the query window. Close the Show Table dialogue box.

- Add **CustomerID, Surname** and **CurrentDue** from **tblCustomer** to the query grid.

- Run the query now, just to see what values are in the **CurrentDue** field before updating. They should be as follows:

CustomerID	Surname	CurrentDue
2	Robson	£8.50
3	Brindley	£6.00
4	Nazarali	£5.00
5	Newbourne	£7.50
6	Carter	£4.20
8	Murphy	£0.00
9	Patel	£5.00
(AutoNumber)		

Figure 5.15: CurrentDue before Update

- Return to Design view and from the menu select **Query, Update Query**. An extra **Update To** row appears in the Query grid.

- In the **CurrentDue** column type *tblDueThisWeek.[DueThisWeek]* in the **Update To** row.

NOTE: You don't need to type the square brackets round the table name because it contains no spaces, but Access will automatically insert the square brackets for you when you press Enter.

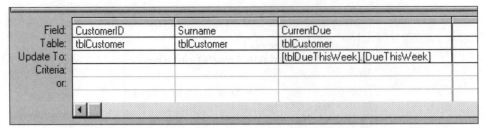

*Figure 5.16: Specifying the new value of **CurrentDue***

- Run the query. You will see a warning message that you are about to update 7 rows – click **Yes** to go ahead with the update. Nothing much appears to happen but the **CurrentDue** fields have been updated.

- Press **F11** to display the Database window. Click the **Tables** tab and open **tblCustomer**. You'll see the updated values in **CurrentDue**.

	CustomerID	Surname	Initia	Title	Address1	Address2	Round	Currentl	PastDue	HolsBegin	HolsEnd
	2	Robson	C	Mr	11 Dales Rd	Broughton	1	£3.85	£17.00	01/01/99	08/01/99
	3	Brindley	J	Mr	1 Chestnut Ave	Broughton	3	£3.70	£12.00	12/12/00	25/12/00
	4	Nazarali	N	Mr	13 Dales Rd	Broughton	1	£4.80	£25.00		
	5	Newbourne	S	Miss	Mill Hse, Mill La	Broughton	2	£4.80	£0.00	01/02/99	28/02/99
	6	Carter	J	Mrs	Bridge Hse, Mill La	Broughton	2	£7.60	£8.40		
	8	Murphy	S	Mrs	15 Elgar Crescent	Broughton	1	£5.10	£0.00		
	9	Patel	J	Miss	3 Elgar Crescent	Broughton	1	£3.90	£3.75	01/01/99	31/12/99
▶	AutoNumber)			Mr			0	£0.00	£0.00		

Figure 5.17: CurrentDue values have been updated.

- Close the table. Save the query as *qupdCurrentDue* and close it.

The **TotalDue** amount can now be calculated by running the query **qryCustomer** created in the last chapter. (You don't need to do this now!) Invoices will be printed using a report based on **tblCustomer**, as described in the next chapter.

Task 5.4: Create tables and queries to handle customer payments

In this task we will first create two tables of identical structure which will hold customer payment details. One table (**tblPayment**) will hold details of this week's customer payments. The second table (**tblArchivePayment**) will be used as an *archive* table, and each week after updating the customer records, payments will be appended to this table and then deleted from **tblPayment**.

We will start by creating **tblPayment**.

- In the Database window select **Tables, Create table in Design view** and click **New**.

- Select **Design View** in the next window.

- Add the following fields:

Field name	Data type
CustomerID	Number (Long Integer)
PaymentAmount	Currency
PaymentDate	Date/Time

- You have to define the key field or fields. In this case the key will consist of the two fields **CustomerID** and **PaymentDate**. This assumes that no customer will make more than one payment on the same date. Select the row for **CustomerID** by clicking in the left hand margin next to the field name, and then hold down the **Ctrl** key while you select the row for **PaymentDate**. Then click the **Primary Key** button on the toolbar.

- Close the table, saving it as *tblPayment*.

Making a copy of a table structure

- Right-click **tblPayment** in the Database window and select **Copy**.

- From the menu select **Edit, Paste**. A dialogue box appears.

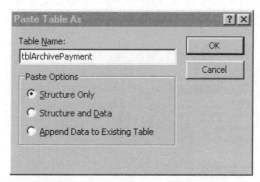

Figure 5.18: Copying a table structure

- Type the name *tblArchivePayment*. We only want to copy the structure, although since there is as yet no data in the table it makes no difference which of the first two options we choose. Choose one of them and click **OK**.

Adding data to the Payment table

- Open **tblPayment** and add data for Newbourne, Robson and Murphy, using the CustomerIDs that are stored in your version of **tblCustomer**, which may be different from those shown below.

In the data set being used here, these are the CustomerIDs of Newbourne, Robson and Murphy. If your ID numbers are different, use the ones for the same customers instead of the ones shown.

CustomerID		PaymentAmount	PaymentDate
(Newbourne)	5	£25.00	12/05/99
(Robson)	2	£19.80	13/05/99
(Murphy)	8	£5.10	13/05/99
	0	£0.00	

*Figure 5.19: Payments to be entered in **tblPayment***

Posting customer payments

This will be done in four steps:

1. Run an update query named **qupdCurrentToZero** to add **CurrentDue** to **PastDue** and set **CurrentDue** back to zero on the Customer table.

2. Run a second update query named **qupdPostPayment** to subtract each customer's payment from their **PastDue** amount.

3. Append the records from the Payments file **tblPayment** to the archive file **tblArchivePayment**.

4. Delete all the records from **tblPayments** to leave the file empty for the next week's payments.

The first two steps involve no new techniques but for the sake of completeness we will go through all the steps.

To create the query **qupdCurrentToZero**:

- Start a new query in Design view and add **tblCustomer** to the query window.

- Select **Query, Update Query** from the menu bar.

- Add the two fields **CurrentDue** and **PastDue** to the query grid.

- Make entries in the **Update To** row as shown below, inserting *0* in the **CurrentDue** column and *[CurrentDue]+[PastDue]* in the **PastDue** column.

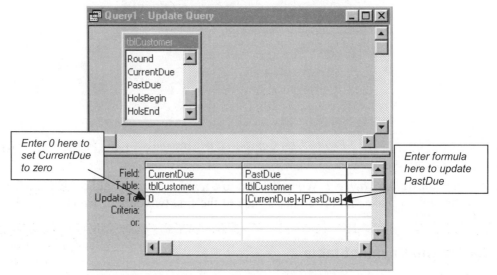

*Figure 5.20: Creating the query **qupdCurrentToZero***

- Run the query and check that the table **tblCustomer** has been correctly updated as shown below. (You can alter the values manually in **tblCustomer** if you have made any errors, to make **CurrentDue** and **PastDue** correspond to the values shown.)

	CustomerID	Surname	Initial	Title	Address1	Address2	Round	CurrentDue	PastDue	HolsBegin	HolsEnd
▶	2	Robson	C	Mr	11 Dales Rd	Broughton	1	£0.00	£20.85	01/01/99	08/01/99
	3	Brindley	J	Mr	1 Chestnut Ave	Broughton	3	£0.00	£15.70	12/12/00	25/12/00
	4	Nazarali	N	Mr	13 Dales Rd	Broughton	1	£0.00	£29.80		
	5	Newbourne	S	Mis	Mill Hse, Mill La	Broughton	2	£0.00	£4.80	01/02/99	28/02/99
	6	Carter	J	Mrs	Bridge Hse, Mill La	Broughton	2	£0.00	£16.00		
	8	Murphy	S	Mrs	15 Elgar Crescent	Broughton	1	£0.00	£5.10		
	9	Patel	J	Mis	3 Elgar Crescent	Broughton	1	£0.00	£7.65	01/01/99	31/12/99
*	(AutoNumber)			Mr			0	£0.00	£0.00		

Figure 5.21: The updated amounts due

- Save the query as *qupdCurrentToZero*

To create the query **qupdPostPayment**:

- Start a new query in Design view and add **tblCustomer** and **tblPayment** to the query window.

- Select **Query, Update Query** from the menu bar.

- Add the **PastDue** field to the query grid and enter *[PastDue]-[PaymentAmount]* in the **Update To** row as shown below.

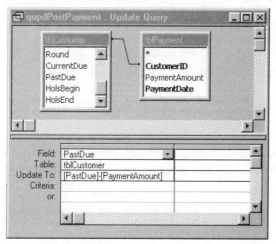

*Figure 5.22: Creating the **qupdPostPayment** update query*

- Display **tblCustomer** and **tblPayments** and make a note of the figures for **PastDue** and **PaymentAmount** so that you know what results to expect after running the query.

- Run the query and check that the results are as you expect. Then save the query as *qupdPostPayment*.

	CustomerID	Surname	Initia	Title	Address1	Address2	Round	CurrentDue	PastDue	HolsBegin	HolsEnd
►	2	Robson	C	Mr	11 Dales Rd	Broughton	1	£0.00	£1.05	01/01/99	08/01/99
	3	Brindley	J	Mr	1 Chestnut Ave	Broughton	3	£0.00	£15.70	12/12/00	25/12/00
	4	Nazarali	N	Mr	13 Dales Rd	Broughton	1	£0.00	£29.80		
	5	Newbourne	S	Miss	Mill Hse, Mill La	Broughton	2	£0.00	-£20.20	01/02/99	28/02/99
	6	Carter	J	Mrs	Bridge Hse, Mill La	Broughton	2	£0.00	£16.00		
	8	Murphy	S	Mrs	15 Elgar Crescent	Broughton	1	£0.00	£0.00		
	9	Patel	J	Miss	3 Elgar Crescent	Broughton	1	£0.00	£7.65	01/01/99	31/12/99
✱	utoNumber)			Mr			0	£0.00	£0.00		

Figure 5.23: Results after running the update query

Creating and running an Append query

The third step described above involves creating a query that will append all the data from **tblPayment** to the end of the data in **tblArchivePayment**. The first time we perform the operation, of course, there is no data in **tblArchivePayment** so the data will simply be added to the empty table.

- Start a new query in Design view and add **tblPayment** to the query window. Click **Close**.

- Double-click the asterisk (*) that appears at the top of the field list in **tblPayment**. This is a fast way of adding all the fields in the table to the query grid. (See figure below.)

- From the menu select **Query, Append Query**. A dialogue box appears asking you to enter the name of the table you wish to append to. Type *tblArchivePayment* and click **OK**.

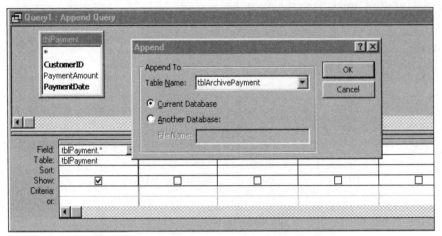

Figure 5.24: Specifying the table in the Append query

- Run the query. You will see a message informing you that you are about to append 3 rows. Click **Yes**.

- Move the query window aside so that you can see the Database window and click **Tables**. Open **tblArchivePayment** to verify that the three records have been appended.

- Save the query as *qappPayment* and close it.

Creating and running a Delete query

Finally, we will run a query that will delete all the records in **tblPayment**.

- Start a new query in Design view, add **tblPayment** to the query window and click **Close**.

- You don't need to add any fields to the query grid to run this query. In a different situation you might want to set criteria, for example deleting all records prior to a specified date, and you would then have to add the **PaymentDate** field to the query grid. But this time, just leave it blank.

- From the menu select **Query, Delete Query**.

- Run the query. You will be asked to confirm that you want to delete three records from the table. Click **Yes**.

- Open **tblPayment** to confirm that all the records have been deleted.

- Save the query as *qdelPayment* and close it.

We've now looked at all the query types except Cross-Tab queries, which are closely related to pivot tables in Excel. Oh well, maybe some other time…

This is probably the most challenging chapter in the whole book, reflecting the fact that queries are central to processing tasks in Access. Make sure you make use of them effectively in your own project!

Chapter 6 – Reports and Charts

Introduction

In this chapter we'll be taking a look at various ways of producing output from your database. We've already had a brief look at *forms* in Chapter 3; forms are useful for inputting data and viewing it on the screen, but if hard copy is required, you need to use an Access report. Although it is possible to print a form, the results are rarely satisfactory for several reasons. For one thing, the screen is a different shape from a standard A4 page, and for another, forms are often designed using coloured text, backgrounds and shading which do not reproduce well when printed.

Access 97 provides several different options for creating a new report including:

- AutoReports
- A Report Wizard
- A Label Wizard
- A Chart Wizard

Task 6.1: Use AutoReport to create reports of newspapers

Creating a columnar AutoReport

AutoReport provides a very quick method of creating a basic report from a table or query but you have very little control over the layout of the report. You can create either a *Columnar* or a *Tabular* report, and we'll try both.

- In the Database window, select **Reports, Create report by using wizard** and click **New**.

- In the New Report dialogue box, select **AutoReport: Columnar** and **tblNewspaper** in the bottom list box.

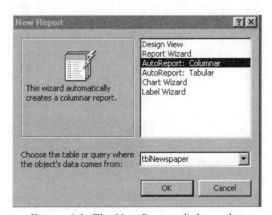

Figure 6.1: The New Report dialogue box

- Click **OK** and the report is automatically created, appearing as shown below.

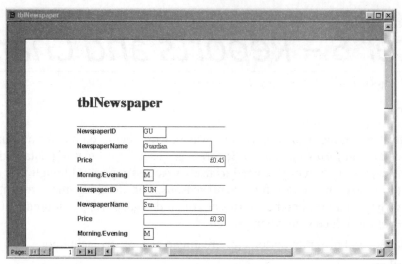

Figure 6.2: A report created using AutoReport: Columnar

The report style comes from the last style you used if you have already created a report using the Report Wizard. If you have not yet created any reports, this report appears in the default **Normal** style.

- As you move the pointer over the report on the screen you will see that it takes the form of a magnifying glass with a minus sign in the middle of it. Left-click the mouse button and the view zooms out so that you can see how the whole page looks.

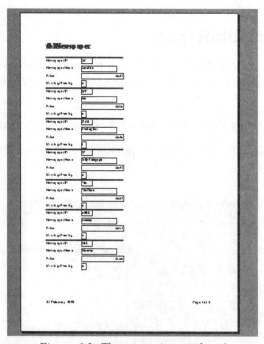

Figure 6.3: The report 'zoomed out'

You will notice that Access automatically adds a footer containing the date and the page number.

- Place the magnifying glass over the bottom left hand corner of the report and click the left mouse button. The view returns to full-size and you can see the date in the footer.

- This is not a particularly attractive looking report, so close it without saving it.

Creating a tabular AutoReport

- In the Database window, select **Reports, Create report by using wizard** and click **New**.

- In the New Report dialogue box, select **AutoReport: Tabular** and **tblNewspaper** in the bottom list box.

- Click OK and the report will be created, looking like the figure below.

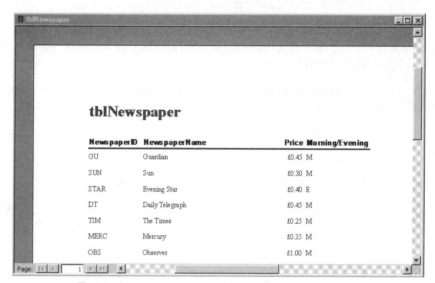

Figure 6.4: A report created using AutoForm: Tabular

- Click the mouse button to zoom out; you may see that the report is laid out in Landscape view.

Editing the report format

This report is in many ways preferable to the columnar format – it uses a good deal less paper when printed, for a start – but it could be improved. You can, for example, change the report title, centre the field for **Morning/Evening** and type your name in the **Page Footer** section of the report.

- Zoom in again if necessary to return to normal view. Then click the **Design View** button on the toolbar. The report appears in Design view as shown below.

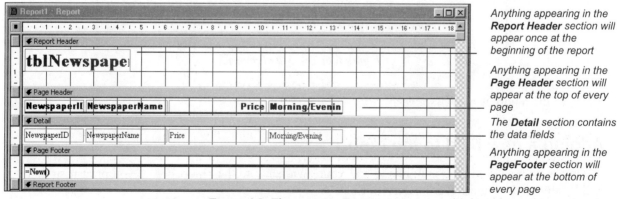

Figure 6.5: The report in Design view

- Click in the default heading box, which says **tblNewspaper**. Black squares known as *handles* appear around the box.

> **NOTE:** When you place the pointer over the larger handle in the top left hand corner, it changes to a pointing finger, and you can drag the entire box to a different location.
>
> When you place the pointer over any of the other handles, it changes to a double-headed arrow and dragging it will change the size of the box.

- Click again in the **tblNewspaper** box and the pointer becomes an insertion pointer. Edit the heading so that it says **List of Newspapers**.

- Click in the text box for **Morning/Evening** in the **Detail** section (not the label in the **Page Header** section). Handles appear around it.

- Click the **Center** box on the Formatting toolbar.

- Return to Print Preview to view your changes.

- The **Price** field is much longer than it needs to be. Return to Design view.

- Select the label **Price**, and hold down the **Shift** key while you select the data field **Price**. Then drag the middle handle on the right of either box to decrease the width of the boxes.

- Return to Page Preview, and the report should look something like the one below.

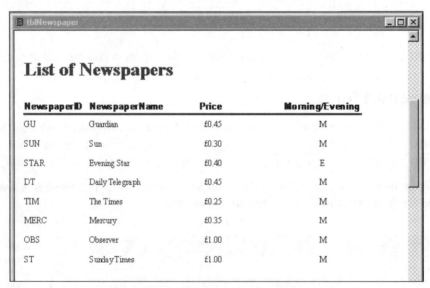

Figure 6.6: The edited report

- Save the report as *rptNewspaper*.

Adding a new field to the report

If you are on a network you may like to add your own name to the report before you print it so that you will be able to distinguish it from everyone else's.

- In Design view, the Toolbox should be visible on your screen. If it is not, click the Toolbox icon on the toolbar. (The toolbox may be 'docked' under the Standard toolbar.)

- From the Toolbox select the **Label** tool and drag out a box in the **Page Footer** section of the report. (In Access 7 the Label tool is slightly different in appearance, a single uppercase A.)

- Type your name in the box.

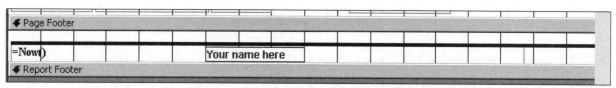

Figure 6.7: Adding your name to the Page Footer

Formatting the report

You may want to make some adjustments to the report layout before you print it. For example, it is shown in Landscape View on the screen, but as it is quite a narrow report, you may prefer to print it in Portrait view.

- From the menu, select **File, Page Setup**.

- Click the **Page** tab and select **Portrait**.

- Click the **Print Preview** button.

The main part of the report is shown in Portrait view, but you will see from the page selector at the bottom of the screen that the report spills onto a second page. Go to page 2 and note that it contains only part of the line in the footer section and **Page 1 of 1**. (Access regards this as a one-page report that just happens to be too wide to print on one sheet of A4 paper.)

You need to move the objects (line and page number) to the left.

- Return to Design view, and scroll to the right so that you can see the edge of the report.

- Select the line in the **Page Footer** section so that handles appear. Place the pointer over the right hand handle so that it becomes a double-headed arrow, and keeping one finger on the **Shift** key, drag it to the left to shorten the line to line up with **Morning/Evening**.. (Keeping **Shift** pressed ensures that the line will move only horizontally so it will not become misaligned.)

  *(In Access 7 it may be hard to see the line. You can select any object in the report using the **Select Object** box at the left end of the toolbar – the line will be called **Line12** or a similar name.)*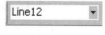

- Select the field **="Page " & [Page] & " of " & [Pages]** in the report footer and drag it to the left to line up with **Morning/Evening**.

- Select the field **Now()** and make it narrower. (Now() is a function giving the current date and time.)

- Click the **Print Preview** button.

- You may get a warning message:

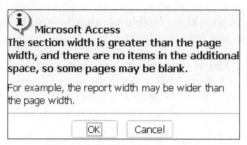

Figure 6.8: Warning message

- Click **OK**. What this means is that you need to make the report area narrower to fit the page.

- Place the pointer over the edge of the report area and drag it to the left, as shown below.

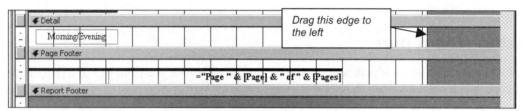

Figure 6.9: Adjusting the report width

WARNING: Before printing, you should check the page selector to see how many pages will be printed. If there is more than one for a short report, probably the Page Footer has spilled on to a second page and the report needs to be made narrower.

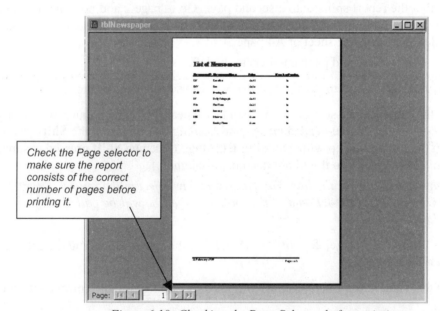

Figure 6.10: Checking the Page Selector before printing

- When you are happy with the report, select **File, Print**.

- Save and close the report.

Task 6.2: Use the Report Wizard to create a customer report

The Report Wizard gives you more control over the design and layout of your report. We'll start by creating a simple customer report.

- In the Database window, make sure **Reports, Create report by using wizard** is selected and click **New**.

- In the New Report dialogue box, select **Report Wizard** and **tblCustomer** in the bottom list box. Click **OK**.

- Add all the fields to the **Selected Fields** list except **CustomerID** and **Address2**, as shown below, and then click **Next**. (It is quickest to click the double arrow between the list boxes to move all the fields to the **Selected Fields** box, and then select and move the two fields you don't want back to the **Available Fields** box.)

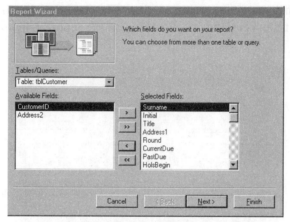

Figure 6.11: Selecting fields for the report

- In the next dialogue box select **Round** and click the arrow between the list boxes to have the records grouped by Round number. Click **Next**.

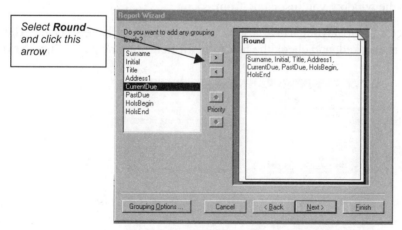

*Figure 6.12: Grouping on **Round***

- Select **Surname** and **Initial** as the two fields to sort on in Ascending sequence.

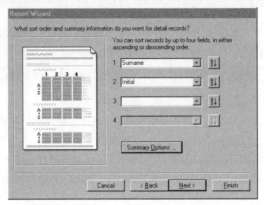

Figure 6.13: Selecting a sort order

- Press the **Summary Options** button in this window. The Summary Options window is displayed. We will display the **Sum** of **CurrentDue** and **PastDue** on the report. Click the appropriate boxes to put check marks in them.

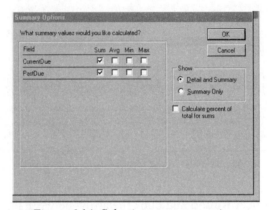

Figure 6.14: Selecting summary options

- Click **OK**, and **Next** in the window you just came from.

- Now you have to select a report layout. Have a look at the options – I have selected **Align Left 1**. Make sure **Landscape** is checked, and check the box to fit all fields on one page. Click **Next**.

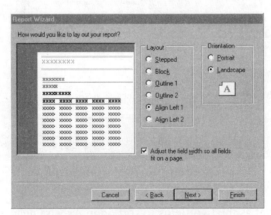

Figure 6.15: Selecting a report layout

- Browse through the styles in the next window. I have selected **Corporate**. Click **Next**.

- In the next window, type *Customer Details* as the title for the report, and click **Finish**.

- The report appears, showing totals for each round and a grand total at the end, as shown below. You can make any alterations that you require by switching to Design View.

Customer Details

Round			1					
Surname	**Initial**	**Title**		**Address1**	**CurrentDue**	**PastDue**	**HolsBegin**	**HolsEnd**
Murphy	S	Mrs		15 Elgar Crescent	£0.00	£0.00		
Nazarali	N	Mr		12 Dales Rd	£0.00	£29.80		
Patel	J	Miss		3 Elgar Crescent	£0.00	£7.65	01/04/00	31/12/00
Robson	C	Mr		11 Dales Rd	£0.00	£1.05		

Summary for 'Round' = 1 (4 detail records)

| **Sum** | | | | | £0.00 | £38.50 | | |

Round			2					
Surname	**Initial**	**Title**		**Address1**	**CurrentDue**	**PastDue**	**HolsBegin**	**HolsEnd**
Carter	J	Mrs		Bridge Hse, Mill La	£0.00	£16.00		
Newbourne	S	Miss		Mill Hse, Mill Lane	£0.00	-£20.20		

Summary for 'Round' = 2 (2 detail records)

| **Sum** | | | | | £0.00 | -£4.20 | | |

Round			3					
Surname	**Initial**	**Title**		**Address1**	**CurrentDue**	**PastDue**	**HolsBegin**	**HolsEnd**
Brindley	J	Mr		1 Chestnut Ave	£0.00	£15.70	12/04/02	17/04/02

Summary for 'Round' = 3 (1 detail record)

| **Sum** | | | | | £0.00 | £15.70 | | |
| **Grand Total** | | | | | £0.00 | £50.00 | | |

27 April 2000   *Page 1 of 1*

Figure 6.16: The report in Print Preview mode

NOTE: You can get rid of the borders round all fields (such as the Grand Total fields above) by returning to Design View and selecting **Edit, Select All** from the menu. Then right-click any field and select **Properties** from the pop-up menu. Set the **Border Style** property to **Transparent**.

- Save the report and close it. It will automatically be named **Customer Details**. Right-click the name in the Database window and rename it *rptCustomer*.

Task 6.3: Produce the Round report for Monday morning

In this task you will create a report named **rptMondayDelivs** that shows, for each Round, which newspapers are to be delivered to each customer on Monday morning. Each round will be printed on a separate page so that it can be given to the paperboy/girl with the newspapers.

Basing a report on a query

First of all we need to create the query which will be used as the basis for the report. The query will be named **qryMondayDelivs** and will pick out all customers who are not currently on holiday and specify which newspapers they have delivered on Monday morning.

- In the Database window select **Queries, Create query in Design view** and select **New**.

- Select Design view and click **OK**.

- In the Show Table dialogue box, select and add **tblCustomer**, **tblDelivery** and **tblNewspaper** to the query grid.

- Make entries so that your query grid looks like the figure below. Note that the query is sorted on **Round** and **Address1** fields. (Sorting on **Address1** is not particularly useful for the application but provides an opportunity later on to demonstrate sorting the report in a different sequence.)

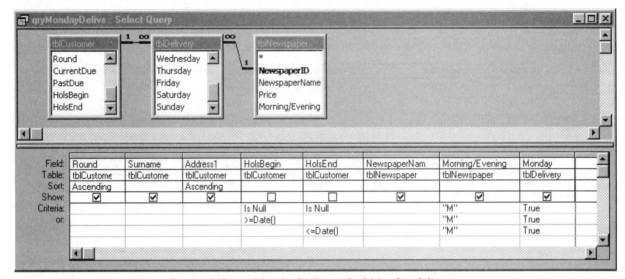

*Figure 6.17: **qryMondayDelivs** to find Monday deliveries*

Note that the criteria pick out all customers who either have no holiday dates recorded, or whose holiday start date is still in the future, or whose holiday end date is past. **HolsBegin** and **HolsEnd** are not needed on the report so deselect the **Show** box for these fields.

- Run the query. Results should be as shown below:

Round	Surname	Address1	NewspaperName	Morning/Evening	Monday
1	Robson	11 Dales Rd	Mercury	M	☑
1	Robson	11 Dales Rd	Sun	M	☑
1	Nazarali	13 Dales Rd	Mercury	M	☑
1	Nazarali	13 Dales Rd	Guardian	M	☑
1	Murphy	15 Elgar Crescent	Guardian	M	☑
2	Carter	Bridge Hse, Mill La	Mercury	M	☑
2	Carter	Bridge Hse, Mill La	Daily Telegraph	M	☑
2	Carter	Bridge Hse, Mill La	Sun	M	☑
2	Newbourne	Mill Hse, Mill La	Mercury	M	☑
2	Newbourne	Mill Hse, Mill La	Guardian	M	☑
3	Brindley	1 Chestnut Ave	Guardian	M	☑

*Figure 6.18: Query results will be used in Round report **rptMondayDelivs***

- Save the query as *qryMondayDelivs* and close it.

The next stage is to create the report based on this query.

- Use the Report Wizard to create a new report based on **qryMondayDelivs**.

- In the next window click the double arrow to add all the fields to the list of selected fields.

- In the next window, scroll through the options in the box labelled **How do you want to view your data?** Select **tblDelivery** and click **Next**.

- Add **Round** as a grouping level by selecting it and clicking the arrow between the boxes. Click **Next**.

- In the next dialogue box, do not add any sorting options. Click **Next**.

- Select **Align Left 1** as the style for the report. Click **Next**.

- Select **Corporate** style for the report. Click **Next**.

- Give the report the title *Monday Deliveries*. Click **Finish**. The report will appear as shown below (it may appear in a slightly different sequence):

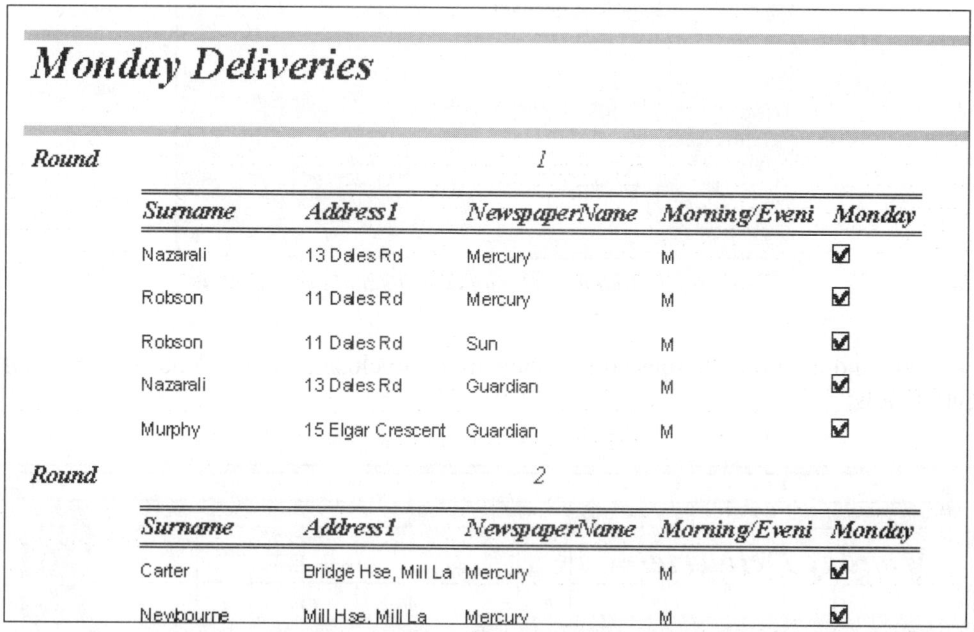

Figure 6.19: The basis of the Monday Morning Round Report

Customising the report

You now need to move fields and labels around until you are satisfied with the result.

- Switch to Design view.

- Click and hold down the mouse button to drag the **Morning/Evening** label and field into the **Report Header** section. If you have trouble with this, click away from the field to deselect it and then try again. (You can also cut and paste controls to move them.)

- Delete the label and field for **Monday** by selecting them and pressing the **Delete** key on the keyboard.

- Adjust the field sizes of **Round** and its label. (See Figure 6.21.)

Sorting and grouping the report

The report needs to be sorted into a more logical sequence. Ideally it should be sorted by surname and address in the order in which the deliveries are made, but this is not possible with the fields on our tables. A design fault! If you were redesigning the system, what extra field(s) would you include?

For the purposes of this exercise, we will sort and group the records by surname.

- Right-click the square at the intersection of the ruler lines and select **Sorting and Grouping**. (Or, click the **Sorting and Grouping** tool on the Report Design toolbar.)

- The Sorting and Grouping dialogue box appears. The report is already sorted on Round. In the second row, select **Surname**, Sort Order **Ascending**.

- In the **Group Properties** at the bottom of the screen, select **Yes** for **Group Footer** for both **Round** and **Surname**. (You need the footers in these two sections to insert a page break between rounds and a line between each address – coming up shortly.)

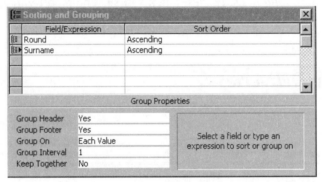

Figure 6.20: Adding sort requirements and group footers

- Close the box and drag the sections so that they are quite close together. Your report should look like the figure below:

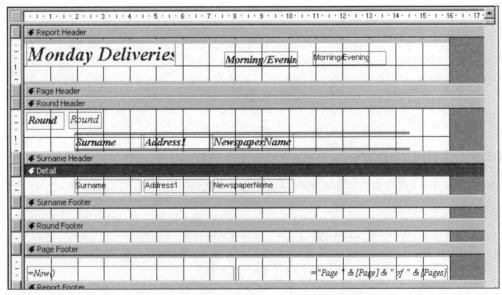

Figure 6.21: The report design after customising

Inserting a page break between rounds

- Click the **Page Break** tool on the Toolbox. (If the Toolbox is not displayed you can display it by selecting **View, Toolbars, Toolbox** from the menu.)

- Click in the **Round Footer** section near the left hand margin. (If the Footer section where you want to put a page break is not visible, you need to insert it as described in the previous section.)

The page break will appear as a short dotted line.

- Use the **Line** tool to insert a line in the **Surname Footer** section – this will separate each customer from the next.

- Switch to Print Preview. Your report should look like the figure below.

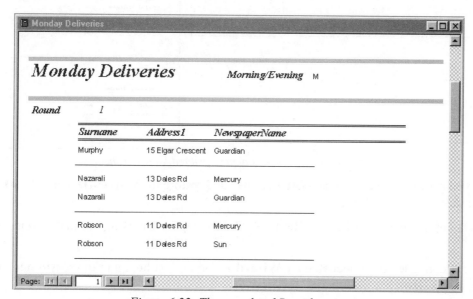

Figure 6.22: The completed Round report

Note that you can prevent repeating the name and address by returning to Design view and selecting **Surname** and **Address1** in the **Detail** section. Then set the **Hide Duplicates** property to **Yes**.

- Save the report and close it. Rename it from **Monday Deliveries** to *rptMondayDelivs*.

> **NOTE:** The default name given by Access to the report will be the title that you specify in the last step of the Report Wizard (e.g. **Monday Deliveries**). When you use the Report Wizard, you may prefer to set the title to the report name (e.g. **rptMondayDelivs**) and edit the heading in the report.

Task 6.4: Print customer invoices

In this task you will print four invoices to a page. The invoices could be printed on special perforated paper and delivered by hand with the newspapers each week. Each page of invoices will be laid out as shown below:

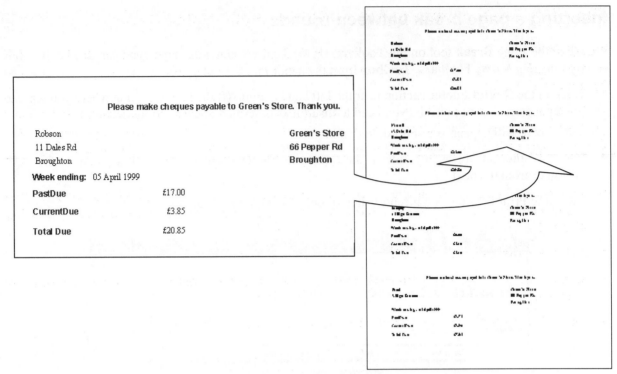

Please make cheques payable to Green's Store. Thank you.

Robson	**Green's Store**
11 Dales Rd	**66 Pepper Rd**
Broughton	**Broughton**

Week ending: 05 April 1999

PastDue	£17.00
CurrentDue	£3.85
Total Due	£20.85

Figure 6.23: Customer invoices printed four to a sheet

- Before you start this exercise, open **tblCustomer** and restore the **CurrentDue** and **PastDue** amounts to those shown in Figure 5.17.

- In the Database window make sure **Reports, Create report by using wizard** is selected and click **New**.

- In the next dialogue box, select **Report Wizard** in the top list box, and **qryCustomer** in the bottom list box. Click **OK**.

- In the next dialogue box move **Surname**, **Address1**, **Address2**, **Round**, **PastDue**, **CurrentDue** and **Expr1**, in that order. Click **Next.**

- Click **Next** in the next dialogue box without adding any grouping levels.

- In the next dialogue box, sort on **Round**. Click **Next.**

- Select a **Columnar** layout. (**Vertical** in Access 7.) Click **Next.**

- Choose **Bold** as the style. Click **Next.**

- Enter *rptInvoices* as the heading for the report. Click **Finish**.

The report is generated and appears on screen. It needs quite a lot of tweaking.

- In Design view, delete the heading and move the **Page Header** section up to the top of the report. Delete all labels except **PastDue**, **CurrentDue** and **Total Due**. Move the field **Now()** from the report footer into the **Detail** section and delete the other item in the report footer.

- You can add new text and move fields around until you are satisfied with the result. The boxes can be removed by choosing **Edit, Select All** and setting the **Border Style** property to **Transparent**. The top and bottom margins can be changed by selecting **File, Page Setup** from the menu.

- When you are satisfied with your report, save and close it. It will automatically be saved as *rptInvoices*.

Task 6.5: Draw a chart of Monday's newspaper deliveries

The Chart Wizard allows you to create output in the form of a chart such as a pie or bar chart. In this example we'll create a bar chart giving an instant picture of the number of each newspaper delivered on Monday morning.

> **NOTE:** To complete this exercise you must have Microsoft Graph installed. Microsoft Graph is not included in the default installation. You can run the Microsoft Access Setup program or the Microsoft Office Professional Setup program again and specify that you want to install the Graph feature only.

- First check that the query on which the chart will be based is correct. In the Database window select the **Queries** tab, select **qryMondaySummary** and click **Design**. The query window should look like Figure 5.3. Make any necessary amendments, save and close it.

- Select **Report**, Create report by using wizard and click **New**.

- In the next window, select **Chart Wizard** and select **qryMondaySummary** as the table or query where the object's data comes from. Click **OK**.

- Select **Quantity** and **NewspaperName** as the fields for the chart, and click **Next**.

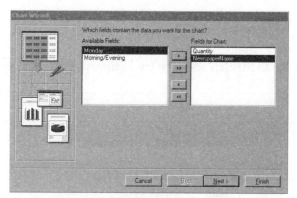

Figure 6.24: Selecting fields for the chart

- Select the first option, **Column chart**, in the next dialogue box and click **Next**.

- You can drag fields around in this to specify which fields go where, but Access has guessed correctly so just click **Next**.

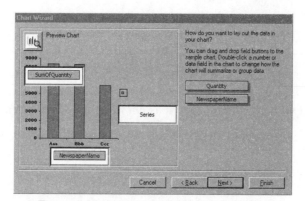

Figure 6.25: Laying out the data in the chart

- Enter *Monday Morning Deliveries* as the title for the chart, and click **Finish**.

The chart appears something like the one shown below.

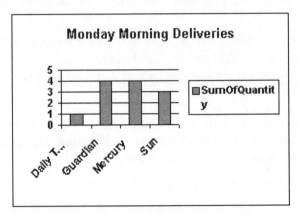

Figure 6.26: The chart produced by the Wizard

- Switch to Design view and select the chart. Drag the middle right hand handle to the right so that the legend fits its box.

NOTE: If this does not work, right-click the chart in Design view and select **Properties**. Change the **Size Mode** property from **Clip** to **Stretch** and then try again. Alternatively, set the **Width** property of the legend to something wider.

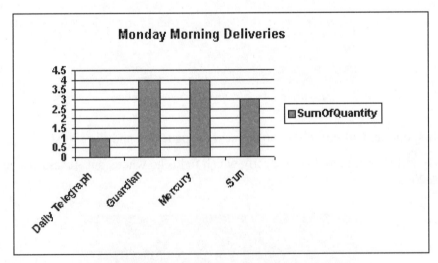

Figure 6.27: The edited chart

- When you are satisfied with your chart, save it as *cht*MondayDeliveries and close it.

Chapter 7 – Macros and Command Buttons

Macros

A macro is a little program that tells Access to perform one or more actions such as running a query, opening a form or printing a report. Once you have written the macro you can save it and run it from the Database window, or you can attach it to an Event Property of a form, report or Command button.

- Open the **NewsAgt** database. If you have not got this to hand, you will need to download **NewsAgt6.mdb** from the web site www.payne-gallway.co.uk or work through Chapters 1 to 6.

Task 7.1:   Create a macro to maximise a form and attach it to the form's On Open Event Property

- In the Database window select **Macros** and click **New**.

- You will see the Macro window. To add an action, you click the drop-down arrow on the first line under **Action** and select an action. The complete list of possible actions, reproduced from the Access Help system, is shown at the end of this chapter.

- Scroll down the **Action** list and select **Maximize**. You can put anything you like in the **Comment** column; it has no effect on the running of the macro, and is used to remind the developer what a particular macro is for.

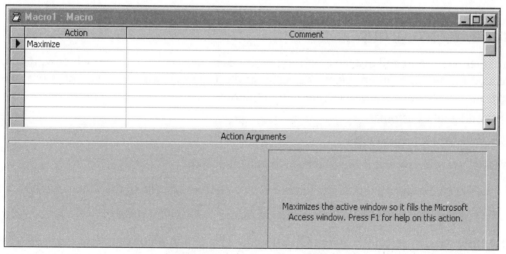

Figure 7.1: The macro window

- Save the macro as *mcrMaximise*, and close the macro window.

We want this macro to run whenever the Customer form is opened. We can do this by attaching the macro to the form's **Open Event** property.

- From the Database window, open **frmCustomer** in Design view.

- At the intersection of the ruler lines in the top left corner of the form there is a little black square. Right-click this square and select **Properties** to open the Properties sheet for the form.

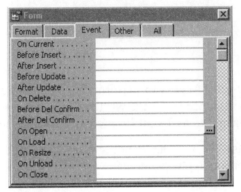

Figure 7.2: The forms Event properties

- Click the **Event** tab at the top of the Properties sheet and click the **On Open** property.

- Click the down arrow to see a list of macros or modules that we could attach to this event. There is only one – **mcrMaximise**, the macro that we have just created. Click this to select it.

- Switch to Form view – the macro runs as soon as the form opens, and the window is maximised.

- Save the form and close it.

Task 7.2:   Create and run macros that are part of a group

In this task you will create two macros which will later be attached to command buttons on a menu.

Creating a macro group

Macros are often very short and instead of storing each macro in a separate macro window, it makes sense to store related macros in a group under one name in the Database window. We will store two macros under one group name which a user will select from in order to:

-      Add a new customer
-      Edit/Delete a customer.

- In the Database window select the **Macros** tab and click **New**.

- Click the **Macro Names** button on the toolbar to add another column to the Macro window.

- In the first line of the new column type the macro name *mcrAddCustomer*.

- In the **Action** column select the action **OpenForm**. This action requires *action arguments*; you have to specify which form is to be opened, in what view (Form, Design, Print Preview or Datasheet), and other optional action arguments as shown below.

- Select **frmCustomer** as the Form Name and leave the other arguments with their default values.

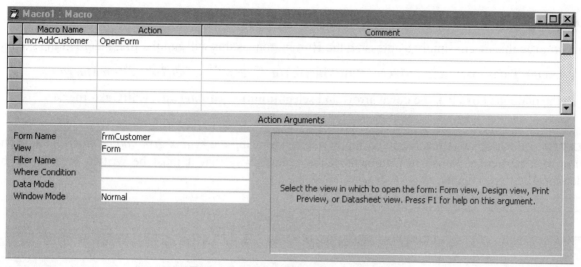

Figure 7.3: Entering Action Arguments

- We want the form to open ready for the user to enter a new record. In the second line of the **Action** column, select the action **GoToRecord**, and in the **Record** Action Argument in the lower half of the window select **New**.

- Click the **Save** tool on the toolbar to save the macro as *mmnuCustomer*. This will be the name of the macro group, in which the first macro is **mcrAddCustomer**.

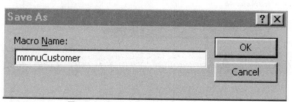

Figure 7.4: Naming the macro

- Run the macro to test it, by pressing the **Run** button on the toolbar.

- Oh dear! We've opened the wrong form. Close the form and edit the macro so that **frmCustomerMain** is opened. Test it again. You will get a warning message that you must save the edited macro before you can run it. Click **Yes** to save it.

- This time, the form should open ready for you to enter a new record. Close the form.

- Now enter the second macro. On the third line in the macro name column enter the macro name *mcrEditCustomer*.

- The first action is once again to open the form **frmCustomerMain**. If you type *o* in the **Action** column Access will guess correctly that you want **OpenForm**. Enter the name of the form in the lower half of the window, under **Form Name**.

- The next action is to position the cursor in the **Surname** field. Type *g* in the **Action** column and Access correctly guesses **GoToControl**. Type *Surname* as the Action argument.

- Save the macro.

When this macro is run, the form will open at the first record with the cursor in the Surname field. The user can then press the **Find** button on the toolbar or use a customised Command button which we will place on the form in Task 7.4.

Running a macro which is part of a group

You can't run this macro simply by pressing the **Run** button, as this will run the first macro in the group.

- From the **Tools** menu select **Macro, Run Macro**. *(In Access 97, select **Tools, Run Macro**.)*

- In the dialogue box click the down arrow and select **mmnuCustomer.mcrEditCustomer.**

NOTE: Each separate macro in a group is referred to using the syntax *groupname.macroname*. (The *syntax* of a particular phrase or statement is the precise way that it must be written in order to be understood by the computer.)

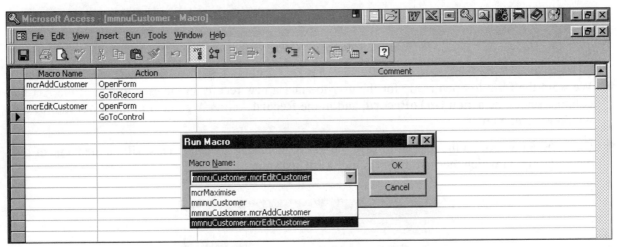

Figure 7.5: Running a macro which is part of a group

- Click **OK**. The Customer form should open with the cursor in the **Surname** field of the first record. In the next task, we'll add a **Find** button which the user can click to open the Find dialogue box.

- Close the form and the macro to return to the Database window.

That completes this task – in Task 7.5 you will attach each of these macros to a command button on a menu.

Task 7.3:   Write macros to (i) calculate and print invoices, (ii) post payments

Macros can be used to perform quite complex processing tasks, by running queries or code modules that have already been created. In this task you will write macros to run the queries you created in Chapter 5. We will just review the processing tasks as outlined just before task 5.3.

(i) To calculate and print invoices:

Run query **qmakDueThisWeek** to calculate this week's amount due from newspapers delivered

Run query **qupdCurrentDue** to update **CurrentDue** field in **tblCustomer**

Run query **qryCustomer** to calculate the total amount due.

Print the invoices, **rptInvoices**.

(We will insert an extra instruction before the last step to warn the user to load the invoice stationery.)

(ii) To post payments:

Run query **qupdCurrentToZero** to add **CurrentDue** to **PastDue** and set **CurrentDue** to zero

Run query **qupdPostPayment** to subtract **Payment** from **PastDue** on **tblCustomer**

Run query **qappPayment** to add payments to archive table **tblArchivePayment**

Run query **qdelPayment** to empty **tblPayments** ready for next week

Display message to user that task is complete.

- In the database window make sure the **Macros** tab is selected and click **New**.

- Click the **Macro Names** button on the toolbar to add another column to the macro window.

- Enter the macros as shown below. The comments in the right hand column specify which query to run at each step. When you enter the instruction **OpenReport**, select **Print Preview** as the **View** in the **Action Arguments** box at the bottom of the screen, so that you don't get hard copy every time you test the macro.

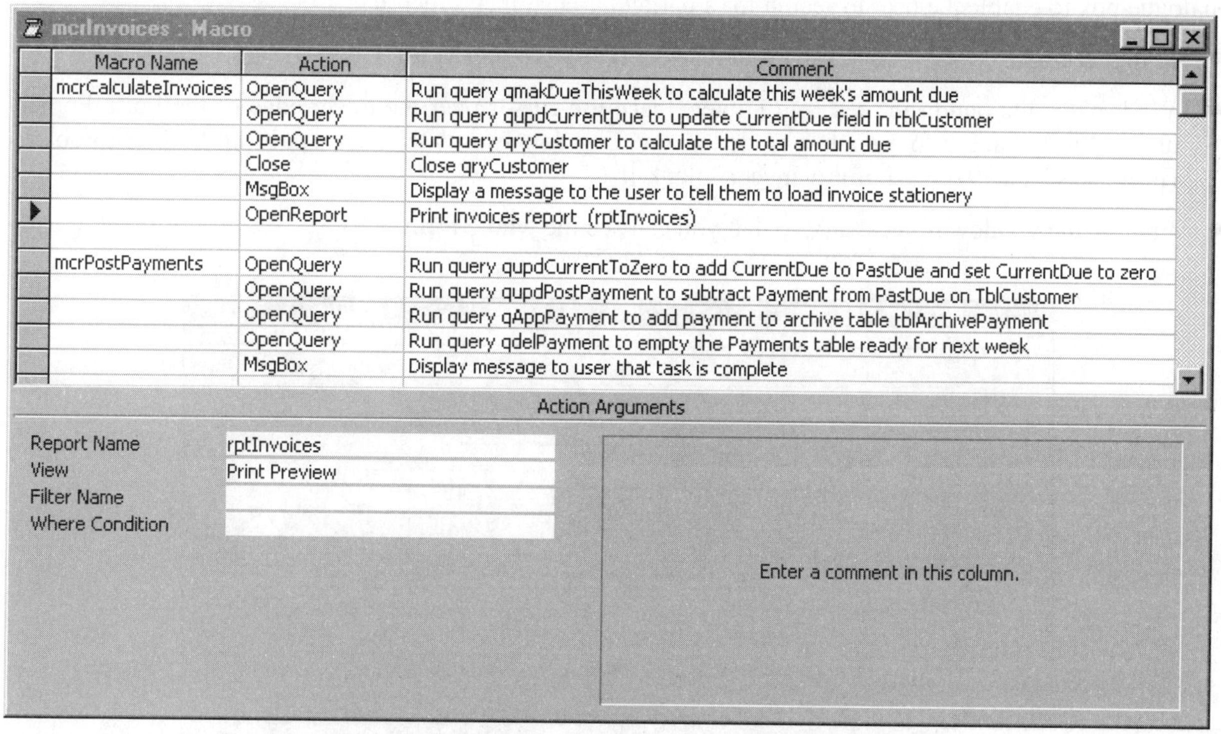

Macro Name	Action	Comment
mcrCalculateInvoices	OpenQuery	Run query qmakDueThisWeek to calculate this week's amount due
	OpenQuery	Run query qupdCurrentDue to update CurrentDue field in tblCustomer
	OpenQuery	Run query qryCustomer to calculate the total amount due
	Close	Close qryCustomer
	MsgBox	Display a message to the user to tell them to load invoice stationery
	OpenReport	Print invoices report (rptInvoices)
mcrPostPayments	OpenQuery	Run query qupdCurrentToZero to add CurrentDue to PastDue and set CurrentDue to zero
	OpenQuery	Run query qupdPostPayment to subtract Payment from PastDue on TblCustomer
	OpenQuery	Run query qAppPayment to add payment to archive table tblArchivePayment
	OpenQuery	Run query qdelPayment to empty the Payments table ready for next week
	MsgBox	Display message to user that task is complete

Action Arguments

Report Name	rptInvoices
View	Print Preview
Filter Name	
Where Condition	

Enter a comment in this column.

Figure 7.6: Macro to handle invoicing and payments

- Save the macro as *mcrInvoices*.

- Test the first macro in the group by pressing the **Run** button.

You will notice that a lot of messages appear on the screen informing you what is happening. This gives you a chance to cancel any of the macros while you are testing. For example you may decide to cancel **qdelPayment** so that you do not have to keep entering new payments for test purposes.

- Test the second macro in the group by selecting **Tools, Run Macro**. Say *No* to the question on the screen.

Command buttons

Command buttons may be placed on forms for the user to click in order to perform some predefined task – for example, you could place a **Find** command button on a form for a user to click instead of using a button on the Access toolbar.

Placing command buttons is one way to customise an application for a user who may not be familiar with the built-in Access tools and menus. You can associate one or more actions with a command button, in either of the following ways:

- Use the Command Button Wizard to select an action for a button;
- Create a button without the Wizard and then use the button's Properties Sheet to select a macro or code to run when the button is clicked.

We'll be using the Command Button Wizard in the next task.

Task 7.4: Add a Find button to the Customer form

In this task you'll add a command button to **frmCustomerMain** which when pressed will open the Find dialogue box to enable the user to search for a particular customer's record.

- In the Database window click **Forms** and select **frmCustomerMain**. Click **Design**.

- We'll place the button in the Form Footer. Place the cursor over the lower edge of the Form Footer and when it changes to a double-headed arrow drag downwards to create space in the Form Footer. (In Access 7 and 97 the subform appears blank.)

- Enlarge the window if necessary so that you can see the whole form.

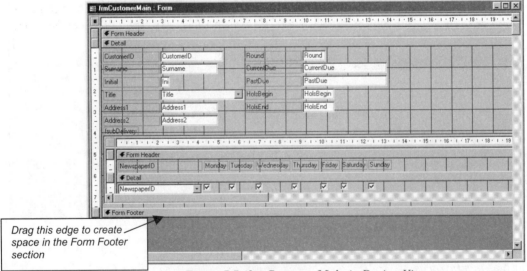

*Figure 7.7: **frmCustomerMain** in Design View*

- The toolbox should be visible – if it is not, select **View, Toolbox** from the menu. Click the **Command Button** tool on the toolbox and drag out a reasonable sized button in the Form Footer. The button is automatically given a caption such as **Command24** because it is the 24th control to be placed on the form. This will be changed later.

- The Command Button Wizard starts up automatically and you will see the following screen:

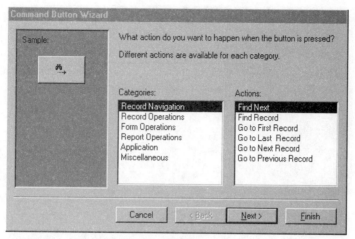

Figure 7.8: The Command Button Wizard dialogue box

> **NOTE:** If this screen does not appear, you probably don't have the **Control Wizards** tool selected on the toolbox. If that is the case, delete your button, select the **Control Wizards** tool, then place another Command button.

- Have a look through the **Categories** list box on the left hand side. The right hand list box tells you what actions are available in each category. When you have finished browsing, select **Record Navigation** in the **Categories** list box and **Find Record** in the **Actions** list box, and click **Next**.

- In the next dialogue box you are asked to choose the picture or text which will appear on your button. If you click **Show All Pictures** you will be able to select from a much larger list. Bear in mind that the user will have to guess what the button does if you choose some obscure graphic like a coffee cup.

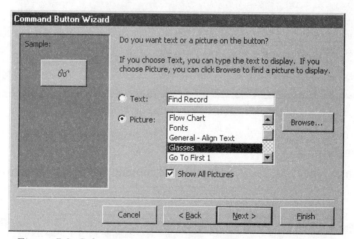

Figure 7.9: Selecting text or graphic for the Command button

- When you have selected a suitable graphic, or selected **Text**, click **Next**.

- You are asked to type a meaningful name for your button – something better than **Command24**. The **Name** is not the same as the **Caption**, but it appears in the Properties sheet when you select the button and it is sensible to give it an identifiable name. Type *FindRecord* and then click **Finish**.

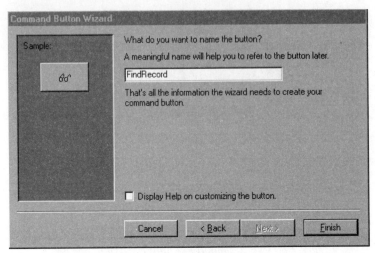

Figure 7.10: Naming the button

- Switch to Form View and try out your button. The Find dialogue box opens, but if the cursor is in the **CustomerID** field, you will be searching for a particular Customer ID, which is probably not very useful. Close the box, tab to the surname field and search for, say, **Carter**.

NOTE: You can use wildcards in a search, so that for example if you enter *c**, Access will find the first customer whose surname begins with **C**.

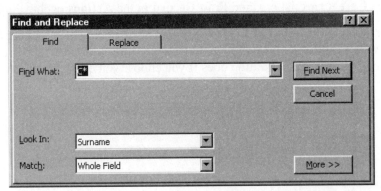

Figure 7.11: Searching for a particular record

- Save and close your form.

That is the end of this task. The next task will combine command buttons and macros on a menu form.

Task 7.5: Create a menu with command buttons

In this task you'll create a menu with two options: **Add a customer**, and **Edit/Delete a Customer**.

- In the Database window select **Forms, Create form in Design view** and click **New**.

- In the New Form dialogue box choose **Design View** and leave the list box at the bottom of the window blank, since this form will not be bound to a table or query. Click **OK**.

A new blank form opens in Design view.

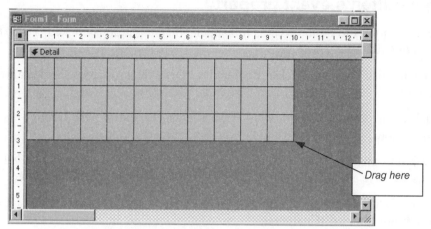

Figure 7.12: Creating a menu form

- Enlarge the window slightly and drag the corner of the form so that it fills the window.

- Click the **Label** tool and drag out a box at the top of the form. Type *Customer Menu* in the box.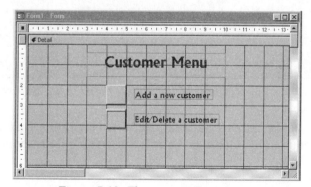

- Click the **Select Objects** tool to select the box and change the font and type size to something suitable.

- Now click the **Command Button** tool on the toolbox and place it on the form (see Figure below).

- In the Command Button Wizard dialogue box click **Cancel**, as we will assign one of our own macros to this button.

- Use the **Label** tool to type a label *Add a new customer* next to the button, and adjust the font and type size.

- You can copy your button and label to create the second menu option. Click in the left hand ruler line opposite the button and its label – this selects everything in line with where you click.

- Press **Ctrl-C** to copy the button and its label, and **Ctrl-V** to paste them. You may need to adjust the position of the second button.

- Edit the text on the second label so that it says *Edit/Delete a customer*, and delete the text on the buttons. Your menu should look something like the one below:

Figure 7.13: The menu in Design view

Defining a button's event property

All we have to do now is to define what is to happen when a button is clicked. To do this we need to set each button's **On Click** Event property.

- Right-click the first button and select **Properties**. (Or, if the properties sheet is already on screen, left-click the button.)

- Click each of the tabs at the top of the Properties sheet and browse through the options. You can change the colour, size, font etc using the various Format properties.

- Click the **Event** tab. Select the **On Click** event and you will see a drop-down list which includes all the macros we have already created. Select **mmnuCustomer.mcrAddCustomer**.

- Select the **Edit/Delete a Customer** button and set its **On Click** Event property to **mmnuCustomer.mcrEditCustomer**.

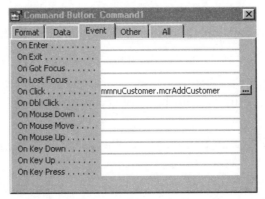

Figure 7.14: The command button's Event Property list

- Click **Form View** on the toolbar to see what your menu looks like.

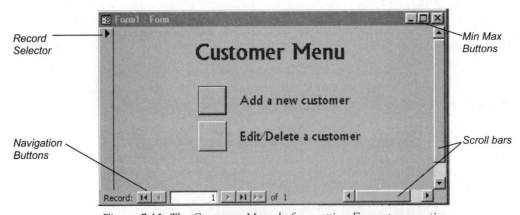

Figure 7.15: The Customer Menu before setting Format properties

A menu form such as this should not have Record Selectors, Navigation Buttons, Min Max Buttons or Scroll Bars. These can be removed by setting the Form's **Format** properties appropriately.

Setting the properties of the form

- Return to Design view and click the square at the intersection of the ruler lines. This brings up the form's properties.

- Click the **Format** tab on the Property sheet, and set **Scroll Bars** to **Neither**, **Record Selectors** and **Navigation Buttons** to **No**, **Min Max Buttons** to **None,** and **Dividing Lines** to **No**.

- Switch to Form view. Your menu should now look something like the figure below.

Figure 7.16: The Customer menu

- Try out the buttons. **Add a new customer** should take you to a new customer form, and **Edit/Delete a customer** should take you to the first record, with the focus in the **Surname** field.

- Save the form as *fmnuCustomer*, and close it.

That completes this exercise.

Using conditions in a macro

You can optionally include conditions in a macro so that the actions will only be taken if the condition is true.

Task 7.6: Use a condition in a macro

In this task you will create a macro which displays a message and beeps if a customer owes more than £20.00. This will then be attached to the **On Current** event of **frmCustomerMain.**

- In the Database window select **Macros** tab and click **New**.

- In the macro window, click the **Conditions** button on the toolbar.

- A new column opens up. Enter the condition *PastDue>20* and press tab to move to the **Action** column.

- In the **Action** column select **Msgbox** as the Action, and in the **Action Arguments** enter the **Message** *Customer owes more than £20.*

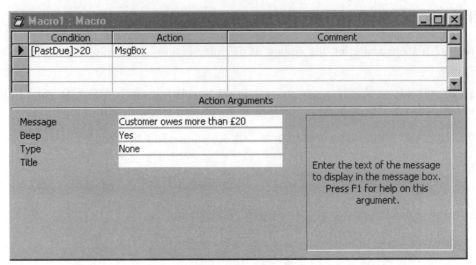

Figure 7.17: A conditional macro

- Save the macro as *mcrOverdue* and close it.

- Open **frmCustomerMain** in Design view and add the macro to the Form's **On Current** Event property.

- Switch to Form view and test the form – the message should appear whenever you display a record where the customer owes more than £20.

- Save and close the form.

Task 7.7: Create a dialogue box to let the user specify an action

Sometimes you want your macro to ask the user a question and then perform an action depending on the reply. In this task this technique will be demonstrated by creating a macro which opens a dialogue box to let the user specify which of two reports is to be viewed on screen, **rptCustomer** or **rptMondayDelivs**. The user can also choose to cancel and not view either of them.

Dialogue boxes

A dialogue box is simply a form with special properties. It is known as an *unbound form* because it is not based on any table or query. It enables you to accept input from the user in the form of text to go on a report, a choice of actions to take, or a simple Yes/No answer to a question such as "Do you want to print the report now?"

Creating an unbound form

- In the Database window select **Forms, Create form in Design view** and click **New**.

- Leave **Design View** selected and click **OK** without selecting a table or query in the bottom list box.

- You will see a completely blank form on your screen, and the Property sheet should open as shown below. (If the Properties sheet is not open right-click the square at the intersection of the ruler lines and select **Properties**.)

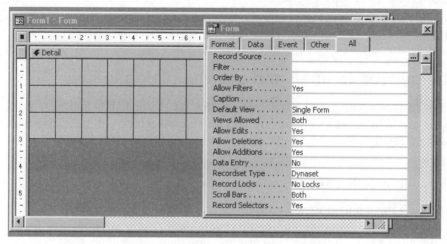

Figure 7.18: Creating an unbound form

- Set the form's **Format** properties as follows:

Property	Setting
Caption	The name that you want to appear in the title bar (e.g. *Report dialogue box*)
Default View	Single Form
Views Allowed	Form
Scroll Bars	Neither
Record Selectors	No
Navigation Buttons	No
Dividing lines	No
Border Style	Dialog *(This is important!)*

- Place a List box on the form.

- In the next window, select **I will type in the values that I want**. Click **Next**.

- In the next window leave the **Number of Columns** as **1** and type the two entries *Customer Report* and *Round Report*. Click **Next**.

- Type *Which report would you like to view?* as the label for your list box. Click **Finish**.

- In the Properties sheet of the List box, set the **Name** property to *WhichReport*.

- Look at the dialogue box in Form view and then adjust the size of the label and list box so that it looks something like the one below.

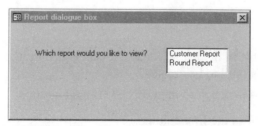

Figure 7.19: First stage in creating a dialogue box

- Save the form, giving it the name *fdlgReport*.

We still have to add **OK** and **Cancel** command buttons but first of all we need to create the macros that the buttons will run.

Creating the macros to open and use the dialogue box

You have to consider what action the user will take to open the dialogue box and view one of the reports. In this example the user will select an option **View/Print reports** which will be added as an extra item to the Customer Menu created in Task 7.5. We'll create the macro first and then attach it to a new command button on the menu.

- In the Database window select **Macros** and click **New**.

- Click the **Macro Names** button to add a macro name. All the macros needed for this exercise will be stored in a macro group named **mcrReports**. The macro window will look like the figure below when you have entered all the macros. The steps are explained below.

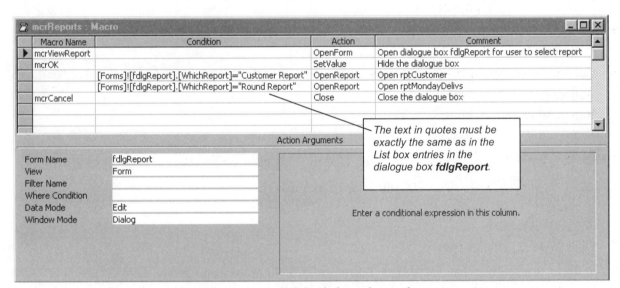

Figure 7.20: Macros to control the dialogue box and report viewing

- Type the name of the first macro in this group, *mcrViewReport* which will open the dialogue box. In the **Action** column, select **OpenForm**, and set the action arguments as follows:

Argument	Setting
Form name	fdlgReport
View	Form
Data Mode	Edit
Window Mode	Dialog

The user will now choose a report in the list box and click an **OK** button on the dialogue box (still to be created) or click a **Cancel** button (still to be created.)

We'll now create the two macros to attach to the **OK** and **Cancel** buttons.

- Type the macro name *mcrOK* in the first column.

- In the **Action** column, select **SetValue**. This action will hide the dialogue box without closing it. Set its Action Arguments as follows, typing them exactly as shown including square brackets:

Argument	Setting	
Item	[Visible]	
Expression	No	(This sets the forms **Visible** Property to **No**.)

- Press the **Conditions** button to open the **Condition** column.

- Enter the condition *[Forms]![fdlgReport].[WhichReport]="Customer Report"* (see Figure 7.20) Take care here – notice the syntax used to refer to the object **WhichReport** on the form **fdlgReport**. The form has to be open in order to refer to the list box, which is why we set its **Visible** property to **No** above instead of just closing it, after the user has selected the report to be printed.

- Enter the action **OpenReport** and set the action arguments as follows:

Argument	Setting
Report name	rptCustomer
View	Print Preview

- On the next line enter the condition *[Forms]![fdlgReport].[WhichReport]="Round Report"*. (You can copy the line above and edit it.)

- Enter the action **OpenReport** and set the action arguments as follows:

Argument	Setting
Report name	rptMondayDelivs
View	Print Preview

- On the next line enter the macro name *mcrCancel*. This macro simply closes the dialogue box.

- Enter the action **Close** and set the action arguments as follows:

Argument	Setting
Object Type	Form
Object Name	fdlgReport
Save	No

- Save the macro, naming it *mcrReports* and close it.

Attaching the macros to command buttons

- Open **fmnuCustomer** in Design view, and place a command button under **Edit/Delete a customer**. Use the wizard to specify **Categories** as **Miscellaneous** and **Actions** as **Run Macro**. The button is to run the macro **mcrReports.mcrViewReport**.

- Copy the text box **Edit/Delete a Customer** and edit the text to *Print Report*.

- Save and close the form.

- The dialogue box needs **OK** and **Cancel** buttons. Open the form **fdlgReport** in Design view.

- Place a command button at the bottom of the form. This button is to run **mcrReports.mcrOK**. Make it show the text **OK**.

- Place a second button called **Cancel** to run the macro **mcrReports.mcrCancel,** and then save and close the form.

- Open the menu form and test the **Print Report** button. If it works, award yourself a Mars Bar!

Task 7.8: Use a dialogue box to capture query criteria

In this final task you will use a dialogue box to ask the user whether they require a Round report for Morning or Evening. The reply will be used as a criteria in **qryMondayDelivs** and also inserted in the Report **rptMondayDelivs**.

- Open a new form in Design view.

- Set all the form properties the same as in the previous exercise. (Set the caption to *Morning/Evening*)

- Place a list box on the form, with the two entries *M* and *E* and a label *Is this a Morning or an Evening Round?*

- Place a command button on the form. In the wizard, select **Report Operations**, **Preview Report**. Specify the report **rptMondayDelivs**. Label it *OK*.

- Place a second command button on the form, which will simply close the dialogue box (form). Select **Form Operations**, **Close Form** and specify **fdlgReport**. Label it *Cancel*.

- The form will look like the figure below. Select **M** in the list box but don't press **OK** – we first have to modify the query and the report.

- Open the Properties sheet for the list box and name it *M/E*.

- Save the dialogue box as **fdlgMorning/Evening** and leave it open in Form view.

NOTE: The dialogue box, i.e. the form created for the user to answer a question, must be open when the query and the report are run, because they use a field (M/E) on this form.

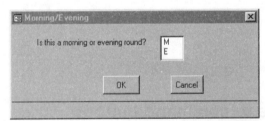

Figure 7.21: Capturing a query criteria using a dialogue box

Using a field from a dialogue box as query criteria

- Press F11 to display the Database window and open the query **qryMondayDelivs** in Design view.

- Replace the criteria "M" in the **Morning/Evening field** with *[Forms]![fdlgMorning/Evening].[M/E]* as shown below. (You can use **Shift-F2** to zoom in. Use **Ctrl-C**, **Ctrl-V** to copy and paste the criteria to the second and third criteria rows to save retyping.)

- Run the query to test it – make sure the dialogue box is open (see note above) and that you have selected **M** in the list box.

- Save and close the query.

- Edit the macro **mcrReports.mcrOK** so that instead of opening **rptMondayDelivs** when the user selects **Round Report**, the macro action is to **OpenForm fdlgMorning/Evening**.

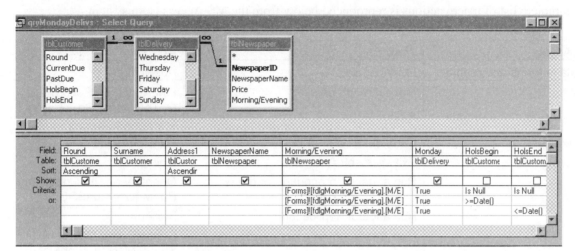

Figure 7.22: Using a field from a dialogue box as criteria in a query

Inserting a field from a dialogue box in a report

- Open the report **rptMondayDelivs** in Design view.

- Delete the field **Morning/Evening** in the report header.

- Place a text box in place of this field and delete its label.

- Set its **Control Source** property to *[Forms]![fdlgMorning/Evening].[M/E]* using the Properties sheet. (You can either type the expression in directly or use the Expression Builder as shown below.)

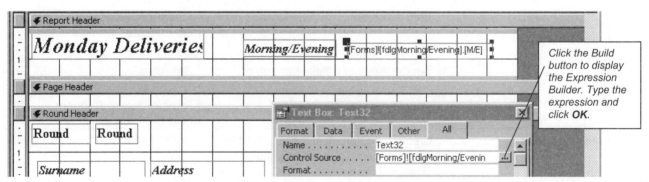

*Figure 7.23: Using a field from a dialogue box in report **rptMondayDelivs***

- Open it in Print Preview mode to make sure **M** is displayed for **Morning/Evening**. If it does not work, check you have the dialogue box **fdlgMorning/Evening** open and **M** selected.

- Save the report and close it.

- Now test your dialogue box by selecting either option and pressing **OK**. Magic!

List of all macro actions in Access

A complete list of macro actions is reproduced below from the MS Access Help system.

Category	Task	Action
Data in forms and reports	Restrict data	ApplyFilter
	Move through data	FindNext, FindRecord, GoToControl, GoToPage, GoToRecord
Execution	Carry out a command	RunCommand
	Exit Microsoft Access	Quit
	Run a macro, procedure, or query	OpenQuery, RunCode, RunMacro, RunSQL
	Run another application	RunApp
	Stop execution	CancelEvent, Quit, StopAllMacros, StopMacro
Import/export	Send Microsoft Access objects to other applications	OutputTo, SendObject
	Transfer data between Microsoft Access and other data formats	TransferDatabase, TransferSpreadsheet, TransferText
Object manipulation	Copy, rename, or save an object	CopyObject, Rename, Save
	Delete an object	DeleteObject
	Move or resize a window	Maximize, Minimize, MoveSize, Restore
	Open or close an object	Close, OpenForm, OpenModule, OpenQuery, OpenReport, OpenTable
	Print an object	OpenForm, OpenQuery, OpenReport, PrintOut
	Select an object	SelectObject
	Set the value of a field, control, or property	SetValue
	Update data or the screen	RepaintObject, Requery, ShowAllRecords
Miscellaneous	Create a custom menu bar, a custom shortcut menu, global menu bar, or global shortcut menu	AddMenu
	Set the state of menu items on a custom menu bar or global menu bar	SetMenuItem
	Display information on the screen	Echo, Hourglass, MsgBox, SetWarnings
	Generate keystrokes	SendKeys
	Display or hide the built-in or custom command bar	ShowToolbar
	Sound a beep	Beep

Chapter 8 – Advanced Form Design

Introduction

In Chapter 3 you saw how to quickly create data entry forms using AutoForm and the Form Wizard. In this chapter we'll look at some of the many ways of customising forms and changing various aspects of a form by altering the properties of the form controls.

> **NOTE:** Any field that accepts, displays or locates data on a form is known as a *control*. Labels, text boxes, drop-down lists, combo boxes and option buttons are all examples of controls.

- Open the **NewsAgt** database. If you have not got this to hand, you will need to download **NewsAgt7.mdb** from the web site www.payne-gallway.co.uk or work through Chapters 1 to 3, and create **tblPayments** as described in Task 5.4.

Before we start a new task, many basic form operations will be reviewed so that you can use this chapter as a reference when creating your own forms. You may like to try some of the techniques by first opening **frmCustomerMain** in Design view and then experimenting with objects on the form. You can then close it without saving it before starting Task 8.1.

Selecting objects

Objects can be selected in several ways.

- Click the object;
- Select the object from the **Object** drop-down list on the Formatting toolbar;
- Click the form selector or the section selector;
- Click on the horizontal ruler to select a column of fields, or on the vertical ruler to select a row of fields.

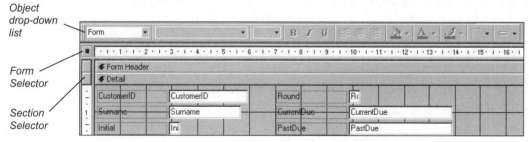

Figure 8.1: Selecting objects

To select multiple objects you can either:

- Hold down the **Shift** key while you click each object, or
- Drag a box around or through the objects; when you release the mouse button, all the objects will be selected.

Moving objects

You can move a control either with or without its label. To move a control with its label, point to it with the mouse and drag. If the object is already selected, point to its border so that the pointer changes to a hand and then drag.

To move just the data field or just the label, point to the top right handle, which is larger than the others. The pointer changes to a pointing hand rather than an open hand. Now drag to the new position.

If you move something by mistake, you can undo the move using the **Undo** button on the toolbar or by selecting **Edit, Undo Move** from the menu bar.

Aligning and spacing objects evenly

To align a group of objects in Design view:

- Select the objects.
- Choose **Format, Align** from the menu bar and then **Left, Right, Top, Bottom** or **To Grid**.

To space objects evenly horizontally:

- Select the objects you want to align.
- Move the left-most object to the place you want it.
- Move the right-most object to where you want it.
- From the menu bar select **Format, Horizontal Spacing, Make Equal**.

To space objects evenly vertically, follow the same steps as above, placing top and bottom objects where you want them and then selecting **Format, Vertical Spacing, Make Equal**.

To make a group of objects the same size:

- Select the objects.
- From the menu bar select **Format, Size** and then choose **To Tallest, To Shortest, To Widest** or **To Narrowest**.

Resizing an area of the form

If you want to increase or decrease the **Form Header**, **Detail** section or **Footer**:

- Select the area you want to resize by clicking on its background or selecting it from the Object drop-down list (see Figure 8.1).
- Point to the bottom border of the area and the pointer changes to a double-headed arrow.
- Drag the border up or down.

You can only add space to the bottom of an area. If you need extra space at the top of an area, you will have to select all the objects and drag them down.

If you have been experimenting with **frmCustomerMain**, remember to close it without saving if you have made changes you do not wish to keep.

Task 8.1: Use form design techniques to smarten up the Customer form

In this task we'll look at many different form design techniques and apply them to the Customer form **frmCustomerMain**.

- Open **frmCustomerMain** in Design view.

We'll start by adding a heading to the form.

- Drag the upper border of the **Detail** section down to make room for the heading in the **Form Header** section.

- Click the **Label** tool on the toolbox and drag out a box in the centre of the **Form Header**.

- Type the title *Customer Details* and tab out of the field.

Changing a heading or label style

- Click the heading to select it (handles appear round the box) and change the font to **Times New Roman, 20 point Bold** and **Centred** using tools on the Formatting toolbar.

- Use the **Fill/Back Color** button to change the background colour of the heading.

Formatting tools

- Use the **Font/Fore Color** button to change the colour of the text.

- Select a border from the **Line/Border Width** drop-down list.

- Change the border colour with the **Line/Border Color** tool.

- Give the heading a shadow or another special effect using the **Special Effect** button.

You can do some additional tidying up, for example:

- Delete the subform label **fsubDelivery**.

- Edit label **Address1**, delete label **Address2**, insert spaces in the labels **CurrentDue**, **PastDue**, **HolsBegin** and **HolsEnd.**

- Set the form's **Record Selectors** property to **No** and **Scroll Bars** to **Neither**.

- Set the form's **Caption** property to *Customer Form*.

Rearranging and resizing fields

Next, we'll rearrange the fields on the form and resize some of them.

- Move the **Round** field and its label to the bottom of the field list, underneath **HolsEnd**. (Click and drag the field and both field and label will move together.)

- Select **CustomerID**, **Title**, **CurrentDue**, **PastDue**, **HolsBegin** and **HolsEnd**. Make them all the same size by selecting **Format, Size, To Narrowest**.

- Rearrange the fields on the form so that they appear something like the figure below. You will need to make use of the techniques described earlier in this chapter to make sure the fields are neatly lined up and evenly spaced.

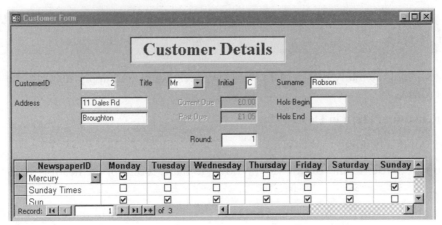

Figure 8.2: The fields rearranged on the Customer form

Inserting an option group

The Round number can be only 1, 2 or 3. We will use an *option group* for this field instead of the text box currently on the form.

- Delete the **Round** text box and its label by selecting it and pressing the **Delete** key.

- Click the **Option Group** button in the toolbox to place an option group in its place.

- The Option Group Wizard dialogue box opens. Enter the labels *Round 1, Round 2, Round* 3 and adjust the width. Click **Next**.

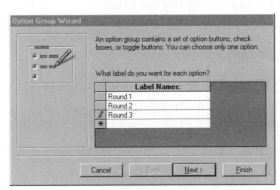

Figure 8.3: The Option Group Wizard

- Leave the default choice as **Round 1** and click **Next**.

- Leave the default values as 1, 2, 3 and click **Next**.

- Click **Store the value in this field** and select **Round** in the list box. Click **Next**.

- Leave the defaults **Option buttons**, **Etched** in the next window and click **Next**.

- Type the caption *Which Round is the customer on?* and click **Finish**.

- With the option group selected, change its **Name** property from **Frame25** or similar name to *Round*.

- Arrange the option buttons in a row and adjust the size of the box around them. Your option group in Form view should look something like the one below:

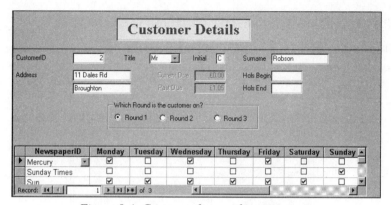

Figure 8.4: Customer form with option group

Changing the tab order

- Switch to Form view and tab through the form. You will find the tab order is all wrong and needs changing.

- Switch back to Design view and select **View, Tab Order** from the menu bar. The Tab Order dialogue box appears.

Figure 8.5: Setting the tab order

- Click **Auto Order** to order the fields from left to right and top to bottom.

Now move **Round** up to below **Address2**, by clicking its left margin to select it and then dragging it to the new location. (If you have not named the option group **Round** it will have a default name like **Frame25**, so drag that instead.) Click **OK**.

- Switch to Form View and test the tab order again. Then return to Design view.

Using the Properties sheet to customise controls

The form and every object on the form has a set of properties which control its appearance and behaviour. To display the property sheet for a selected object, you can use any of the following methods:

-    Click the **Properties** button on the toolbar;
-    Right-click the object and select **Properties** from the shortcut menu;
-    Select **View, Properties** from the menu bar.

We'll set some of the properties for **CustomerID**, **PastDue** and **CurrentDue**.

- Select the **CustomerID** control and display its Property sheet. (Make sure you have selected the text box and not the label. Note that text boxes, labels and other objects are all referred to as *controls*.)

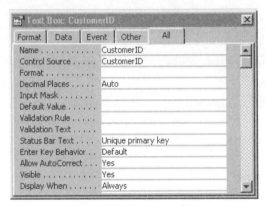

Figure 8.6: Property sheet

- Make sure the **All** tab is selected on the Property sheet, and scroll down to the **Tab Stop** property.

- Since the user can't change the **CustomerID**, we could arrange for the cursor to go straight to the next field. Change the **Tab Stop** property from **Yes** to **No**.

- The **CurrentDue** and **PastDue** fields will be updated automatically by running Update queries. It should not be possible for the user to change either of these fields. Select **CurrentDue** and change its **Tab Stop** property to **No**. Then change its **Enabled** property to **No**. This will make it impossible for the user to change its value. Make the same changes to the **PastDue** properties.

- Switch to Form view and try out the changes. You will see that the two fields **CurrentDue** and **PastDue** are greyed out.

NOTE: The **Tab Index** property controls the tab order. You can change the tab order manually instead of using **View, Tab Order**.

Changing a form's record source

Sometimes you create tables and forms and then decide to rename a table or query on which a form is based. When you next try to open the form you will get an error message like the one below:

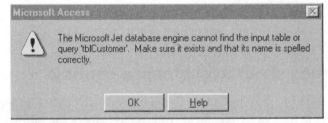

Figure 8.7: The record source for a form cannot be found

To correct this you need to change the Form's **Record Source** property to match the new table or query name. You don't need to do this now.

Task 8.2: Smarten up the Newspaper form

In this task we'll look at combo boxes and list boxes, add a combo box which will help a user to find a particular record, and insert a graphic on the Newspaper form.

Combo boxes and list boxes

These two types of control are similar but have some differences. For example:

- A list box shows all or some of the values in the list, with the selected value highlighted.

- A combo box only shows the current value, and you have to click the drop-down arrow to see a list of values. Another important difference is that a list box only allows you to enter a value from the list. With a combo box, you have the option to either use the list to limit field values or not.

Using a combo box to find a record

You can use a combo box or a list box to find a record. We will place a combo box on **frmNewspaper** which the user can use to search for a particular Newspaper record. This is an alternative method to the **Find** button which we placed on **frmCustomerMain** for finding a particular record.

- Open **frmNewspaper** in Design view. If necessary make it larger so that there is room at the bottom of the form to add the new combo box.

- Click the **Combo Box** tool and click near the bottom of the form to place the box. (The top left corner of the combo box will be positioned at the point where you click.)

- In the first step of the Wizard, select **Find a Record on my Form based on the value I selected in my combo box**. Click **Next**.

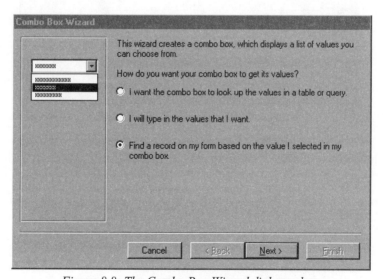

Figure 8.8: The Combo Box Wizard dialogue box

- Move **NewspaperID**, **NewspaperName** and **Morning/Evening** to the list of selected fields.

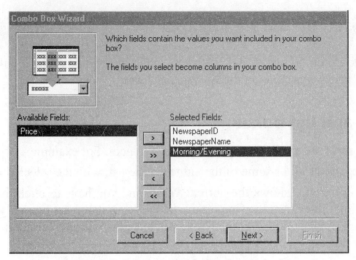

Figure 8.9: Selecting fields for the combo box

- In the next window, uncheck the **Hide Key Column** checkbox and adjust the width of the columns. Click **Next**.

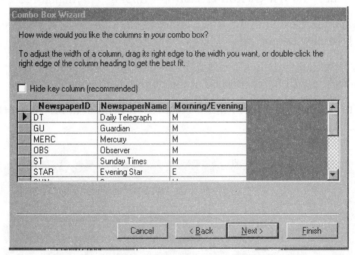

Figure 8.10: Adjusting column widths

- In the next dialogue box, choose **NewspaperID** as the field that uniquely identifies the row. Click **Next**.

- In the next dialogue box, select **Remember the value for later use**. Click **Next**.

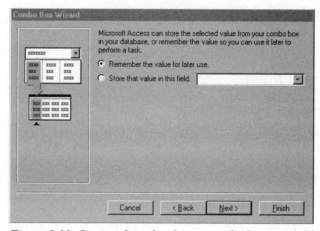

Figure 8.11: Storing the value from a combo box in a field

- In the next dialogue box give the combo box the label *Find Newspaper* and click **Finish**.

- Adjust the size of your combo box and its label.

- Switch to Form View to test your new box.

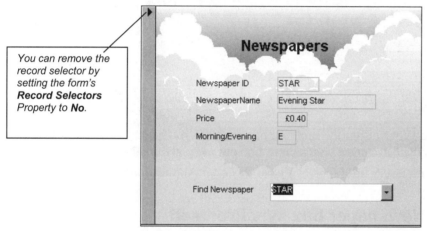

Figure 8.12: Using a combo box to find a record

Inserting a picture on a form

You can add graphic elements such as pictures, lines and boxes to forms to make them more attractive. We'll add a picture to the Newspaper form to draw attention to the **Find** combo box.

- Open **frmNewspaper** in Design view. Make it larger if necessary to make room for a picture.

- Click the **Image** button on the toolbox and drag out an area on the form in the position shown in the figure below. When you release the mouse, an Insert Picture dialogue box will open.

- You can now insert a picture of your own. In Access 2000 it is not so simple to select and insert a clip art picture as it was in Access 97, since you have to know the file names or browse endlessly. In Figure 8.13 I have inserted a clip art picture from C:\Program Files\Common Files\Microsoft Shared\Clipart\Bd00028_.wmf. (In Access 97, select a graphic file from **C:\Program Files\Microsoft Office\Clipart\Popular** or some other source and click **OK**.)

- You now need to shrink the picture to fit its frame, and probably also adjust the size of the frame. In the image's Property sheet change the **Size Mode** property to **Zoom**.

Adding a box to the form

You can use boxes to separate areas of the form.

- Select the **Rectangle** tool and drag out a box around the data fields.

- Use the **Special Effects** tool on the toolbar to create a special effect. You should end up with a form that looks something like the one in the figure below.

- Save your form and return to the Database window.

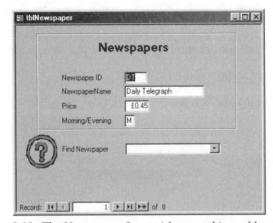

Figure 8.13: The Newspaper form with a graphic and box added

We haven't looked at all the controls on the toolbox, but now that you have a good idea of how some of them work, you can use the help system if you want to find out more about other types of control.

We'll finish this chapter with a very brief look at Visual Basic for Applications.

Keeping the Find Newspaper box synchronised

You will notice that in the above form, the value in the **Find** box is not synchronised with the current record on the screen. If, for example, you use the **Find Newspaper** box to find the Guardian, and then click the **Next Record** navigation button at the bottom of the Form window, the **Find Newspaper** box will still display GU when the Mercury record is on screen. It doesn't really matter, but it could confuse a user and it would be better if the two boxes showed the same data item.

Unfortunately in Access you can't do anything remotely clever without getting into a bit of programming. The good news is that this particular problem is not very difficult to solve!

- Switch to Design view.

- Select the new **Find Newspaper** combo box and make a note of its name, which you are going to need in a moment. You can do this by looking at its **Name** property in the Properties sheet. It will probably be called **Combo10** or **Combo11**.

- Click the box at the intersection of the ruler lines to select the form. We are going to add some code to the **On Current** event property of the form to make the value in the **Find Newspaper** box equal to the current value of the **NewspaperID** field.

- Click the **Event** tab in the Property sheet.

- Click the **Build** Button (3 dots) at the right hand side of the **On Current** event property.

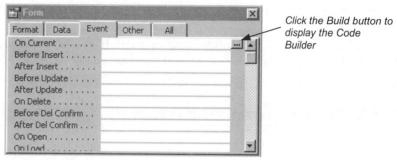

Figure 8.14: The Form's Event properties sheet

- A new dialogue box opens. Select **Code Builder**, and click **OK**.

- Access opens the Form module for the form and displays the Visual Basic code. Note that the procedure headed Sub Combo_AfterUpdate() was created automatically by the Combo Box Wizard. We are going to add one line to the procedure Private Sub Form_Current().

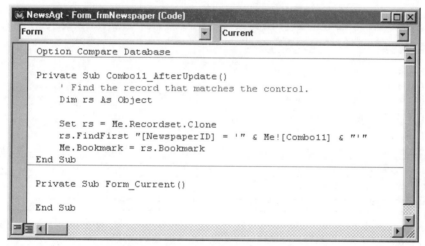

Figure 8.15: The Visual Basic code window

- Underneath the statement **Dim rs as object** (in Access 97, underneath the heading **Private Sub Form_Current ()**) add the line

      Combo11 = NewspaperID

  (Substitute the name of your combo box if it is different.)

  This sets the value of the combo box equal to the current value of **NewspaperID**.

- Save and close the code window.

- Click the **Form View** button on the toolbar. Test the effect of the code by pressing the **Next Record** button at the bottom of the Form window – the combo box should now stay synchronised with the current record.

We'll be looking at Visual Basic again in Chapter 11.

Creating a form from a query

Sometimes you need to combine fields from more than one table on a form. This can be done by first running a query with all the required fields in the query grid, and then creating the form based on the query instead of on a table. *It is important to make sure the query works before you do this, so test your query thoroughly first!*

It is a good idea to create all forms from queries rather than tables because of the extra flexibility it will give you to add extra fields from other tables if you find you need to modify your design.

Task 8.3: Create a form for customer payments

In this task you will first of all design a query named **qryCustomerPayments** to combine fields from **tblCustomer** and **tblPayments**, and then design a form named **frmPayments** based on this query.

- In the Database window select **Queries, Create query in Design view** and click **New**.

- Accept **Design View** in the next dialogue box and click **OK**.

- Add **tblCustomer** and **tblPayment** to the Query window and close the Show Table dialogue box.

- Add fields to the query grid as shown below. Note that **CustomerID** is placed from **tblPayments**.

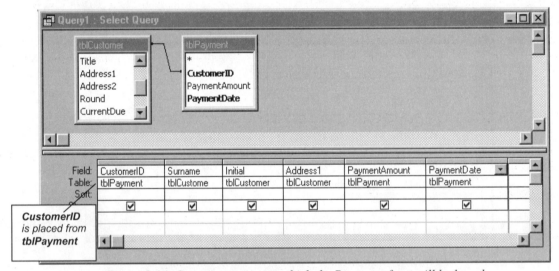

Figure 8.16: Creating a query on which the Payments form will be based

- Run the query to test that it works correctly, and then close it, saving it as *qryCustomerPayments*. (If the Payments table is empty, one empty row will appear.)

Creating the Payments form

- In the Database window click **Forms, Create form by using wizard** and click **New**.

- In the next dialogue box select **AutoForm: Columnar**, and select **qryCustomerPayments** in the bottom list box.

- The form is automatically created. (There may be no records to display.)

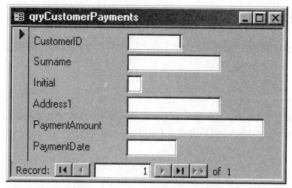

Figure 8.17: The automatically generated Payments form

Design considerations

You need to consider the manual procedure that will take place when a customer comes into the shop to pay. Will the customers present their invoices with the Customer ID (Account number) and Payment amount printed on them, from which the information will be entered? Will the payment be entered into the computer straight away? This is unlikely especially in busy periods. You would need to interview the user (probably the owner of the shop) to find out how the system works.

Depending on how and when the data is entered, and what source document is used, the user of a form such as this may want to be able to locate a particular customer from their surname without necessarily knowing their ID number.

This requires a slightly different technique from that used in Task 8.2 since you are looking up a customer surname not from records already on the Payments table, but from records in the Customer table. We will convert the Surname field into a combo box and put it at the top of the form.

Using a combo box to look up a record from another table

- With the form in Design view, delete the **Surname** label and field and move the **CustomerID** label and field down in its place.

- Place a combo box at the top of the form.

- In the first step of the Wizard, select **I want the combo box to look up the values in a table or query**. Click **Next**.

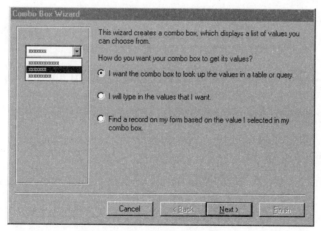

Figure 8.18: Combo Box Wizard

- In the next dialogue box select **tblCustomer**, and click **Next**.

- Move **CustomerID**, **Surname** and **Address1** to the list of selected fields and click **Next**.

- Leave the default **Hide Key Column** checked and click **Next**.

- Check **Store that value in this field**, and select **CustomerID** in the list box, as shown below. Click **Next**. (Note that you are looking up the record by Surname, then selecting the correct record and storing the corresponding CustomerID in the CustomerID field of the Payments table.)

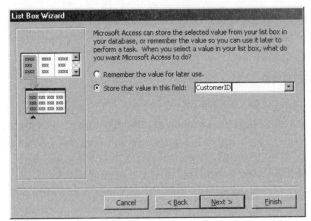

*Figure 8.19: Storing **CustomerID** in the Payment record*

- Specify *Surname* as the label for the combo box and click **Finish**.

- The new combo box appears at the top of the form. You can test it out – having selected a customer you can either enter a payment amount and date, or simply press **Esc** to abandon the record.

- The names do not appear in alphabetical order in the list, which is inconvenient. In the Properties sheet for the combo box, click in the **Row Source** property and the **Build** buttton (3 dots) will appear. Click this to open the query and set **Sort** order to **Ascending** in the **Surname** field. Close the query, answering **Yes** when asked if you want to save the changes made to the SQL statement and update the property.

- The tab order needs to be corrected; select **View, Tab Order**. Select **Auto Order** in the dialogue box and click **OK**.

- You should not allow edits or deletions using this form, which is for additions only. Click the square at the intersection of the ruler lines and change the form properties **Allow Edits** and **Allow Deletions** to **No**.

- Change to Form view and test your form. Try editing a record and adding a record for a customer chosen from the combo box. Try adding a record for a non-existent customer who is not in the list – Access will not allow you to, and you get an error message **The text you entered isn't an item in the list**.

- Close the form when you are happy with it, saving it as *frmPayments*.

TIP: To make all the forms in an application look consistent, define a form called for example **frmTemplate** with all the basic properties. Then make a copy of this for each new form that you need.

Chapter 9 – Rounding off an Application

Introduction

When you have created all the tables, forms, reports, queries, macros and modules that you need in your database, you will probably want to round it all off by creating a customised user interface so that the user does not need to see the Database window at all.

To complete the exercises in this chapter you will need to have created most of the tables, forms and other objects in earlier chapters. Otherwise, download **NewsAgt8.mdb** from the web site www.payne-gallway.co.uk

You saw briefly in Chapter 7 how you can create a menu form with buttons which when clicked perform functions such as opening a form or report. Access has a special tool to create a menu known as a *switchboard*.

One of the tasks that you will perform when you carry out your project design is to decide what the user interface will look like, and this will include designing the menu structure. In the first instance this needs to be done with a pencil and paper.

The menu structure for the Newsagents database

The basic menu structure for the application developed in this book will be as shown below. (Two items included in the sample project, printing receipts and Round sheets, are not included below as the relevant reports and macros have not been created.)

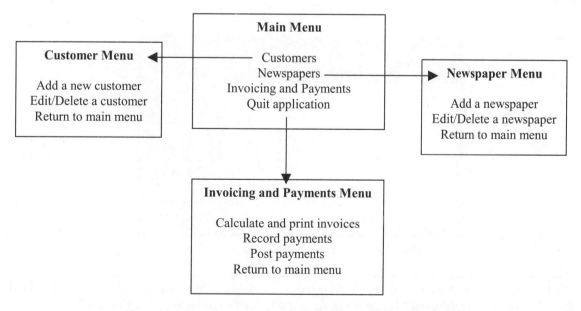

Figure 9.1: Menu structure for Newsagent's database application

Task 9.1: Create a switchboard for the Newsagent application

In this task you will create the menus ("switchboards") as described above using the Access Add-in **Switchboard Manager**, available from the **Tools, Add-Ins** menu. If you have not got this add-in on your system you will have to create your menus as described in Chapter 7.

Creating a switchboard

When you create the menu structure, you must start by creating the submenus and specifying what action will take place when, for example, the user selects **Customers** from the main menu or *switchboard*. When all the submenus have been specified, you can create the main switchboard and perhaps add a graphic.

To start the Switchboard Manager:

- Select **Tools, Database Utilities, Switchboard Manager** (In Access 97, **Tools, Add-Ins, Switchboard Manager**).

- You will see a message:

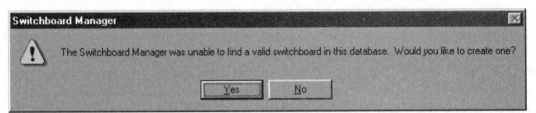

Figure 9.2: Creating a new switchboard

- Click **Yes**. The Switchboard Manager automatically adds a page called **Main Switchboard (Default)** to its window.

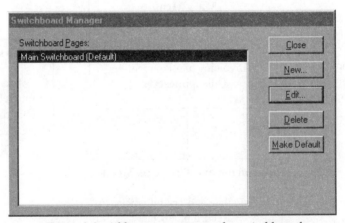

Figure 9.3: Adding a new item to the switchboard

NOTE: Any time you want to display this window in order to edit your switchboard, select **Tools, Database Utilities, Switchboard Manager** (In Access 97, **Tools, Add-Ins, Switchboard Manager**).

Creating the submenus

- Click **New** to add a new switchboard page (this will be the first submenu).

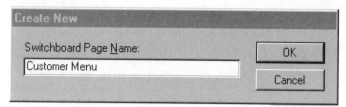

Figure 9.4: Naming the switchboard page

- Type the name *Customer Menu* and press **OK**.

- Add a second new page and name it *Newspaper Menu*.

- Add a third new page and name it *Invoicing and Payments Menu*.

- In the Switchboard Manager window select **Customer Menu** and click **Edit**. The Edit Switchboard Page window appears.

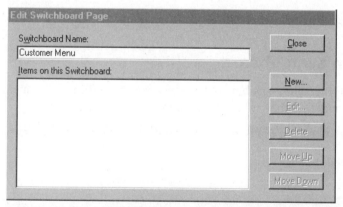

Figure 9.5: The Edit Switchboard Page

- Click **New**. Make entries in the dialogue box as shown below. Click **OK**.

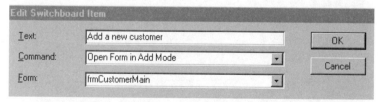

*Figure 9.6: Specifying the action for **Add a new customer***

- Click **New** again in the Edit Switchboard Page window. Type the text *Edit/Delete a customer*, select the command **Open Form in Edit Mode** and specify **frmCustomerMain** as the form to open. Click **OK**.

- Click **New** a third time in the Edit Switchboard Page window. Make entries as shown below and then click **OK**.

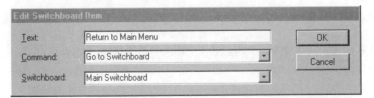

*Figure 9.7: Specifying the action for **Return to Main Menu***

- That completes the **Customer** switchboard. Click **Close** to return to the Switchboard Manager window.

- Create the **Newspaper** switchboard in the same way, by selecting **Newspaper Menu** and clicking **Edit**. Use **frmNewspaper** to Add a newspaper, and Edit/Delete a newspaper.

- Create the **Invoicing and Payments Menu** in the same way as described above. The actions associated with the menu items are as follows:

Calculate and print invoices	Run macro **mcrInvoices.mcrCalculateInvoices**
Record payments	Open Form **frmPayments** in Add mode
Post payments	Run macro **mcrInvoices.mcrPostPayments**
Return to Main Menu	Go to Switchboard **Main Switchboard**

- Click **Close** on the Edit Switchboard Page window, and **Close** on the Switchboard Manager window.

Viewing the main switchboard

We have now created all the submenus but we have not yet created the main menu or switchboard. You can have a look at the empty switchboard before adding the menu items to it.

- In the Database window click **Forms** and select **Switchboard**. Click **Open**.

- The empty switchboard opens.

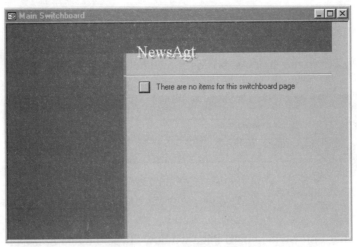

Figure 9.8: The empty switchboard

When we have finished placing the menu items on this switchboard we will change the title and place a graphic.

- Close the form.

Creating the main menu (switchboard)

- Select **Tools, Database Utilities, Switchboard Manager** (In Access 97, **Tools, Add-Ins, Switchboard Manager**) from the menu bar.

- Make sure **Main Switchboard (Default)** is selected in the Switchboard Manager window and click **Edit**.

- Click **New** in the Edit Switchboard Page window to add a new item to the main menu.

- Enter the text *Customers*, and select **Customer Menu** as the switchboard to go to, as shown below.

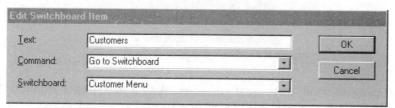

Figure 9.9: Editing a switchboard item

- Click **OK**, and then add the other 3 items on the main switchboard. Note that command for the final item "Quit Application" is **Exit Application**.

- When you have added all the menu items your Edit Switchboard page should look like the figure below:

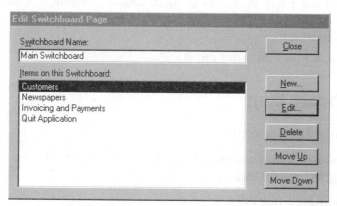

Figure 9.10: The main switchboard items

NOTE: You can change the order of switchboard items by selecting the item you wish to move and clicking **Move Up** or **Move Down**. Try it now!

- Close this window and the next one so that you are back in the Database window.

- Open the Switchboard form to test it.

Testing the switchboard

At this stage you should discover a few things that don't work properly. When you open a form in Add mode, the other records in the table are not displayed and therefore the **Find** buttons that we placed in **frmCustomerMain** and **frmNewspaper** return an error message.

- On the main switchboard, select **Customers**. On the next menu select **Add a new customer**.

- Click the **Find** button that you placed on the form earlier. You will get an error message:

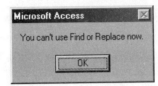

Figure 9.11: Error message from Access

You will get an even more alarming message if you select **Add a newspaper** from the **Newspaper** menu and then press the **Find** button that was placed on that form. Press **End** in the error message box and close the form.

There are several solutions to this problem. You could, for example:

- Use slightly different forms for Adding and Editing a record, with no **Find** button on the form used for adding a customer or a newspaper;

- Not have separate options for adding, editing or deleting a customer, but lump them all together and place custom buttons on the form to enable the user to select an option;

- Run a customised macro instead of using the built-in options to **Open Form in Add Mode** or **Open Form in Edit Mode**. Look back at Figure 7.5 and you will recall that we have already written macros.

We'll select the last option for the **Customer** menu.

Editing a switchboard item

- Close any open forms and switchboards.

- Select **Tools, Database Utilities, Switchboard Manager** (In Access 97, **Tools, Add-Ins, Switchboard Manager)** from the menu bar.

- Select **Customer Menu** and click **Edit**.

- In the Edit Switchboard Page window select **Add a New Customer** and click **Edit**.

- In the Edit Switchboard Item window select the command **Run Macro**. Select the macro **mmnuCustomer.mcrAddCustomer**.

- Close all the windows until you are back in the Database window. Open the Switchboard form and test the **Add a New Customer** option. This time the **Find** button should work correctly.

Customising a switchboard form

We can add a graphic to any or all of the switchboards, change their colours and appearance, change the titles etc. We will add a graphic to the main switchboard and change its title.

- Make sure the **Forms** tab is selected in the Database window and open **Switchboard** in Design view.

- Right-click the title **Newsagt** and select **Properties** to open its Properties Sheet.

- Change the **Caption** property to *Newsagent's Database*.

- There is a 'shadow' caption underneath, so move the top caption aside and alter the caption in the shadow. Then move the top caption back to its original place.

- Click the green background to the left of the menu. At the moment the **Picture** property is **None**.

- Click the ellipsis (…) next to the **Picture** property to open the Insert Picture dialogue box.

- Enter the name of a graphics file. You can use one of the ones you find in **C:\Program Files\Microsoft Office\Office\bitmaps\dbwiz**. I've chosen **Ordproc**.

- Switch to Form view to see the effect of your changes.

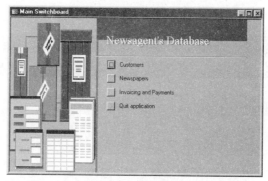

Figure 9.12: The edited main switchboard

- Save and close the form.

That ends the task of creating a switchboard. Next we'll look at creating an Autoexec macro so that your menu opens automatically when you load the application.

Task 9.2: Creating an Autoexec macro

Any macro that is named **AutoExec** will execute automatically as soon as the database is loaded. We will create one that minimises the database window and opens the Switchboard form.

- In the Database window click **Macros** and click **New**.

- Enter the two commands as shown below.

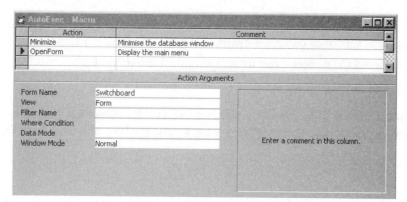

Figure 9.13: Creating an AutoExec macro

- Save the macro, naming it *AutoExec*.

- Close the macro window, and close the database.

- Open the database again. The switchboard should appear automatically.

Setting Startup options

You can set various options such as the name that appears in the Title Bar at the top of the screen, from the **Tools, Startup** menu. You can also specify a form (like a switchboard) to be displayed on starting an application – this could be used instead of creating an AutoExec macro.

- From the menu bar select **Tools, Startup**.

- A dialogue box appears.

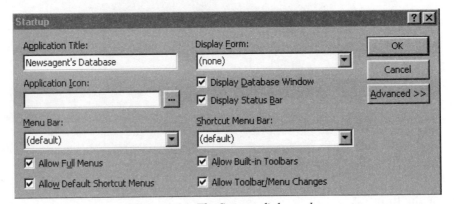

Figure 9.14: The Startup dialogue box

- Type *Newsagent's Database* as the application's title. Leave the other defaults and click **OK**.

- The title bar will now show the new title.

NOTE: If you uncheck **Display Database Window** in the Startup dialogue box, the Database window will be hidden. If you subsequently need to display it, select **Window, Unhide** from the menu bar.

Security

You can add a password to your database so that it is secure from unauthorised users. You will probably not be able to do this on a school or college network, but you can do it on a standalone computer.

In order to set the password the database has to be open in exclusive mode.

- Close the database.

- Click **File, Open Database**. In the Open window, select the **NewsAgt** database and select **Open Exclusive** as shown below. (In Access 97 check the **Exclusive** box, and then click **Open**.)

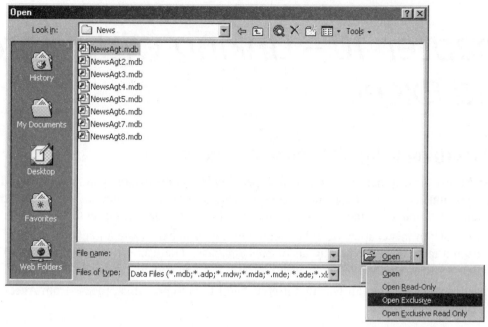

Figure 9.15: Opening a file in Exclusive mode

- From the menu select **Tools, Security, Set Database Password**.

- Type a password, e.g. *news* and type it a second time to verify it. Click **OK**.

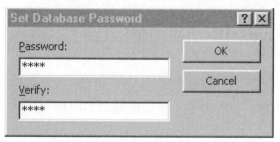

Figure 9.16: Setting a password

WARNING: If you forget the password you will not be able to use the database again. Be warned!

- Close the database and open it again. You will be asked to enter the password:

Figure 9.17: Entering the password

- You can get rid of the password using **Tools, Security, Unset Database Password**.

Chapter 10 – Linking with Word and Excel

Mail merging using data held in Access

If your Access project includes tasks such as printing letters or memos, you may want to do this in Word, which has much better document-processing capabilities than Access. OLE (Object Linking and Embedding) automation is the mechanism that Windows provides for doing this.

In the first task in this chapter we'll be looking at how you can create a mail-merge letter in Word, using fields from a table or query held in an Access database. The user will be able to load Word to create a new letter or use an existing letter and send it to selected customers.

The disadvantage of using OLE is that it is difficult to automate this process from Access without using Visual Basic code.

- Open the **NewsAgt** database. If you have not got this to hand, you will need to download **NewsAgt.9.mdb** from the web site www.payne-gallway.co-uk or work through Chapters 1 to 3.

Task 10.1:   Create a mail merge letter in Word to send to selected customers

In this task we will use the **Office Links** button in Access to jump to Word and create a letter to all customers informing them of a change in opening hours.

- In the Database window select **Tables** and select **tblCustomer**.

- Click the arrow on the **Office Links** button to display the list of options, and select **Merge it with MS Word**.

- The Microsoft Word Mail Merge Wizard opens.

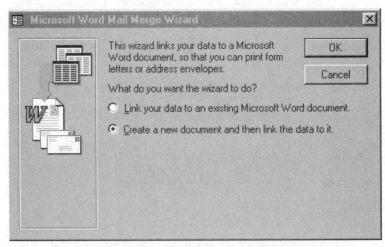

Figure 10.1: The Mail Merge Wizard

- Select the option **Create a new document and then link the data to it**. Click **OK**.

- Word opens in mail merge mode. Create a standard letter as shown below. To insert a field from the Access query, click on the **Insert Merge Field** button and select the required field from the drop-down list.

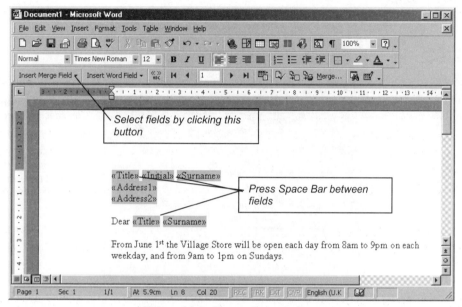

Figure 10.2: The mail merge letter

- Click the **View Merged Data** button to see what the letter will look like when merged with the data. The first letter should appear as shown below.

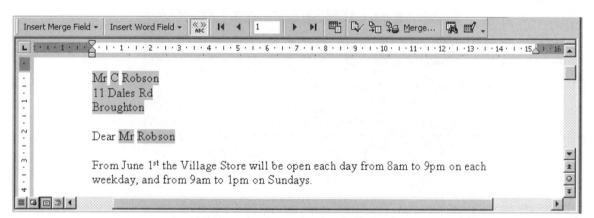

Figure 10.3: The letter with merged data

- Click the **View Merged Data** button again to return to the standard letter. Make any corrections necessary and save it in the same folder as your Newsagent's database application as *Newsletter.doc*.

- Close Word, and you will be returned to your Access database.

- Test out the Mail merge by clicking the Office Links button again. This time, select the first option in the Mail Merge Wizard dialogue box, **Link your data to an existing Microsoft Word document**.

- Select the document **Newsletter.doc**.

- Word opens again with the standard letter on the screen.

- Click the **Mail Merge Helper** button to display the Mail Merge dialogue box. Check that the correct document and data file are specified.

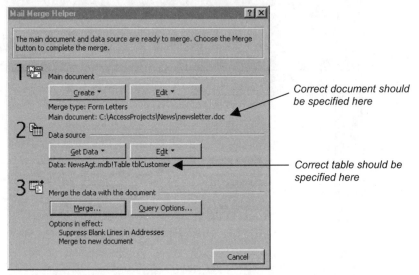

Figure 10.4: Mail Merge Helper

- Click **Merge...** to merge the letter with your data.

- Click **Merge** in the dialogue box as shown below.

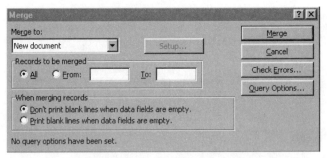

Figure 10.5: Merging the data

- The letters appear on the screen. You could print one letter if you wish, but don't waste paper printing them all at this point!

- Close the letters without saving them, and then close Word to return to Access.

- Close the database window.

If you need to include a mail merge in your project, you can follow through steps such as we have just done to set up a letter, and give instructions in the User Manual for the user to be able to run the mail merge. Without creating a Visual Basic module you cannot easily automate this process any further.

- Close your database without closing Access.

NOTE: You can place a Command Button on a form which opens Word. **Run Application** is one of the actions which you can attach to a button using the Command Button Wizard.

Importing data from Excel

There are some situations where it may be convenient to import data from a worksheet into Excel, perhaps in order to perform queries on it or use it in a database application.

In the next task we will use Excel to create empty records which will be used to contain holiday cottage bookings for the next season. Projects involving bookings systems of one kind or another – for hairdresser's appointments, sports hall facilities, flying lessons or holidays – are quite often attempted by students. One of the major problems is how to create the blank booking records so that the user can see at a glance which times or dates are still available. It is much easier to create a large number of such records in Excel and then import them into Access ready for the new season, month or whatever, than to create them directly in Access.

Task 10.2: Create empty booking records in Excel and import them into Access

- Start Excel and open a new spreadsheet.

    Records need to be entered for a 6-month season starting on Sunday 4th April 1999 – Sunday 26th September 1999, for each of 3 different cottages. Some of the records for the first cottage are shown below:

    Adjust column width by dragging this border

	A	B	C	D	E	F
1	Week Number	Date	Cottage	Customer ID	Number in Party	
2	1	04/04/99	1			
3	2	11/04/99	1			
4	3	18/04/99	1			
5	4	25/04/99	1			
6	5	02/05/99	1			
7	6	09/05/99	1			
8	7	16/05/99	1			
9	8	23/05/99	1			
10	9	30/05/99	1			
11	10	06/06/99	1			
12	11	13/06/99	1			
13	12	20/06/99	1			
14	13	27/06/99	1			
15	14	04/07/99	1			

Figure 10.6: The first few Bookings records

The data for cottages 2 and 3 will be entered beneath the data for cottage 1.

- Type the headings as shown and adjust column widths to accommodate them.

- Type the data in Row 2 as shown.

- In Cell A3 enter the formula $=A2+1$. Copy the formula down to row 27 by clicking the cell and dragging the square at its bottom right corner.

- In cell B3 enter the formula $= B2+7$. Copy the formula down to row 27.

- Copy cell C2 down to row 27.

Now you can prepare the details for cottage 2, using copy and paste wherever possible.

- In A28 enter the formula $=A2$. Copy the formula down to row 53 to enter all the week numbers. (The cells will automatically fill with formulae **=A3, =A4** etc)

- In cell B28 enter the formula $=B2$. In B29 enter $=B2+7$ and copy the formula down to row 53.

- In cell C28 enter *2*, and copy down to row 53. This specifies that all these rows refer to cottage 2.

You can repeat this process to get empty booking records for Cottage number 3, or skip this step!

You will notice that all you have to do to create empty records for the year 2000 is to change the date in cell B2. Try it!

- Save the spreadsheet in a convenient folder as *EmptyBookings99.xls* and close Excel.

Importing records into Access

The next step is to import these records into a new Access database.

- Open a new, blank database in your current folder and name it *Bookings.mdb*.

- Right-click the Database window and select **Import...**

- In the Import window, select the folder where you saved the Excel file. Select Files of type **Microsoft Excel (*.xls)** in the dialogue box near the bottom of the screen.

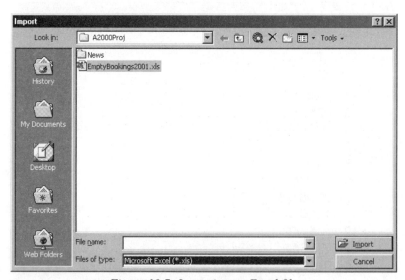

Figure 10.7: Importing an Excel file

- Select **EmptyBookings2001.xls** and click **Import**.

- The Import Spreadsheet Wizard opens as shown below. Leave the defaults and click **Next.**
  (In Access 7 this window does not appear, so skip this step.)

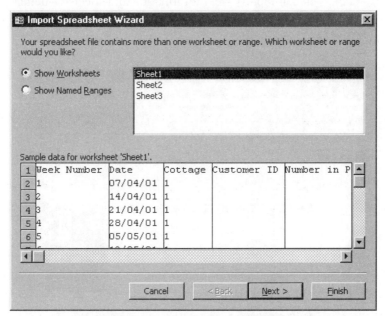

Figure 10.8: The Import Spreadsheet Wizard

- In the next dialogue box, leave **First Row Contains Column Headings** checked and click **Next**.

    In the next dialogue box you have the choice of whether to create a new table or store the data in an existing table. *(In Access 7 this window does not appear, so skip this step.)*

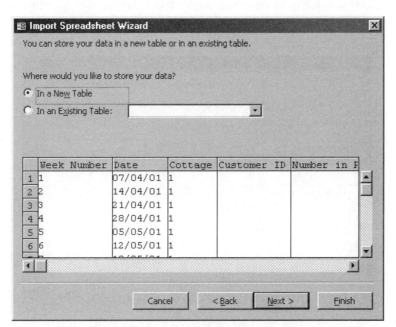

Figure 10.9: Selecting where to store data

- Select **In a New Table**. (Note that if you needed to, you could add new empty records for the next period to an existing table.) Click **Next**.

- In the next dialogue box, you can modify field information and specify whether certain fields are not to be imported. Select **Number in Party** by clicking its column header and change its **Indexed** property to **No**. Click **Next**.

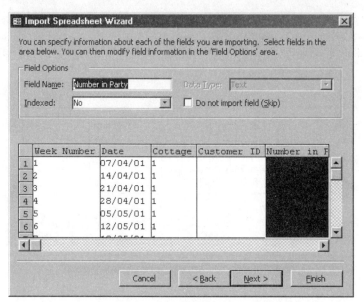

Figure 10.10: Specifying which fields are indexed

- In the next dialogue box you are asked to select a primary key. The key field will consist of two fields, **Date** and **Cottage**, but you can only set a single field as the key in this Wizard. Click **No Primary Key** – we will define the Primary key later. Click **Next**.

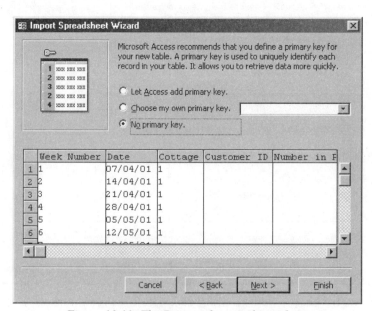

Figure 10.11: The Primary key can be set later

- In the next dialogue box give the table the name *tblBookings* and click **Finish**.
- Click **OK** in the message box 'Finished Importing File'.

- Open the table in Design view. You need to set the Primary key – select **Date** and hold down the **Shift** key while you select **Cottage**. Then click the **Primary Key** button.

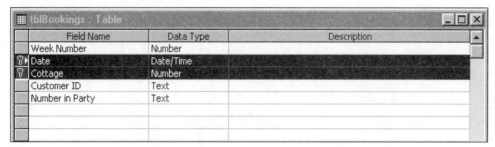

Figure 10.12: Defining the Primary Key

- Save and close the table.

Appending imported records to an existing table

You can now try appending the next year's records to the existing table.
(You cannot do this in Access 7. You would have to import the data to a new table and then use an Append query to append the data to an existing table.)

- Edit the Excel spreadsheet, changing the date in cell B2 to *02/04/00*. Save the amended sheet in the same folder as before, naming it *EmptyBookings2002*. Close Excel.

- In the Database window, right-click and select **Import...**

- Follow through the steps of the Wizard, but this time select the table **tblBookings** as the table in which to store your data.

The new set of records will be added to the original imported records.

This of course is only the beginning – you now have a basic Bookings table, and you will have to create other tables, queries and forms as required. You could consider, for example, opening a dialogue box when a customer wants to make a booking to ask for a desired range of dates or times. The answers could be used as criteria in a query on which a booking form could be based.

That ends this task – we'll look next at exporting data to Excel.

Analysing data in Excel

Although it is possible to summarise data in Access, it is sometimes easier to perform statistical analyses or calculations in Excel. If for example you wanted to produce a graph comparing the number of holiday bookings each month in 1999 and 2000, it would probably be easier to do this in Excel.

We have no data to analyse at present, but to illustrate how to export data to Excel, we'll export the table *tblBookings* that you have just created.

- In the Database window select the table **tblBookings**.

- Select **Analyse it with MS Excel** from the **Office Links** drop-down list on the toolbar. The table appears as a worksheet in Excel.

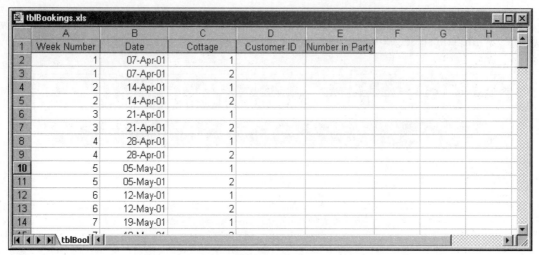

Figure 10.13: The table opened as a .xls file in Excel

Any changes you make to this spreadsheet will not change the original table.

Exporting data

As well as importing data into an Access database, you can export it to different files, including other Access databases or to an Excel spreadsheet.

- Select the table to be exported. Select **File, Export** (In Access 97, **File**, **Save As/Export)** from the menu bar.

- (In Access 97, select **To an External File or Database** and click **OK**.)

- Change the **Save As Type** to the type of file you want to export to.

- Change the folder if necessary and enter a name for the new file.

- Click **Export**.

infotech

Chapter 11 – An Introduction to Visual Basic for Applications

Introduction

Many processing tasks simply cannot be accomplished in Access except by running modules written in Visual Basic for Applications (VBA), the programming language that Access uses. (VBA is very closely related to Visual Basic and the language is often referred to using the terms interchangeably.) It is impossible in a book of this size and scope to go into much detail about the language or the programming techniques that are used by experienced programmers, and indeed you may feel that you do not want to include Visual Basic programming in your Access project. Many operations can be performed using command buttons and macros, which have already been covered. This chapter will give you a feel for what you may be able to accomplish using VBA.

Visual Basic Modules

Visual Basic code is stored in *modules*. Each form and report in a database has its own attached form module or report module, and most VBA code that you write will belong to an individual form or report. You can also write code that applies to more than one form or report and is stored in a *standard module*, which is a separate object in the Database window.

Visual Basic code comes in units called procedures, each performing a single task. You saw an example of a Visual Basic procedure in Chapter 8. The procedure consisted of just one line and kept a combo box synchronised with the record currently on screen. Many procedures consist of just a few lines.

The following diagram illustrates the relationships between Forms, Reports, Modules and Procedures.

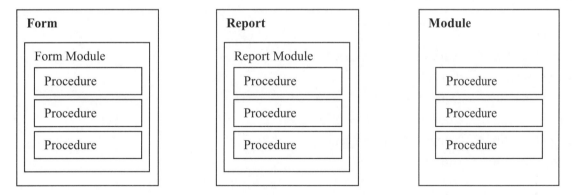

Figure 11.1: Relationships between Forms, Reports, Modules and Procedures

We'll create a fast prototype for a brand new database to practise some new techniques. If you don't want to bother with creating the tables, relationships and forms that we need before getting on to the VBA programming, you can download **Snackbar.mdb** from the web site www.payne-gallway.co.uk and skip straight to the coding.

A stock control application

The application that we will create in this chapter is a very basic stock control system for a snack bar at a Youth Club. The stock control system will consist of just two tables: **tblProducts** which will contain details of each product and **tblTransactions** which will contain details of each stock transaction. Transactions can be one of the following types:

Sale   Goods are sold and the quantity in stock is decreased by the amount sold;

Purchase   Goods are purchased by the snack bar, and the quantity in stock is increased by the amount purchased;

Write-off   Goods are damaged, lost or stolen and the quantity in stock is decreased accordingly;

Refund   Goods are returned to stock and the quantity in stock is increased accordingly;

Amendment   Used to correct errors in data entry.

The purpose of this application is to maintain a database showing details of each product and how many of that product are currently in stock. This will be done by recording every stock transaction and updating the master file in real time.

What is the relationship between the two entities **Product** and **Transaction**?

Creating the tables

- Open a new database and name it *Snackbar.mdb*.

- Create two tables in Design view structured as follows:

tblProducts

StockID	AutoNumber (Primary key)
StockDescription	Text (50)
CostPrice	Currency
SellingPrice	Currency
QuantityInStock	Number (Long Integer)

tblTransactions

TransactionNumber	AutoNumber (Primary key)
TransactionType	Text (50)
TransactionDate	Date/Time
StockID	Lookup Wizard (see below)
TransactionQuantity	Number (Long Integer)
TransactionAmount	Currency

When you select Lookup Wizard as the field type for **StockID**, a dialogue box will open.

- Choose the option **I want the lookup column to look up the values in a table or query** and click **Next**.

- Choose **tblProducts** in the next dialogue box and click **Next**.

- Move **StockID** and **StockDescription** from **Available Fields** to **Selected fields**. Click **Next**.

- Leave the default **Hide Key Column** selected in the next dialogue box. Click **Next**.

- Leave **StockID** as the label for your Lookup column and click **Finish**.

- Click **Yes** when asked if you want to save the table, and name it *tblTransactions*.

- You may see a message: **The Lookup wizard was unable to create the relationship**. Click **OK**.

- Close the table.

Creating the relationships between the tables

- Click the **Relationships** button to open the Show Table dialogue box.

- Add both tables to the Relationships window and then close the dialogue box.

- Drag **StockID** from **tblProducts** to **StockID** in **tblTransactions**. In the dialogue box, check **Enforce Referential Integrity** and click **Create**. This is a *one-to-many* relationship – always drag the common field from the **One** to the **Many** side of the relationship.

- The relationships window should appear as shown below:

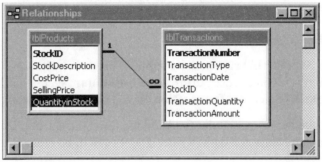

Figure 11.2: Creating the one-to-many relationship

- Save and close the relationships window.

- Open **tblProducts** and add records as shown below.

	StockID	StockDescription	CostPrice	SellingPrice	QuantityinStock
	1	Trebor softmints	£0.15	£0.32	20
	2	Mars Bar	£0.15	£0.30	20
	3	Maltesers Standard	£0.21	0.39	20
	4	Walkers Cheese & Onion Crisps	£0.10	£0.30	20
	5	Walkers Bacon Flavoured Crisps	£0.10	£0.30	20
	6	Coca Cola can	£0.10	£0.49	20
	7	Seven Up can	£0.12	£0.49	20
*	(AutoNumber)		£0.00	£0.00	0

Record: 3 of 7

Figure 11.3: Products data

- Save and close the window.

Creating data entry forms

The next stage in this quick prototype application is to create some data entry forms.

- Select **Forms, Create form by using Wizard** and click **New**. In the New Form dialogue box select **AutoForm: Columnar** and select **tblProducts** in the list box **Choose the table or query...**

- The form will be created as shown below:

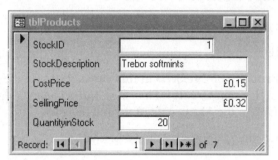

Figure 11.4: The Products form

- Save the form as *frmProducts*.

- Create a new form for the **tblTransactions** table. This time, choose **Form Wizard** instead of **AutoForm: Columnar**. (If you choose **AutoForm: Columnar** Access will not automatically insert a lookup field for **StockID**.) Select **tblTransactions** in the bottom list box and click **OK**.

- In the next few dialogue boxes, put all the fields on the form and select a **Columnar** layout. Choose a **Standard** background and leave the default title. The form will be created as shown below:

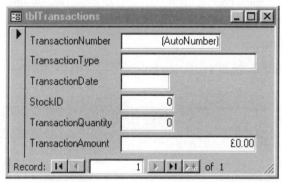

Figure 11.5: The Transactions form

- Save the form as *frmTransactions*.

We'll replace the field **TransactionType** with a list box so that the user can select from the five transaction types.

- Switch to Design view, or open **frmTransactions** in Design view if it is not currently open.

- Click the **TransactionType** field and delete it.

- Click the **List Box** tool on the toolbox and click in place of the field you have deleted. (The top left corner of the list box will be positioned where you click.)

- In the List Box Wizard dialogue box, select the option **I will type in the values that I want** and click **Next**.

- Type in the values as shown below, and then click **Next**.

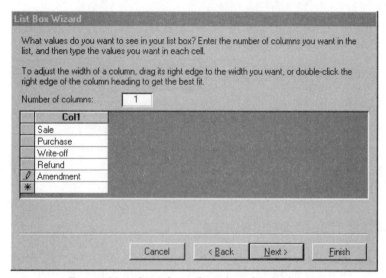

Figure 11.6: Specifying the values for the list box

- In the next dialogue box, select **TransactionType** in the box **Store that value in this field**. Click **Next**.

- Enter **Transaction Type** as the label for the list box. Click **Finish**.

- Adjust the position and size of the fields so that in Form view, all the values in the list box can be seen.

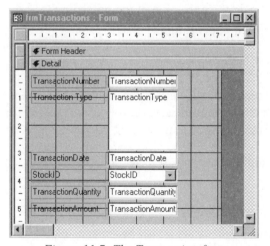

Figure 11.7: The Transaction form

- Check the form in Form view and when it is satisfactory, save the form again.

- Try entering a record as shown below. (We will write VBA code to calculate **TransactionAmount** automatically.)

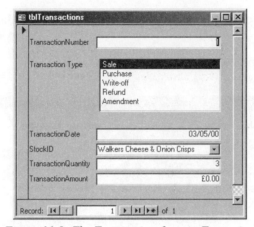

Figure 11.8: The Transaction form in Form view

We're ready to start programming!

Planning a Visual Basic procedure

We need to write one or more procedures which will be triggered when the user enters transactions using the above form. The procedure(s) will calculate the sterling amount and automatically put it into the field **TransactionAmount**. The **QuantityInStock** will then be adjusted in **TblProducts**.

The amount will be calculated by multiplying **TransactionQuantity** by either the **CostPrice** or the **SellingPrice** held on **tblProducts**, depending on the type of transaction. To start with, the procedure will assume that the transaction type is a Sale, and when that is working correctly the procedure will be expanded to cope with all transaction types.

When you plan a VBA procedure, you have to think about three separate issues:

- What tasks will the procedure carry out?
- How do you code the procedure in VBA?
- What event will trigger the execution of the procedure?

The basic task that has to be carried out is simple:

```
Make TransactionAmount equal to SellingPrice multiplied by TransactionQuantity.
Subtract TransactionAmount from QuantityInStock
```

However, a bit more detail is required, because in the first statement, for example, **SellingPrice** comes from **tblProducts**, and **TransactionAmount** is a control on the current form. We will first of all have to make sure that the procedure knows which item's selling price we are referring to.

One way to do this is to wait until the user has selected a particular **StockID**, and then run a procedure to perform the following tasks:

```
Make sure frmProducts is open
Set the focus in the StockID field
Find the record with the same ID as the one the user has selected in frmTransactions
Set focus back in frmTransactions
```

This procedure could be attached to the **On Exit** event on the **StockID** control.

As soon as the user tabs out of the **TransactionQuantity** field, a second procedure to calculate **TransactionAmount** and update the **QuantityInStock** can be run.

A VBA procedure to find a record

We'll create the first procedure and then take it apart to see how it works.

- Switch to Design view or open **frmTransactions** in Design view if it is not already open.

- Right-click the combo box **StockID** and select **Properties** to open its Properties sheet.

- Make sure the **Event** tab is selected and click the **Build** button (3 dots) for the **On Exit** property. In the next dialogue box select **Code Builder** and click **OK**.

- The VBA module window opens with the first and last lines of the procedure already written. Type the following lines of code (excluding the first and last lines which are already there):

```
Private Sub StockID_Exit(Cancel As Integer)
    Dim StockNum As Long
    StockNum = StockID
'frmProducts must be open so that the right record can be found
    DoCmd.OpenForm "frmProducts"
'Set focus in StockID field and find the record
    StockID.SetFocus
    DoCmd.FindRecord StockNum
'Return to frmTransactions
    Forms![frmTransactions].SetFocus
End Sub
```

- Save the code and close the code window.

- Switch to Form View and enter a new transaction. As soon as you tab out of the **StockID** field, the Products form will open at the correct record. If it doesn't, check your code and try again!

Now we'll dissect this program so see how it was all put together.

Sub and End Sub

These two lines designate the beginning and end of the procedure. You'll see similar lines at the beginning and end of every event procedure – they are added automatically and you really don't need to think about them.

The Dim statement

Dim stands for *Dimension*. This statement tells Access about a variable that you're going to use in the procedure. A variable is a temporary place to store information in a computer's memory. A Dim statement includes the name of the variable and the type of data it will store.

For a list of all the data types select **Objects, Data Types** and then **See Also**, **select Data Type Summary** in the Help index.

In this instance we are going to use a variable **StockNum** to store the value of **StockID** in **frmTransactions**, which being an AutoNumber field has the data type Long Integer.

Assignment statements

An assignment statement sets the value of a variable to an expression on the right hand side of the = sign. You can optionally put the word Let at the start of an assignment statement.

For further help look up **Assignment statements, Let Statement** in the Help index.

Comments

Any line beginning with an apostrophe ('), by default shown in green text, is a comment and has no effect on the running of the program. You should always use comments to explain what your procedure does.

The DoCmd object

You'll be seeing a lot of the keyword DoCmd if you get into VBA programming. It is an *object*, along with other objects such as forms, reports and controls. Each object has its own set of *methods* – for example a Form has methods to Open, Close, Maximise and Minimise, and a control has a SetFocus method.

OpenForm and FindRecord are methods of the DoCmd object. You can see a complete list of all the methods that you can use with the DoCmd object as follows.

- Switch to Design view in the form **frmTransactions**.

- Return to the VBA code window by clicking the **Build** button for the **On Exit** event of the **StockID** control.

- Click the **Object Browser** button.

- In the Object Browser window, select **Access** in the top list box, and **DoCmd** in the **Classes** list box.

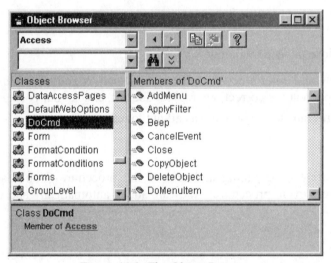

Figure 11.9: The Object Browser

Using the Object Browser is the best way of finding the command you are looking for.

NOTE: To use the Object Browser, first load any module and then the **Object Browser** button will appear on the toolbar. If you have no modules to load, select the **Modules** tab in the Database window and click **New**.

Referring to forms, subforms, reports and subreports

The final statement of the procedure

```
Forms![FrmTransactions].SetFocus
```

sets the focus (see below) back in the form **frmTransactions**.

To refer to an open form or report you type the name of the **Forms** or **Reports** *collection* (i.e. the word **Forms** or **Reports**) followed by an exclamation mark (!) and the name of the form or report.

To refer to a subform named **fsubCust** in a form named **frmCust**, for example, write

```
Forms![FrmCust]![fsubCust].Form
```

If the focus is currently in **frmCust**, you can write instead

```
Me![fsubCust].Form
```

For more information on referring to forms look up **Objects, referring to in Expressions** in the Help system.

The *focus* allows an object to receive user input, and is often shown by a dotted outline around a control. Only one object at a time can have the focus. It can be changed by clicking or tabbing into a control or form, or by the **SetFocus** method which moves the focus to the specified form or the specified control on the active form.

A second VBA procedure

This procedure calculates the transaction amount and the new stock quantity. It will be attached to the **On Exit** property of the **TransactionQuantity** control.

- With the form open in Design view, display the Properties sheet for **TransactionQuantity**.

- Click the **Build** button for the **On Exit** Event property.

- Select **Code Builder** and click **OK**.

- Type the following lines of code in the procedure:

```
' calculate the transaction amount
    TransactionAmount = TransactionQuantity * Forms![frmProducts].SellingPrice
' subtract transaction quantity from QuantityInStock on frmProducts
    Forms![frmProducts].QuantityInStock = Forms![frmProducts].QuantityInStock _
    - TransactionQuantity
```

> **NOTE:** To continue a long statement onto a second or third line, type a space followed by an underscore and then press **Enter**. Do not split a statement in the middle of a word or identifier.

- Save and close the code window.

- Test the form. As soon as you tab out of the **StockID** control, **frmProducts** should open. As soon as you tab out of **TransactionQuantity**, the **TransactionAmount** should be calculated and **QuantityInStock** should be updated on the Products form **frmProducts**. (You may need to position your windows so that both forms are visible on screen.)

*What happens to **QuantityInStock** if you click in **TransactionQuantity** and then tab out of the field again? This is discussed near the end of this chapter.*

You may notice some things about the form which could be improved. For example you want the focus to move straight to **TransactionType** when a new Transaction form is displayed ready for data entry. Does this involve a procedure or simply changing the property of the **TransactionNumber** control?

We now need to add some extra code to this procedure to cater for all the different types of transaction. So far, your two procedures should look like the ones shown below:

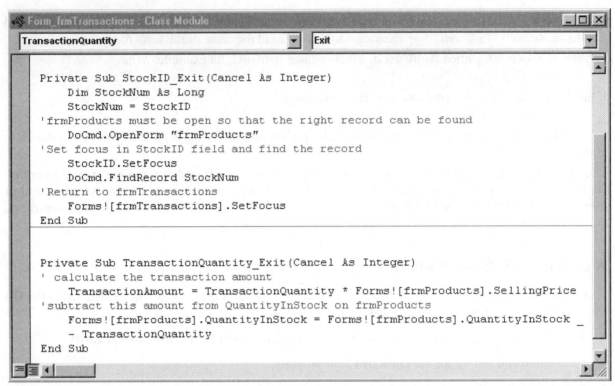

Figure 11.10: VBA code window

Selection statements in VBA

Selection statements are used in programs to select alternative courses of action depending on the value of an expression or variable. In the example that we are looking at, the action to be taken depends on the transaction type, as summarised in the action list below:

Transaction

Type	Transaction Amount	Calculation of new Quantity in stock
Sale	TransactionQuantity * SellingPrice	QuantityInStock - TransactionQuantity
Purchase	TransactionQuantity * CostPrice	QuantityInStock + TransactionQuantity
Write-off	TransactionQuantity * CostPrice	QuantityInStock - TransactionQuantity
Refund	TransactionQuantity * SellingPrice	QuantityInStock + TransactionQuantity
Amendment	TransactionQuantity * CostPrice	QuantityInStock + TransactionQuantity

There are two kinds of selection statement that we could use: **If..Then..Else** or **Select Case**. When there are several possible cases to be tested, it is more efficient to use a **Select Case** statement. You can get extra information on both these statements from the Access Help system, but for now, you can amend your procedure **Sub TransactionQuantity_Exit** as shown below.

TIP: Use **Shift-tab** to move the indent position to the left.

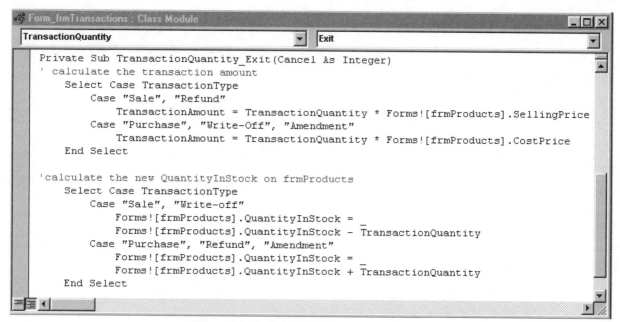

Figure 11.11: Using the Select Case statement

When you test this procedure, you may notice that it seems to work correctly but that if you go back and change the quantity before moving to a new record, the quantity in stock will be adjusted again, which is incorrect. In order to prevent this happening, you need to attach the second part of the procedure, which calculates the new **QuantityInStock** on **FrmProducts**, to the **After Update** property of the form (**not** the **TransactionQuantity** control).

You also need to make sure that the user cannot edit or delete any transactions that have already been accepted. (This can be done by setting the Form properties **Allow Edits** and **Allow Deletions** to **No**.) If the user makes a mistake an **Amendment** must be entered to cancel out the incorrect transaction and then the original transaction reentered. It needs to be made clear whether an amendment results in items being returned to stock or removed from stock – maybe two different transaction types are required instead of one for amendments.

This discussion illustrates the importance of:

- very careful systems design;

- thoroughly testing all your procedures and trying to anticipate what could possibly go wrong;

- getting the user to test the system, which will usually reveal all kinds of unexpected events that had not occurred to you, and result in some changes to your design.

Debugging code

If you find that your procedures don't work as expected, Access has several tools to help you find logic errors. Look up **Debug window** or **Debugging Code** in the Help system for more details.

Part 2

Tackling the Project

In this section:

Chapter 12 -   Project Ideas
Chapter 13 -   The Systems Life Cycle
Chapter 14 -   Writing the Project Report

Chapter 12 – Project Ideas

Introduction

Access is a good choice of software for a major project, if you intend to select a problem that can be implemented as a database. Be careful not to put the cart before the horse though; you must show in the Design section that you have considered a number of approaches to solving the problem you have identified and have made a considered choice. This may mean looking at alternative software packages such as a spreadsheet, a commercially written package such as Sage Accounting software or a specialist package used by say, doctors, hairdressers or sports centres for handling appointments or bookings. It may also mean looking at alternative models (solutions) within Access. You must be prepared to justify your choice of Access database and/or model and, if you cannot, choose a different project or use the software that you have identified as being the most suitable for the job.

Finding a real user

It is absolutely essential when tackling a major project to find a real user with a real problem to be solved. The 'problem' may be a task that is currently being performed manually, but that could be done better using a computer. It could be that a manual system just cannot produce the required information. For example, manual appointment systems generally involve writing the customer's name in a large Appointments book. The last time I went to the dentist, a few months ago, I made an appointment for about 6 months ahead, but I've lost the card telling me when it is. The only way the receptionist can tell me is by thumbing through all the appointments over a three-month period, since I really can't remember when my last visit was. A computerised booking system should be able to produce this information instantly!

You need to start looking for a project idea towards the end of the first year of a two-year course. Ask your parents to help – maybe there is a suitable problem for computerisation at their workplace. If you have ever had a part-time job, or have one now, perhaps you can think of some aspect of the job that would work better with the aid of a database.

Another idea is to find out how things work at your doctor's or dentist's surgery, or at your local sports centre, cinema or newsagents. It is not a requirement of the project that the solution you produce is actually adopted by the organisation; but you should get the user to try out the finished project and give you some feedback.

Input-Process-Output

Take heed of these words written by the Principal Moderator in the Report on the Examination 1998: "An increasing number of projects were seen where the candidate concentrated upon the user interface but the solution did not actually do anything. Functionality of input/processing/output took second place to cosmetics... splash screens, combo boxes, list boxes, menus and buttons calling macros were created to provide an impressive front end but little or no real data processing was done."

Such projects will not score very good marks. You should, therefore, look for an application in which data is

♦ **input**, preferably on a regular basis (daily, weekly, monthly or even annually),

♦ **processed** in some way (using various types of queries, macros or modules) and finally

♦ **output** in the form of a screen or printed report of some kind. The output may show on screen the answer to a query or it may be a report that is produced on a regular basis.

Look for a project that includes cyclic characteristics, processing which is repeated on a regular basis which will provide potential for clearing down or archiving data.

Using a relational database

Access is a particularly suitable package for a database project because it is a *relational* database. In order to score high marks your project must exploit this fact, by using at least two or three tables which are related by means of common fields. It is absolutely essential to thoroughly understand the theory of database design including the definitions of entities, attributes and relationships. These topics are briefly covered in Chapter 1. The dentist's appointment system mentioned above, for example, could involve tables for Patients, Appointments and Patient Records. How are these three entities related? The answers to such questions are rarely simple and generally the statement of the problem will need further clarification. Does a patient have just one patient record, or is a patient record defined as the record of a particular treatment, visit or tooth?

As well as understanding how the entities are related, you must have a clear understanding of how the system will work. For example, what happens to appointment records when the date of the appointment is past? Do they stay on the file, or are they moved to an Archive file or simply deleted? How far in advance can a patient book?

Using advanced features of Access

As well as using related tables, you must demonstrate an advanced knowledge of the various features of Access. These could include:

♦ a customised interface including a front end menu;

♦ data entry screens including list boxes or combo boxes, command buttons to perform tasks such as moving between records, finding/deleting particular records or returning to a menu;

♦ validation of input data or use of masks;

♦ forms with subforms;

♦ queries involving parameters input by the user;

♦ update, append or delete queries to perform processing tasks;

♦ summary reports or forms based on the results of queries involving several tables;

♦ use of macros or modules written in Visual Basic for Applications;

♦ security features such as passwords in a multi-user environment;

♦ links to other packages such as Word or Excel.

Some possible topics for projects are described below – read them to get an idea of the sort of 'problem' you are looking for, and then find a real user for your own project!

Booking systems

Booking systems for holiday cottages, badminton and squash facilities, theatre productions, hairdresser's appointments and so on are quite a popular choice for a database project. You need to be sure you understand what the objectives of the system are and whether a database is the right solution. For a hairdresser, are there any real advantages in a computerised booking system? Would they be better to get a specialised package written specifically for hairdressers?

You need to consider what advantages a computerised system will give the user, and what the disadvantages are. It may be that extra information on customers can be held in a database which will be useful in some way. On the other hand a hand-written appointments book may be very quick and convenient.

You need to think out how you are going to record bookings or appointments. Are you going to have blank booking records for a month, season or year ahead, which will be edited as bookings are made? Or are you simply going to add new bookings to the database as they are made? If so, will you be able to tell customers what times, dates, seats etc are free? You might like to consider creating a set of blank appointment records in Excel and then importing them at intervals to your Access database. Such a system is explained in Chapter 10.

Order entry systems

Database software can be successfully used to record details of customers and orders for goods or services of some description – really anything from spectacles to garden furniture, from legal services to building work. The entities involved may be Customers, Orders, Order Lines and Payments. The entity Order Line is necessary if an order may consist of more than one item or 'order line'.

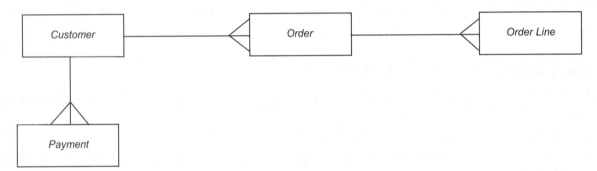

Figure 12.1: An E-R diagram for a Customer Orders database

Stock control systems

A small-scale stock control system can be quite successful, but do not attempt to redesign the Tesco or Woolworth stock control. The sweetshop at a cinema or club, or a school or college shop, is more likely to be the source of a suitable project. The entities involved will probably be Stock and Transaction, linked by a one-to-many relationship. The main point to grasp about a stock control project is that it is essential to maintain an Audit Trail, by which it is possible to see exactly why there are say 50 Mars Bars left in stock when you had 100 a week ago. You must never allow the user simply to go in and edit the quantity in stock – it must always be changed by updating the stock file from a transaction. Stock may be sold, purchased, returned, spoilt or 'adjusted' because of an error or because a physical check of the stock on the shelves does not agree with what the database says – but every stock movement in the database must be traceable. A very simple stock control application is implemented using some simple Visual Basic programming in Chapter 11.

You would have to be clear about what the output from the system was to be: it is not sufficient to create a system which simply tells you how much stock you have. The user might require the system to produce a weekly reorder report of items which were running low, a report of best-selling or slow-moving items, or a monthly profit report.

League tables

Basketball, football or other Sports Leagues can be suitable topics for a project. You need to have personal experience of how the league tables work, how many teams there are in the league, how many fixtures there are each season and so on. You must have a clear idea of the objectives; are you tracking individual players or teams? What is the input, processing and output? What will be done in your system at the start and end of each season?

General information systems

It is impossible to describe in general terms many of literally thousands of database applications that individual students come up with every year. In the next chapter we'll look at how to tackle each stage of the project by looking at a particular example. You may know someone who wants to keep information on club members, students, customers, patients, pets, plants, meals, books, videos (best avoided – it's been done to death), cars or houses. Just remember that there has to be some *point* to having a database – **there must be some information produced that is more than simply a list of the data that you entered**.

Inappropriate projects

Finally, here's some advice on what *not* to choose.

♦ Payroll, which is a very complex business and, unless you have first-hand experience of a payroll system, best avoided;

♦ Problems with too much scope such as an attempt to computerise an entire major business, taking in stock control, ordering, invoicing, paying suppliers, payroll and so on;

♦ Essays comparing different software or describing how to customise and install software;

♦ Projects which would be better tackled using other software, e.g. a spreadsheet or accounts package.

Chapter 13 – The Systems Life Cycle

Introduction

Project work and theory should go hand-in-hand on any course and this one is no exception. In order to produce a satisfactory project report you need to know something about the systems life cycle and the techniques used in each stage. The basic stages in the traditional cycle (excluding ongoing maintenance) form the basis of what you are expected to do for your project, and they are shown in diagrammatic form below.

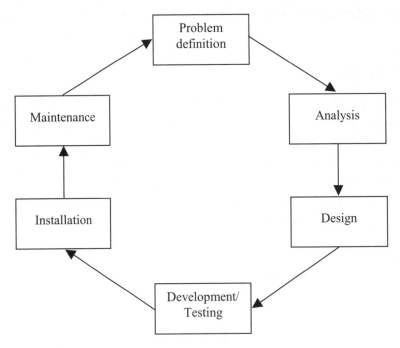

Figure 13.1: The Systems Life Cycle

Problem definition

In the last chapter we talked about choosing a suitable project. In a working environment, of course, the Systems Analysts would not be casting about looking for suitable projects to keep them busy – some alert manager or employee would perceive the need for change or innovation and be suggesting ways in which I.T. could drive the company forward. In that case, as in your current situation, the first requirement is to *identify a valid problem* in writing, clearly and unambiguously. This document is sometimes referred to as the *Terms of Reference*.

In the example below, a student has been given an idea for a project and has written the statement of the problem as shown. This document can then be shown to the teacher to make sure that the project is suitable before embarking on further Analysis.

Sample project idea

A Student Training Database

A large company offers training to students who are or will be studying for a degree in Engineering. Some start their training immediately after 'A' Levels, before starting their degree course the following year, and others do a year's training in the middle of their degree course. All students also do work placements in the summer vacations so that a total of 18 months training is completed before graduating.

The training is divided into six placements each lasting 3 months:

♦   2 manufacturing placements

♦   2 product design placements

♦   1 business placement

♦   1 applied engineering technology course.

The placements are completed in different locations in Great Britain and Europe.

The Recruitment Department needs to be able to keep track of students on placement. They need to know, at any time, where they are and who their supervisor is. They need to be able to send out details of placements to students who will be starting a new placement in the next quarter.

The database needs to record whether students have sent back their feedback forms and appraisal forms from their last placement, so a mailshot can be sent to students who have not sent in reports to remind them to do so.

The output required is:

♦   aa printout showing the training plan for any particular student;

♦   a mailshot to selected students;

♦   a screen report of where a particular student is at a given date.

It would also be useful to be able to perform various analyses on the data to show, for example:

♦   the percentage of female students;

♦   the percentage of students from ethnic minority groups;

♦   the percentage of students living in different areas of the country.

Reading through this statement of the problem, a teacher will be able to see that:

♦   This is a project for a real user – it is not the sort of topic anyone could easily make up;

♦   It can be satisfactorily implemented in Access;

♦   It has input, processing and output requirements;

♦   It will probably involve two or three related tables;

♦   It is an open-ended project and has plenty of scope for gaining top marks.

The identification and statement of the problem in IT terms is an essential part of any Analysis.

Analysis

During this stage you will be expected to:

♦   Investigate and report on the existing system and problems associated with it;

- Recognise the requirements of the intended user and the capabilities and limitations of the resources available;

- Specify objectives for the new system (e.g. better customer service, faster and/or more accurate operation, ability to handle increased volume of business, better management information);

- Identify the information flow and data dynamics of the problem;

- State and justify which applications package you intend to use, by describing the features of the software that make it a suitable choice and, if appropriate, any limitations to be overcome. (You may feel this fits better into the Design Section and if so you can refer the reader to that section.)

- Identify the user's current IT skill level and training needs;

- Specify the performance criteria (quantitative and qualitative) of the new system;

- Prepare a plan for implementing the new system within a set time scale.

Finding out about the current system

There are basically three ways of finding out about the current system, any or all of which you might use in your project work:

1. Interviews

Fix up an interview with the prospective user of the system, who may or may not be known to you – quite likely it could be a parent or friend. You should first of all make a list of questions you intend to ask, and write down the answers. It is not necessary or recommended to include a transcript of the interview in your project report – just summarise the findings, making it clear how you got your information.

Here are some general suggestions for questions that might form the framework of an interview. Of course, you have to be flexible and follow a line of questioning, but it helps to have a basic plan if you are not going to waste your own time and that of the interviewee.

- Can you give me a brief description of the problem you had in mind? (You may not need to ask this if you have already written a statement of the problem.)

- How does the current system work?

- How would the new system be different?

- Have you any sample input documents I could look at, and possibly have a copy of?

- What form would the output take? Would hard copy be required? How should it be laid out? Have you any samples I could look at or have a copy of?

- What volume of data is involved (e.g. how many invoices daily, how many club members, how many transactions weekly?)

- Are records ever removed from the system to be 'archived'?

- What hardware and software do you have available for the new system?

- How expert are you (or whoever will use the new system) at using PCs, Windows, Excel or whatever software is installed?

- Is any of the data confidential?

These general questions need to be supplemented by questions specific to your particular project, once you have written up the statement of the problem and had it passed by your teacher. Do not, however, put off doing any work on your project until you have interviewed the user; the more you work on the design before you have a second interview, the more clear it will be what questions you need to ask.

For example, think about what further information you would need on the Student Training Database in order to do detailed design work. You may decide you need to ask:

- What information needs to be held about each student?
- What information needs to be held about each placement?
- Does information need to be held about each supervisor? (You need to know whether Supervisor is a separate entity in the database.)
- Who inputs the student and placement details, and who decides and inputs the training plan for each student?
- Who uses the data analyses (e.g. percentage of female students)? Do these need to be hard copy?
- Will the user have sufficient skills to be able to perform new analyses as the need arises?
- Will the mailshots always be sent to the student's permanent address, or do they notify the Recruitment Department of their new address each time they move to a new placement?

Maybe you can think of other questions that need to be asked.

2. Questionnaires

Questionnaires are useful in some circumstances if the new system has a large number of potential users. The questionnaire has to be very carefully worded in order to obtain exactly the information you require, and of course many people won't bother to fill them in. Don't include a hundred copies of returned questionnaires with your project – one sample is enough, with a summary of the results.

3. Observation and inspection of documents currently used

Spending some time with the user or in the user's organisation is always a good way of finding out how things actually work. If you have firsthand experience of the task that you intend to computerise you are likely to understand the problems associated with it, and the pitfalls to avoid in your new system.

Possibly the single most important part of the Analysis in your project work is showing the relevant source documents to your teacher and explaining them. If you can do this with ease you probably have a good understanding of the scenario. If however you are unable to describe the purpose of your source documents, you probably need to stop and take some advice from your teacher.

From the teacher's point of view, it is often very difficult to grasp what a student's project is all about from a written or verbal explanation. Laying a source document in front of them will, at the very least, shed some light on what you are going to attempt.

Data flow diagrams

One important task of systems analysis is to find out:

♦ where the data originates,

♦ what processing is performed on it and by whom,

♦ who uses the data,

♦ what data is stored and where,

♦ what output is produced and who receives it.

One way of recording all this information is to use a **data flow diagram (DFD).** You should include such a diagram in the Analysis section of your project report.

There are only four symbols used in data flow diagrams, and they should not be confused with any other type of flowcharting symbols.

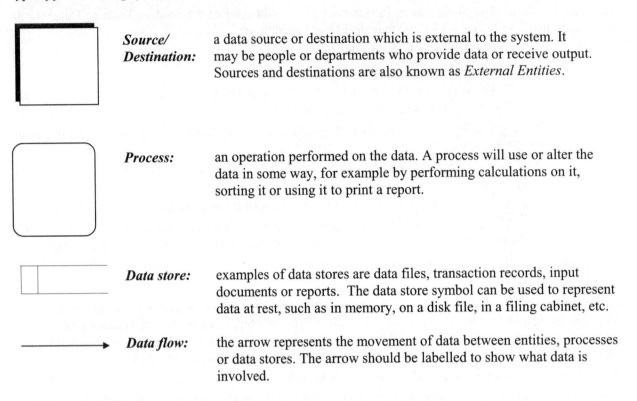

Source/ ***Destination:***	a data source or destination which is external to the system. It may be people or departments who provide data or receive output. Sources and destinations are also known as *External Entities*.
Process:	an operation performed on the data. A process will use or alter the data in some way, for example by performing calculations on it, sorting it or using it to print a report.
Data store:	examples of data stores are data files, transaction records, input documents or reports. The data store symbol can be used to represent data at rest, such as in memory, on a disk file, in a filing cabinet, etc.
Data flow:	the arrow represents the movement of data between entities, processes or data stores. The arrow should be labelled to show what data is involved.

Figure 13.2: Symbols used in Data Flow Diagrams

When drawing data flow diagrams, you should stick to the following conventions:

- Do not draw data flow lines directly between data stores and external entities: there should be a process box between them to show the operation performed (e.g. print a report).

- Label the data flow lines so that it is clear what data is being transferred.

Levelled DFDs

It is often impossible to represent a complete business system in a single diagram, so two or three levels of data flow diagrams may be used, each showing more detail. The top level, a 'Level 0 DFD' is also sometimes referred to as a context diagram, and represents the whole system as one process box.

Example: *Student Training Database*

The external entities in this example are the Recruitment Department, Students and possibly Management, if the statistical analyses are passed to Management in a different department. Supervisors could be regarded as external entities too, if they receive reports from this system telling them which students they will be supervising. However this has not been mentioned as part of this system so it is not really necessary to include them.

In the diagram below, the same external entity 'Student' has been shown three times – there is no hard and fast rule here, and you simply need to draw the diagram in as clear a manner as possible.

The context (Level 0) data flow diagram (DFD) can be drawn as follows:

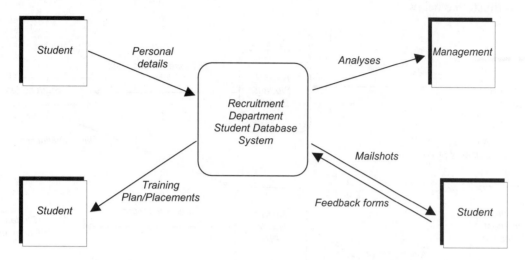

Figure 13.3: A context diagram or top level DFD (Level 0)

A Level 1 DFD can then be drawn showing a process to handle each incoming data flow and a process to generate each output data flow.

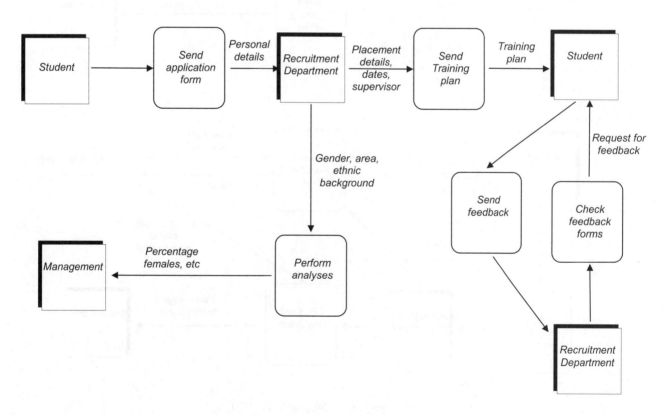

Figure 13.4: Level 1 DFD

A Level 2 DFD may show part of this system in greater detail, and could be included in the Design section of your project. The next level of detail may show data stores and more detail of the processing involved, as illustrated below:

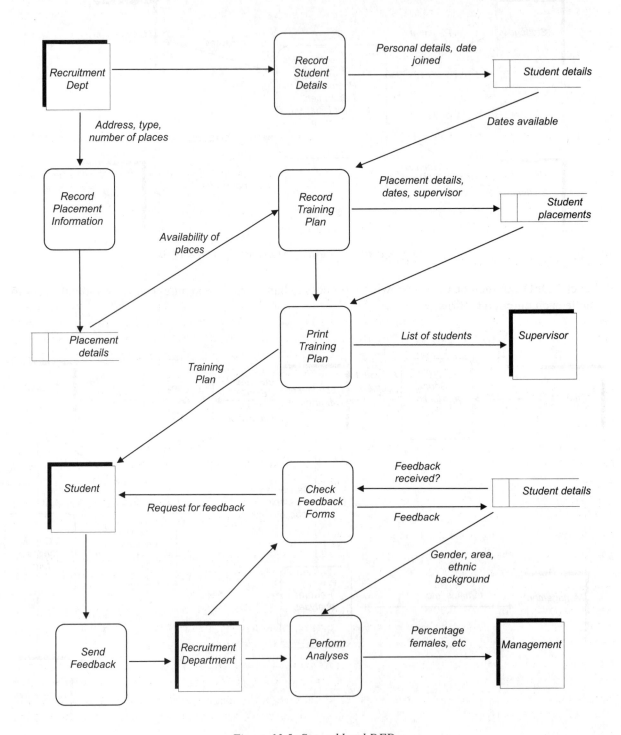

Figure 13.5: Second level DFD

Identifying tasks and subtasks

From the information gathered in interviews with the user, a list of all the tasks that the user will be able to perform using your system can be written down.

Here is a sample list:

1. Add, edit and delete student details.

2. Add, edit and delete placement details.

3. Add, edit and delete training plans.

4. View and print training plan for a particular student.

5. View and print a list of names of students going to a particular placement in a particular period, to send to the supervisor.

6. Send a mail merge letter to all students who have not sent back their feedback forms for a particular period.

7. Perform analyses of student data to find percentage of females, percentage from minority ethnic groups, percentage from each county. Print reports/charts.

Specifying performance criteria

If you are working to the AQA Mark Scheme for a major project, you will notice that the Implementation earns quite a small fraction of the overall 90 marks for the project. In other words, the implementation is only a small part of the project and no matter how clever your solution is or how many advanced features you have included, you will not necessarily end up with a good mark if you ignore the Mark scheme. You would be foolish not to spend time, for example, deciding on and writing down criteria against which you will be able to evaluate your project when the implementation is complete.

Performance criteria can be either *qualitative* ("easy", "fast", "clearly laid-out") or *quantitative* ("A student record can be located in under 10 seconds", "the system will run on a 486 with 16Mb of memory").

For example, you might specify that your system will make it "easy to enter the Training Plan for a particular student". You could be more specific, stating that it should be possible to enter the whole training plan for a student on a single screen input form.

You could specify that the user should be able to "easily edit the mail merge letter and send it to a selected group of students", or perhaps that "it should take no longer than 30 seconds to load Word from Access and open the mail merge letter in order to edit it".

You could specify that "in order to ensure that the Analysis by County is accurate, it should be impossible for the user to enter a County in different formats such as Hants, Hampshire". This shows some insight into possible errors in data entry.

Another criteria might be that "a user with some experience of Excel should be able to perform the required analyses with some help from the user manual". Maybe, on the other hand, you want to specify that the user should be able to perform the analyses just by selecting menu options.

Basically, you should think through what the user wants and try and write down as many meaningful performance criteria as you can. Avoid writing statements such as "It should be quick and easy to enter a new student record" – of course it should, we all know that, but it doesn't mean much! The more carefully you think out the performance criteria, the easier it will be to gain marks in the Evaluation section of the project.

Design

The systems designer will consider

♦ **possible solutions:**	A range of different approaches to solving the problem;
♦ **output:**	content, format, sequence, frequency, medium (e.g. screen or hard copy) etc;
♦ **input:**	documents, screens and dialogues;
♦ **files, tables or workbooks:**	contents, record layout, organisation and access methods;
♦ **processing:**	the programs and procedures needed and their detailed design;
♦ **security:**	how the data is to be kept secure from accidental corruption or deliberate tampering or hacking;
♦ **testing strategies:**	how the system is to be thoroughly tested before going 'live';
♦ **hardware:**	selection of an appropriate configuration.

Consideration of possible solutions

Having justified your choice of Access in the Analysis Section, you need to show that you have considered different ways of tackling the problem. This means considering whether you should, for example, do everything within Access or implement some parts of the project in say, Word or Excel. You have to choose between different user interfaces; for example, will you have a Switchboard created with an Access wizard, another type of menu system, pull-down menus, a customised toolbar? Will the processing be done by means of queries, by using macros or by writing VBA modules?

User Interface

A good user interface design is an important aspect of a successful system. The design must take into consideration:

♦ **who** is going to use the system – members of the public, experienced computer users or novices;

♦ **what tasks** the computer is performing; e.g. repetitive tasks or variable tasks such as switching between a word processor, spreadsheet and database.

In particular, careful **screen design** can make a huge difference to the usability of a system. When designing an input screen, the following points should be borne in mind:

♦ The display should be given a title to identify it;

♦ It should not be too cluttered. Spaces and blanks are important;

♦ Items should be put into a logical sequence to assist the user;

♦ Colour should be carefully used;

♦ Default values should be written in where possible;

♦ Help facilities should be provided where necessary.

Database design

In a database project, the most crucial aspect to get right is the definition of the required normalised tables. A good way of approaching database design is to first of all identify the entities and draw an entity-relationship diagram to show how they are related. If you have any many-to-many relationships, extra 'link' tables need to be introduced.

When you have drawn the entity-relationship diagram, make a list of what attributes need to be held for each entity. Familiarise yourself with the rules of normalisation and make sure that you have no repeating fields, partial key dependencies or non-key dependencies. If you do, you need to introduce extra tables. If you don't understand these terms, re-read Chapter 1!

Example: *Student Training Database*

We'll go through the steps involved in designing the database tables for the Student Training Database.

Step 1: *Make a list of the likely entities* – the people, places or things that we need to hold data about. The obvious ones are:

> Student
>
> Placement
>
> (Possibly Supervisor?)
>
> (Possibly Training Plan?)

Step 2: *Decide what the relationships are between the entities.*

> A student can go on many placements. Can a placement have several students? You need to be clear what the entity **Placement** really is. It is simply a particular type of placement (Manufacturing, Product Design, etc) in a particular department at a particular address, perhaps with a particular manager in charge. Therefore several students may go on the same placement, at the same or different times.
>
> How does **Supervisor** fit in? What information needs to be held about supervisors? Can a student have more than one supervisor? After further discussion with the user, you may decide that although Supervisor is an entity, the only attribute of Supervisor that is relevant to this application will be his or her name so it is not worth creating a separate Supervisor table.
>
> Is **Training Plan** an entity at all? What are its attributes? A Training Plan is all the placements that a single student will be sent to. Leave it out for the moment.

Step 3: *Draw the Entity-relationship diagram.*

> There is a many-to-many relationship between Student and Placement.

> Because this is a many-to-many relationship, you will need an extra *link* table in the middle. The link table will specify the Student ID and the Placement ID. If you think about it carefully, this is also where the Supervisor fits in, as an attribute of a particular student placement. What other attributes does a particular student placement have? We'll come back to that later. It seems that this link table is closely related to the Training Plan – in fact maybe that is what it is.
>
> When you introduce the link table, you turn the crow's feet round the other way. You can spend some time thinking about this but it's always true!

> I've called the link table **StudentPlacement** but it could be called **TrainingPlan**. (I prefer not to have spaces in the middle of Entity names as this avoids any problems when referring to them in a VBA module).

Step 4: *For each entity specify the attributes and their characteristics, validation rules etc.*

You can use a preprinted form for this, or design your own.

TABLE NAME: STUDENT

Attribute name	Data Type	Default Value	Description, Validation, Comments
StudentID	AutoNumber (Long Integer)		Key field
Surname	Text (30)		
FirstName	Text (30)		
Title	Text (4)		Mr, Mrs, Ms
HomeAddress1	Text (50)		
HomeAddress2	Text (50)		
HomeAddress3	Text (50)		
County	Text (20)		
HomePostCode	Text (9)		
UniAddress1	Text (50)		
UniAddress2	Text (50)		
UniAddress3	Text (50)		
UniPostCode	Text (9)		
DateOfBirth	Date		>=1/1/1979
Gender			M or F
Ethnic group	Text (10)		
EngType	Text (6)		ImechE or IEEE
StartYear	Integer		
DateOfFirst Placement	Date		>=1/1/1999

Figure 13.6: The STUDENT table

The other tables will be defined in a similar way. You should make a final check that the tables are normalised – show them to your teacher if you have any doubt.

Designing the menu structure

You should include a hand-drawn design for your menu structure, showing the main menu and submenus, or the pull-down menus if you are using them. You will see an example in the sample Newsagent's Database project.

Tasks and subtasks

The major tasks identified in the Analysis section need to be broken down into subtasks, if necessary, and the steps necessary to perform them described. For example:

Task 3: Add, edit and delete training plans.

The steps involved in completing this task are:

1. Design a query which combines data from the three tables.
2. Design a form with subform based on this query.
3. Add command buttons to the form to add a new record, find a record, delete a record, print the training plan, return to menu.
4. Write macros to maximise the form and attach the macro to the form's On Open event.

Plan for implementation

You should include hand-drawn designs for your input and output screens and reports. You may also need to show what the data capture documents look like – these may be available from the user or you may need to design them yourself.

You are also required to show a plan of how your time will be spent. A Gantt chart can be drawn to give a diagrammatic representation of your plan. An example is shown below – you can use a wordprocessor or spreadsheet to enter the dates and tasks and draw the bars by hand. Notice there is some overlap of tasks.

Plan for Implementation of Student Training Database

Month ending	01/10/99	01/11/99	01/12/99	01/01/00	01/02/00	01/03/00	01/04/00
Interview user	■						
Write up Analysis	■						
Design tables		■					
Design menus		■					
Design input forms			■				
Design reports			■				
Design test plan			■				
Write up Design				■			
Implement quick prototype				■			
Show to user					■		
Adjust design if necessary						■	
Add advanced form features						■	
Write macros						■	
Implement menus						■	
Test system						■	
Write user manual						■	
Show to user						■	
Make final adjustments						■	
Write evaluation							■
Annotate and complete documentation							■

Figure 13.7: A Gantt chart

Module or macro design

You need to specify what modules or macros you will be using in your system. One way of doing this is to write out the steps involved in **pseudocode** – a halfway stage between ordinary English statements and statements written in a particular programming language. It is a useful technique for describing the steps in an algorithm without having to know the syntax of the language.

Typical pseudocode constructs include the following:

> **If.. Then.. Else.. Endif**
>
> **Case.. Of.. EndCase**
>
> **For.. To.. EndFor**
>
> **Repeat.. Until..**
>
> **While.. Do.. Endwhile**
>
> **Procedure.. EndProc**

For example, pseudocode for a macro to 'find student details' could be:

> **Procedure** FindStudent
>> Open frmStudent
>>
>> Set focus in Surname field
>>
>> Allow user to enter required name (user can press Find Button)
>>
>> Find Record
>
> **EndProc**

The code will be automatically generated when you create the macro. You cannot view or print macro code in the same way as you can view and print a VBA module, although you can use **Tools, Analyse, Documenter** to show details of all the macros you have created. This creates a large quantity of hard-to-follow documentation and is generally not recommended.

Security

It may be appropriate to include a discussion of security, especially if the system involves confidential data. You can implement a password in Access, though probably not on a school or college network.

Test strategy

A test strategy will typically include:

- **Module testing** to test every macro or procedure in the system under different conditions, using valid, invalid and extreme data;
- **Functional testing** to ensure that the test tries each menu item under different conditions;
- **System testing** to test the system from beginning to end;
- **User testing** which is likely to throw up errors and weaknesses if you have not fully understood the requirements of the system. Sometimes a user has provided an original specification which was ambiguous or not tightly defined and it is only at this stage that they realize how to provide a more detailed requirements list.

Prototyping

Prototyping involves building a working model of a system in order to evaluate it, test it or have it approved before building the final product. When applied to computer systems this could involve, for example, designing basic forms using wizards, a user interface or front end with buttons that don't actually do anything, and a sample report showing what will be produced (or at least the headings) when the processing has been done. The user can then experience the 'look and feel' of the input process and suggest alterations before going any further.

Sometimes prototypes are simply discarded before the real system is started, and in other cases the prototype may be developed into a working system.

Prototyping is a useful development tool, especially when you are inexperienced with the software and are still experimenting with Access's capabilities, but it should not be used as a substitute for thinking out the design before you start on the implementation. Even prototypes have to be designed properly.

Development

This stage involves the actual implementation of your design using the computer. The word 'implementation' is confusing because it is sometimes used to mean doing the practical computer work involving creating workbooks or templates and writing formulae, macros etc and other times it means actually getting the system up and running on the user's hardware.

In the mark scheme for the project, 'Implementation and Testing' implies the former – getting the project to actually do what it's supposed to do.

Testing is an important part of development and should be done in accordance with the test strategy and test plan written in the Design phase.

Installation

This involves installing the system on the user's computer – this will very likely not form part of your project, although user testing and obtaining user feedback should be done.

Evaluation

An evaluation of what has been achieved and how well the system meets the performance criteria is an essential part of the system life cycle. Go carefully though all the performance criteria that you specified in the Analysis section and decide honestly how well they have been satisfied. There may be good reasons why you have ended up doing things a different way from how you originally planned. Feedback from the user is very useful at this stage as well as at other stages in the project – but make sure it is genuine. Some constructive criticism from the user, and suggestions for improvement, should be included if possible.

Chapter 14 – Writing the Project Report

Introduction

This chapter will give you some advice on how to set about writing the project report. Remember that the moderator will not actually see your system running – the report has to provide all the evidence of what you have achieved.

It will help you to look at the sample project as you will see how the report could be laid out and get some idea of what should be included in each section.

The mark scheme

Turn to the Appendix at the end of this book, which contains the AQA instructions and guidance for project work for the 2001-2002 specification. You will see that the Criteria for the Assessment of a Major Project is divided into the following categories:

-	Analysis	(18 marks)
-	Design	(16 marks)
-	Implementation	(15 marks)
-	Testing	(15 marks)
-	User Guide	(8 marks)
-	Evaluation	(10 marks)
-	Report	(8 marks) (Total 90 marks)

You could organise your project report into these six major sections (the last category, Report, is for the overall presentation) but you may choose to vary this.

The new specification and mark scheme as given in Appendix B is effective from September 2000 and you must be sure you are working to the correct one.

Spend some time familiarising yourself with the mark scheme so you know exactly what you are aiming for. Ultimately the decision on how best to structure the report is yours.

Creating an outline for your project

You will need to word process your report. If you are going to use Microsoft Word, you may like to follow the steps in the task below to get started on the report.

Word has a useful feature called **Outlining**. This feature enables you to create an outline for your entire project, breaking it down into sections and subsections, which you can then fill in as you build up your project. You can easily add, delete or rearrange headings at any stage, and at the end of it all you will be able to create an automatic Table of Contents.

Task 14.1: Create an outline for your project

In this task you will use Word's Outline feature to create an outline for your project. You can do this even before you have selected your project. It will help you to get a clear idea of the kind of task you should be setting yourself.

- Open a new document using the Normal template and save it as *Project.doc*.

- Click the **Outline View** button at the lower left corner of the Word window.

Figure 14.1: The Outline view button

- The Outline toolbar pops up, the Style box displays Heading 1 style, and a fat minus sign appears in the left margin.

Figure 14.2: The Outline toolbar

- Type your first heading ***Statement of the Problem*** and press Enter.

- Type the next heading, ***Analysis***. It also gets Heading 1 style, just like the first heading.

- Type the first subheading, ***Description of the current system***. Since you want it to be a subtopic, click it and then click the **Demote** tool on the outline toolbar. That makes it a Heading 2 style.

- Type the other headings for the Analysis section. These could include those shown below. At this stage your screen should look something like Figure 14.3.

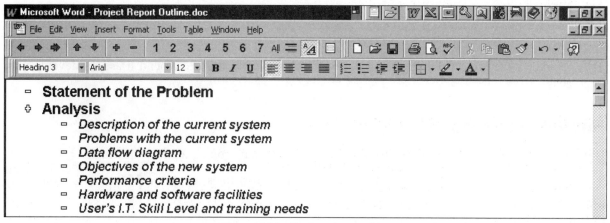

Figure 14.3: Outline for Analysis

- Now enter the headings for the remaining sections. You must decide what headings are most suitable for your own particular project – one suggestion is given below.

Design

Solution design

Consideration of possible solutions

Reason for choice of solution

Tasks and subtasks

Design of the database

Design of menu system

Design of input forms

Design of reports

Design of queries

Design of macros and modules

Security considerations

Test strategy

Test plan

Plan for implementation

Implementation and Testing

Commentary on implementation
Test results

Evaluation

User Guide

Technical Manual

This completes the project outline. Naturally, you will probably want to amend it as you develop your own ideas.

Reordering topics

If you decide that you want to change the order of topics in your project, do the following:

- Select for example *Design of queries*. To move it up two lines, click the **Move Up** button twice.

Adding numbers to the headings

- Select **Format, Bullets and Numbering**.

- Click the **Outline Numbered** tab and select a numbering format or customise one to your own liking. Your outline will appear something like Figure 14.4.

Note: If you decide to move your outline headings up or down it's a good idea to remove the numbers first and then reapply them.

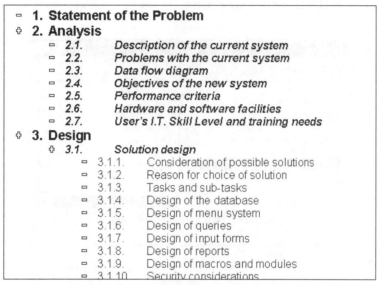

Figure 14.4: Adding numbers to an outline

Turning the outline into a document

The outline IS the document. Just click the **Normal View** button at the bottom of the window, and start entering text. You may want to change the indent and make a new style for the document text.

Adding a header and footer

You should add a header and footer to your project documentation. For example, the header could contain the Project title and the Section title, and the footer could contain your name and the page number.

- Insert page breaks between each of your major sections by pressing **Ctrl-Enter** wherever you want a page break.

- With the cursor at the beginning of the project outline, select **View, Header and Footer**. A toolbar appears:

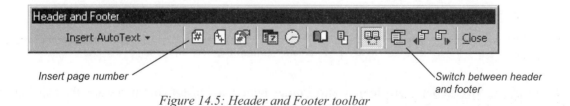

Figure 14.5: Header and Footer toolbar

- On the left hand side of the header, type your project title.

- Tab twice to get to the right hand side of the header. We need to insert a field here so that the name of the section is inserted.

- Select **Insert, Field**. In the **Categories** box select **Links and References**. In the **Field Names** box, select **StyleRef**.

- After the word **STYLEREF**, enter the style name *"Heading 1"* in quotes as shown in Figure 14.6.

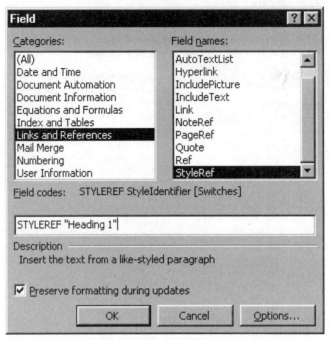

Figure 14.6: Inserting a field into the header

- Click **OK**. The header should appear as in Figure 14.7.

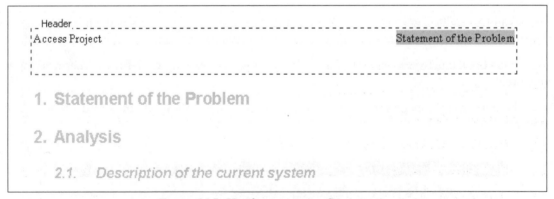

Figure 14.7: Header containing Section name

- Click the **Switch between Header and Footer** button and insert your name and the page number.

Inserting a Table of Contents

You can now insert a Table of Contents at the beginning of your project. This can be automatically updated at any time by clicking in it and pressing F9.

- Insert a page break in front of the heading **Statement of the Problem**.

- Click the **Normal View** button in the bottom left of the Word window (or select **View, Normal**).

- With the cursor at the beginning of the document, click **Insert, Index and Tables**.

- Click the **Table of Contents** tab. Leave the other defaults as shown in Figure 14.8.

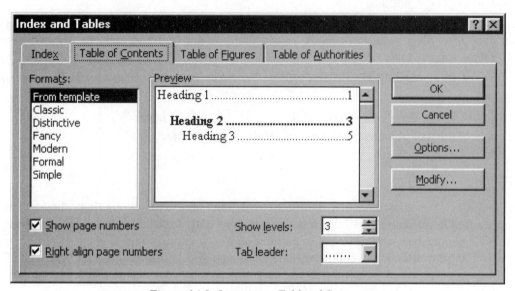

Figure 14.8: Inserting a Table of Contents

- The table of contents will appear as shown below.

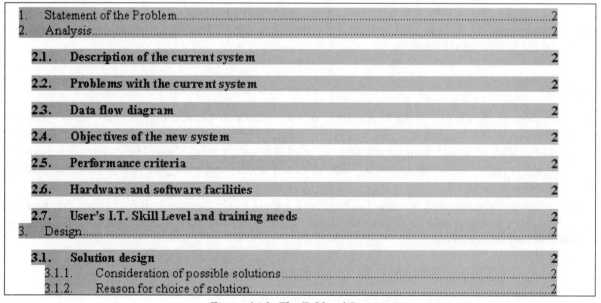

Figure 14.9: The Table of Contents

- You can change the styles of TOC1, TOC2 etc which are used in the Table of Contents using **Format, Style**.

- You can also change the styles of Heading 1, Heading 2 etc.

That's about it for your project outline. In the next few paragraphs we'll flesh out each section.

Analysis

In the last chapter advice was given on how to find out information about the current system, and how to draw a data flow diagram to show where data comes from, what data is stored and what processes are performed on it to get the output.

Try to write a good clear list of objectives and performance criteria, as the success of your project may depend on this. After all, if you don't really know what you are trying to achieve, how will you know whether you have achieved it?

"The objective of my system is to create a user-friendly system which will be more efficient, save time and be easy to use."

Does this tell you what I am setting out to build?

For an example of a list of objectives, have a look at the sample project.

Design

For a major project, you must consider alternative solutions and justify your final choice. The design should be specified in sufficient detail that a competent third party (even a second party) could implement it. You MUST do some design work on paper before you start implementing. If you feel you are unable to do so, then you are not sufficiently competent in Access and you should go back and complete Part 1 of this book! Planning is essential, even though you may have to alter your design if it doesn't work.

Implementation

Keep a diary of how the implementation goes, and include this in a 'Commentary on Implementation'. This provided valuable evidence that you have actually done the work. Explain why you have performed a task in a certain way or why you have not implemented something as you originally designed it. It is perfectly acceptable to include evidence of difficulties encountered in implementation, and to discuss reasons for the difficulties if possible.

Testing

You must show evidence of testing in the form of screenshots or printed output. This output must be cross-referenced to the original test plan – it is a complete waste of time and paper including page after page of output with no meaningful comment as to what it is supposed to show. Handwrite on the output, use a highlighter pen or any other means to help the reader understand what your test is designed to show, and how it actually shows it.

It is important to show user involvement in the testing – quite likely the user will find errors that you had not noticed. If it is impossible or impractical to get the user to test your system, find a substitute, for example a fellow student.

Evaluation

Refer back to the objectives and performance criteria and state to what extent these have been achieved. Also give some suggestions as to how the system could be enhanced, or what its weaknesses were – it's no good pretending that a rather feeble project is exactly what the user always wanted for Christmas, the moderator is unlikely to be fooled. Much better to show that you realise there are weaknesses and write about how you feel it could be improved. Honesty pays!

Remember that it is the success of the IT tasks and solutions that are to be evaluated and not your own performance.

User documentation

This is for a non-technical user and should explain clearly all the functions of your system. Use plenty of screenshots to illustrate the text. These can also provide valuable evidence of the fact that your system actually works. Many moderators look at the User Guide early in the moderation process to help them understand the project better.

Technical documentation

A separate section or manual for technical documentation might include installation instructions and information about hardware requirements. You should also include any VBA listings appropriately annotated, and descriptions of macros used. Page after page of output generated using **Tools, Analyse, Documenter** is not really useful, though you could include a maximum of two pages, hand annotated where necessary to explain what it shows.

This section could also list any error messages and advise what action to take if they occur, and possibly give a helpline number (yours!) for the user to ring if they are really stuck.

Handing it in

You must include a title page and a Table of Contents, and number every page, by hand if necessary.

Don't spoil it all by handing in your project as a collection of loose pages paper-clipped together, or stuffed into a single plastic pocket intended for a single sheet. Take pride in what you have achieved – spend 50p on a plastic folder in which the pages can be securely held.

Heed this advice from the 1998 Examiner's report:

"All projects must be securely bound; a thin folder or punched holes and treasury tags work well. Slide binders are often inhibiting to reading all the text, or they come off in the post. Ring binders, lever arch files and individual plastic pockets must not be used at all. They add unnecessary bulk and weight. The practice of using multiple sheets in poly pockets should cease."

Don't forget to include a signed cover sheet giving your name, candidate number and centre number.
Good luck!

Appendix A

Sample Project

Newsagent's Database

Major Project by:

A. Student

Any College

2001

Table of Contents

*You MUST number your pages and include a Table of Contents. This one was created automatically using Word's **Insert, Index and Tables**.*

Statement of the Problem **5**

    Introduction 5

    User requirements 5

Analysis **5**

    Initial investigation 5

        Volume of data 5

        Deliveries 5

        Holidays 6

        Payments 6

        Integration with existing accounts system 6

        Supplier orders and payments 6

        Hardware and software 6

        User skill level 6

    Data flow diagram (Level 1) 7

    Objectives of the new system 7

    Performance Indicators 8

    Consideration of solutions 9

    Final choice of software 9

    Database design 10

        Entity-relationship diagram 10

        Table design 10

        Form Design 10

        Report design 11

        Query design 12

        Macro design 13

        Menu design 14

        Security 15

    Test strategy 15

    Test plan 15

        User testing 18

    Schedule of Activities 18

        Plan for implementation 18

Implementation and Testing **19**

    Test results 19

    Commentary on Implementation 23

Evaluation *24*

Performance criteria 24

Enhancements...25

User Manual *26*

Introduction..26

Starting the system 26

Security and passwords 26

The main menu 26

The Customer menu...26

The Newspaper menu 26

The Invoicing and Payments menu...27

    Calculate and print invoices 27

    Print receipts 28

    Record payments..29

    Post payments 29

    Quit application...29

Backups...29

Technical manual *30*

Macros..30

    Processing invoices (mcrInvoices)......................................30

    Processing Round Sheets (mcrRoundSheets)......................31

Queries 32

Statement of the Problem

Introduction

Green's Store in Broughton is a small independent newsagent's which sells a range of products as well as newspapers and magazines. At the moment customers have to come to the store to pick up their newspapers as there is no system of deliveries. However, the business is expanding and Mr Green would like to offer a delivery service to customers. He has a computer which is used for keeping the store accounts, but feels that a separate system would be needed to handle the proposed newspaper deliveries.

User requirements

Specifically he would like a system which will:

♦ Hold details of customers, newspapers and deliveries;

♦ Print a 'round sheet' showing which newspapers are to be delivered to each customer on a given round each day;

♦ Print a summary report each day showing the total number of each newspaper required for each round;

♦ Calculate each customer's weekly bill and add it to their outstanding balance;

♦ Print each customer's weekly invoice;

♦ Print a receipt and update the customer's record when payment is received.

Analysis

Initial investigation

Mr Green was interviewed to find out more detail about the proposed new delivery system.

Volume of data

There will initially be in the range of 100 -150 customers divided into 3 rounds. There are about 20 different newspapers and magazines that would be regularly delivered.

Deliveries

Some newspapers and magazines are delivered only weekly. Customers will not always have a daily paper delivered every day of the week; for example some customers only want the local paper on Thursdays when houses for sale are advertised, or on Saturdays when they have more time to read it.

Each day a Round report is needed to give to the boy or girl doing the deliveries, so that they know which newspapers to deliver to each address. In addition a summary report is needed so that the correct number of newspapers is given to the paperboy/girl.

Holidays

Provision has to be made to suspend deliveries when a customer goes on holiday. Mr Green thinks it will be sufficient to record one holiday period. When a customer notifies the shop that they are going on holiday, the shop assistant will record this in a log book or diary and this will be transferred to the computer at a convenient time at the end of the day. If the customer notifies the store of more than one holiday period the second holiday will be entered in the diary, but not recorded in the computer system until after the first holiday is over.

Payments

Customers will be sent a weekly invoice with the delivery of their Saturday newspapers or, if they do not have a newspaper on Saturday, the following Monday. It is anticipated that customers will come to the store in person to pay their invoices, and be handed a receipt. Not all customers will pay every week so there has to be a system of specifying 'Past Due' amounts on the invoice. No interest will be charged on late payments.

Integration with existing accounts system

Each week a report of all payments made will be printed. The total amount paid will be entered under a special account to the existing accounts system. The payments will then have to be stored in a separate file (Archive File) to provide an Audit Trail. At the end of each year the Archive file will be stored safely and a new file started.

Supplier orders and payments

The actual ordering of the newspapers and magazines, and payment for them, will not form part of this system. This will be handled by the existing accounts system.

Hardware and software

Include a discussion of the hardware, which version of the software you will be using for development and which version the user has, if different.

Mr Green currently has a Pentium PC with 32Mb memory, a 4Gb hard disk and a laser printer. He has Windows 95 and Microsoft Office 97 loaded on the system as well as his Accounts package. This hardware will be quite adequate to implement a suitable system.

Development work will be carried out partly on a school network and partly on a standalone Pentium similar to the one described above. All the files will need to fit on a 3½" floppy disk for easy transportation between home and school. (They may need to be compressed.) The school network stations are 120MHz Pentium PCs with 16Mb of RAM attached to a laser printer.

A discussion of possible solutions and software packages will be found in the Design Section.

User's skill level

The user's skill level is relevant to the final design.

Mr Green uses a PC for his accounts and is familiar with Windows, including Explorer which he uses for file management. He also uses Excel and Word but has not used Access.

Data flow diagram (Level 1)

The following diagram illustrates in outline the process of documenting deliveries, invoicing and payments.

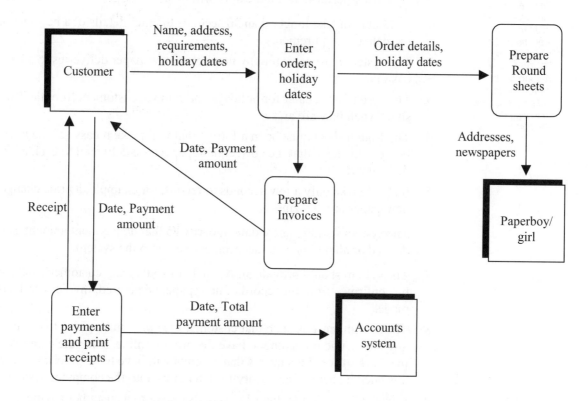

Objectives of the new system

The system must perform the following functions:

♦ allow customer details and newspaper deliveries required to be recorded and edited quickly and accurately;

♦ allow one holiday period to be logged in advance so that no deliveries will be made or recorded during that period;

♦ produce a list sequenced by Round which will be given to each newspaper boy or girl to refer to when they deliver the newspapers;

♦ produce a daily summary sheet showing the total quantity of each newspaper required for that day's deliveries;

♦ calculate the weekly amount due from each customer and print an invoice;

♦ allow easy recording of customer payments and the production of a receipt which can be handed to the customer at the time of payment;

♦ provide a summary of weekly payments which can be entered into the existing Accounts system. Full integration is not planned at this stage.

Performance Indicators

The Performance Indicators will be used to 'benchmark' the new system.

A good set of performance indicators is crucial to writing the Evaluation!

The following performance indicators will be used:

1. It should not take longer than 30 seconds to enter details of a new customer and the delivery requirements.

2. The system must cater for any number of newspaper deliveries to a particular customer.

3. The system must cater for holidays and remove customers from the Round sheet when they are away.

4. The Round sheet must be in a format that will make it easy for the newspaper boy/girl to check that the correct newspapers are delivered to each address on their round.

5. It should take only a few seconds to record, for example, a price change for a newspaper or magazine.

6. The system should ensure data integrity so that no payment amount can be deleted or altered once it has been entered onto the system.

7. The system should provide an Audit Trail so that any customer's balance can be confirmed from the record of newspapers delivered, invoices and payments made.

8. The system must be such that customer receipts can be given to customers at any time without needing to have the printer online, since the computer is kept in a back office. This means that receipts will have to be preprinted and amended by hand if necessary for later entry into the computer system.

9. It must take no longer than 15 seconds to record a customer payment.

10. The system should be usable by someone with no experience of using database software.

Design

Consideration of solutions

There are various possible methods of administering the new delivery system.

1. **Manual system**. This would be extremely time-consuming, requiring a list of newspaper deliveries to be produced each day either using a wordprocessing package or by hand. The calculation of weekly invoices would be very lengthy and error-prone. It would be impractical to even contemplate using a manual system.

2. **Spreadsheet system**. This would enable the list of customers to be held on one sheet and their deliveries on another sheet. The calculation of invoices could be automated to some extent. However it would be difficult to design a data entry form so that customer details and delivery details could be entered in one operation. It is also much harder to format reports in Excel.

3. **A system specifically designed for newsagents**. There are off-the-shelf packages available to newsagents and as every newsagent has similar requirements, this might be a very good solution. The package would be well tested and documented and would be drawing on the experience and feedback of thousands of newsagents over several years. It seems likely that after a trial period, Mr Green may well decide to invest in such a package. I have interviewed another newsagent who uses this type of software and observed the system and have picked up some ideas for my own tailor-made system.

4. **Use the existing Accounts system**. This does not have the specific capability to produce round reports, and customer orders would have to be re-entered each week, so it is not suitable.

5. **Access database**. This system can be conveniently implemented using Access, which is a relational database already installed on the user's computer and available on the school network for development work.

Final choice of software

This system will be implemented using Access 97. This package is ideal as it includes many features which can be used in customising the application, such as:

Summarise the advanced features that you plan to use.

- ◆ Ability to relate tables through a common field;

- ◆ Ability to create a customised menu system;

- ◆ Sophisticated form design capabilities;

- ◆ Sophisticated report facilities with the ability to format text, set margins and page layout, import a company logo if desired and preview before printing;

- ◆ Ability to prevent user from making accidental changes to payment records;

- ◆ Ability to perform processing tasks through the use of queries and macros;

- ◆ Ability to link to Word if the user wants to create standard letters to customers.

Database design

Entity-relationship diagram

There are four entities in the database related as shown in the following diagram.

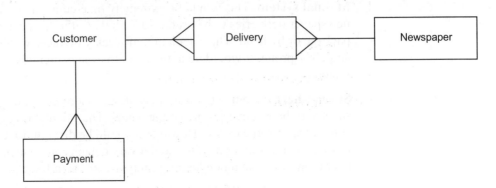

Table design

The four tables are defined as follows:

*(see Part 1, Figure 1.7 for **tblCustomer, tblDelivery** and **tblNewspaper**)*

tblPayment

Field name	Data type	Description/Validation
CustomerID*	Number (Long Integer)	Must exist on tblCustomer
PaymentAmount	Currency	
PaymentDate*	Date/Time	Part of key field, together with CustomerID

There will be a fifth table named **tblPaymentArchive** with exactly the same structure as **tblPayment**. This will be used to hold payments that have already been used to update the customer records.

Form Design

Show hand drawn designs for each of your forms

There will be 3 forms for data entry:

frmCustomerMain   a form with a subform, used to input customer details and which newspapers they want delivered each day of the week; (Source: **tblCustomer** for main form, **tblDelivery** for subform.)

frmNewspaper   a form to add and edit details of each newspaper. (Source: **tblNewspaper**.)

frmPayment   a form to enter customer payments; (Source: **qryCustomerPayments**, a query which combines the customer name and address from **tblCustomer** with the payment amount and date from **tblPayment**.)

There will also be two dialogue boxes:

fdlgWeekday   Asks the user which day of the week it is, and whether a Morning or Evening report is required, before printing the Round report.

fdlgPrintSummary   Asks if a Summary report is required listing quantities of each newspaper required for the day

Report design

The following reports will be required:

rptMondayDelivs   Reports based on a query **qryMondayDelivs.** A dialogue box asks the user to enter the Round number and whether this is a Morning or Evening delivery, and then sets the query criteria for Morning/Evening based on the reply. (See below under Queries.) It then prints the name and address of each customer on that round and which newspapers they want delivered.

Include the original hand drawn designs for each of your reports - not scanned as shown here.

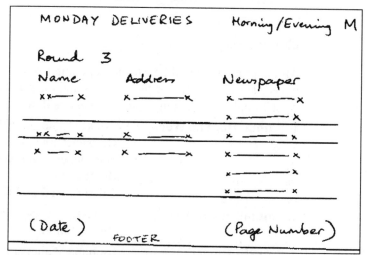

RptTuesdayDelivs, rptWednesdayDelivs etc are similar to the above.

rptMondaySummary   A report based on a query **qryMondaySummary** which shows the total number of each newspaper required for each round on Monday. Similar reports will be produced for each day of the week.

rptInvoice   A report based on **qryCustomer** which prints a weekly invoice for each customer. The invoices are printed 4 to a page on perforated paper.

rptReceipt   Also produced from **qryCustomer** and printed on perforated stationery, this report shows in alphabetical order by name, the name, account number, date and payment amount of each customer twice, side by side, separated by perforations. When the customer pays their bill, the right hand strip is torn off and handed to them. The left side is used as the input document to enter the payment. The design is shown below.

GREEN'S STORE Gregory A/C 57 W/E 29/05/99 £12.50	GREEN'S STORE Gregory A/C 57 W/E 29/05/99 £12.50
GREEN'S STORE Heathcote A/C 15 W/E 29/05/99 £6.00	GREEN'S STORE Heathcote A/C 15 W/E 29/05/99 £6.00
GREEN'S STOR [This part used to input payment] Jones A/C 123 W/E 29/05/99 £17.50	GREEN'S STORE [This part given to customer] Jones A/C 123 W/E 29/05/99 £17.50

Query design

All the processing will be carried out using macros running queries of different types. The calculation of the invoices and the posting of payments requires the most complex processing, and the steps are described below.

1. **qmakDueThisWeek**   (Make Table query) At the end of each week, the **CurrentDue** amount is calculated from this week's newspaper deliveries and a new table **tblDueThisWeek** is created with fields **CustomerID** and **DueThisWeek**.

2. **qupdCurrentDue**   (Update query) Puts current due amount on **tblCustomer**.

3. **qryCustomer**   (Summary query) Adds **CurrentDue** and **PastDue** to calculate the **TotalDue**.

4. Customer invoices are produced and printed from this query. The invoice report will be named **rptInvoices** and the summary report **rptInvoiceSummary**.)

5. Customer payments are recorded each day and stored in table **tblPayment**.

6. **qupdCurrentToZero**   (Update query) Adds **CurrentDue** to **PastDue** and sets the **CurrentDue** back to zero ready for the coming week.

7. **qupdPostPayment**   (Update query) is run once a week to subtract each customer's payment from their **PastDue** amount.

8. **qappPayment**   (Append query) is run to add the week's payments to an archive table.

9. **qdelPayment**   (Delete query) is run to delete all the week's payments from the **Payment** table.

In addition, the following queries will be required to produce the Round sheets and the Summary of each day's deliveries:

10. **qryMondayDelivs, qryTuesdayDelivs**, etc. These queries set criteria to find customers who are not on holiday and who have newspapers delivered on the particular morning/evening.

11. **qryMondaySummary, qryTuesdaySummary** etc. These queries create a count of the number of newspapers delivered to each customer each day. These queries are used as the source for the daily summary reports.

Macro design

Macros are used to handle the printing of the Round report (**rptMondayDelivs**, etc) and daily summaries (**rptMondaySummary**, etc)

mcrRoundSheet — This is a macro group which contains 3 macros:

mcrAskWhichDay — Open a dialogue box and ask which day of the week it is and whether it is Morning/Evening.

(This is run when the user selects Print Round Sheets from the Newspaper menu)

mcrPrintRoundSheet

Hide the dialogue box;

Print the report for the specified day;

Open a second dialogue box to ask if a summary report is required;

*(This is run when the user clicks OK in the **fdlgWeekday** dialogue box.)*

mcrPrintSummary — Print the summary for the specified day.

*(This is run when the user clicks OK in the **fdlgPrintSummary** dialogue box)*

Macros will be used to perform the processing of payments.

mcrInvoices — This macro group will contain two macros as follows:

mcrCalculateInvoices to calculate and print invoices:

Run query **qmakDueThisWeek** to calculate this week's amount due from newspapers delivered and save on **tblDueThisWeek**;

Run query **qupdCurrentDue** to update **CurrentDue** field in **tblCustomer**;

Run query **qryCustomer** to calculate the total amount due;

Display a message to load correct stationery;

Print the invoices, **rptInvoices**.

*(This is run when the user selects **Calculate and Print Invoices** from the **Invoicing and Payments** menu.)*

mcrPostPayments Post payments:

Run query **qupdCurrentToZero** to add **CurrentDue** to **PastDue** and set **CurrentDue** to zero;

Run query **qupdPostPayment** to subtract Payment from **PastDue** on **tblCustomer**;

Run query **qappPayment** to add payments to archive table **tblArchivePayment**;

Run query **qdelPayment** to empty the Payments table ready for next week;

Display message to user that task is complete.

*(This is run when the user selects **Post Payments** from the **Invoicing and Payments** menu)*

Menu design

The menu system will be created using Access's Switchboard add-in, and will have the following structure.

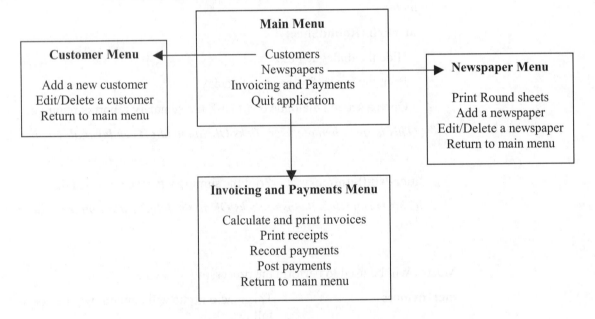

Notes on the implementation of the menu:

The first three items on the main menu will open submenu forms.

On the **Customer** menu:

♦ **Add a new customer** will open **frmCustomerMain** in Edit mode so that all customer records are available, but the form will open ready for a new record to be entered.

♦ **Edit/Delete a customer** will open the form in Edit mode at the first record with the focus in the Surname field. The user can then press a customised **Find** button on the form to locate a specific record.

On the **Newspaper** menu:

♦ **Print Round Sheets** will run macro **mcr.RoundSheet.mcrAskWhichDay.**

♦ **Add a new newspaper** will open **frmNewspaper** in Edit mode so that all newspaper records are available, but the form will open ready for a new record to be entered.

♦ **Edit/Delete a newspaper** will open the form in Edit mode at the first record with the focus in the **NewspaperName** field. The user can then press a customised **Find** button on the form to locate a specific record.

On the **Invoicing and Payments** menu:

♦ **Calculate and print invoices** will run **mcrInvoices.mcrCalculateInvoices**

♦ **Record Payments** will open **frmPayments** in Add mode so that no existing payments are available. This prevents any existing payments being accidentally or fraudulently changed.

♦ Post Payments will run macro **mcrInvoices.mcrPostPayments.**

The main menu will appear automatically, and the main database window will be hidden, when the application is loaded. This will be done by setting the appropriate options using **Tools, Startup**.

Security

The database will be password protected since it is important that no one except Mr Green has access to the database. Transactions such as a change in delivery requirements, recording of holidays etc will be written down as they occur in the shop and entered into the computer by Mr Green. Customer payments will be handled as already described, with data entry to the computer being done daily by Mr Green, and posting of payments done weekly.

Test strategy

The test strategy will include:

♦ Testing of each individual object (form, report, query, macro) as it is created;

♦ Functional testing to test each menu item and command button under different circumstances;

♦ Testing the effect of inputting invalid and extreme data;

♦ System testing by running through a sequence of tests which test the system as a whole, checking results of each option against known expected results;

♦ End-user testing to establish whether the system meets the end-user's requirements.

Test plan

The following tests are a sample from the system testing which include at least one test for each menu option. It is impractical to show all the tests that need to be performed to show that all options work correctly under every circumstance.

Test No.	Test	Expected result
1.	Test password.	Only "news" accepted.
2	Test Main Menu options.	Correct submenu opens each time. Application closes when Quit selected.
3.	Add all newspapers from Data set 2.	All newspapers added correctly.
4.	Delete the record for The Banner.	Record successfully deleted.
5.	Select Add Customer. Enter Customer 1, Robson (see data set 1.) and newspaper Mercury on Monday. Return to menu.	Form should open at a new record, focus in Surname field.
6.	Test Edit/Delete. Delete Robson.	Record deleted.
7.	Add all records from data set 1.	All records added starting at Customer ID 2. (PastDue and CurrentDue cannot be inserted or edited in Form View as they are calculated fields. Add them in Table view for test purposes.)
8.	Print Round report for Monday morning.	In Round 1 Robson has Sun, Nazarali has Gu and Merc, Murphy has Gu. In Round 2 Carter has Merc, Telegraph and Sun, Newbourne has Merc and Gu. Brindley is the only customer in Round 3, delivery Gu.
9.	Print Summary report for Monday morning.	2 Sun, 4 Gu, 3 Merc, 1DT, 1 Star (evg)
10.	Calculate and print invoices.	Invoices printed 4 per page.
11.	Print receipts.	Receipts printed in Surname order.
12.	Record payments from test data set 4.	Payments stored in **tblPayments.**
13.	Post Payments.	Current due added to PastDue, current due set to zero, payment subtracted from TotalDue. e.g. Robson should owe £1.05. Payment records transferred to Archive table and Payment table emptied.
14.	Test Quit Application option.	Database should close.

Test data set 1: Customers

Surname	Initial	Title	Address1	Address2	Round	Current Due	PastDue	HolsBegin	HolsEnd
Robson	C	Mr	11 Dales Rd	Broughton	1	£3.85	£17.00	01/01/99	08/01/99
Brindley	J	Mr	1 Chestnut Ave	Broughton	3	£3.70	£12.00	12/12/00	25/12/00
Nazarali	N	Mr	13 Dales Rd	Broughton	1	£1.80	£25.00		
Newbourne	S	Miss	Mill Hse, Mill La	Broughton	2	£4.80	£0.00		
Carter	J	Mrs	Bridge Hse, Mill La	Broughton	2	£7.60	£8.40		
Murphy	S	Mrs	15 Elgar Crescent	Broughton	1	£5.10	£0.00		
Patel	J	Miss	3 Elgar Crescent	Broughton	1	£3.90	£3.75	12/02/99	12/06/99

Test Data set 2: Newspapers

NewspaperID	NewspaperName	Price	Morning/Evening
DT	Daily Telegraph	£0.45	M
GU	Guardian	£0.45	M
MERC	Mercury	£0.35	M
OBS	Observer	£1.00	M
ST	Sunday Times	£1.00	M
STAR	Evening Star	£0.40	E
SUN	Sun	£0.30	M
TIM	The Times	£0.25	M
BAN	The Banner	£0.30	E

Test data set 3: Deliveries

Customer ID	NewspaperID	Monday	Tuesday	Wednesday	Thursday	Friday	Saturday	Sunday
Robson	Mercury	No	No	No	No	No	No	No
Robson	Sunday Times	No	No	No	No	No	No	Yes
Robson	Sun	Yes	Yes	Yes	Yes	Yes	Yes	No
Brindley	Guardian	Yes	Yes	Yes	Yes	Yes	Yes	No
Brindley	Observer	No	No	No	No	No	No	Yes
Nazarali	Guardian	Yes	Yes	Yes	Yes	Yes	Yes	No
Nazarali	Mercury	Yes	Yes	Yes	Yes	Yes	Yes	No
Newbourne	Guardian	Yes	Yes	Yes	Yes	Yes	Yes	No
Newbourne	Mercury	Yes	Yes	Yes	Yes	Yes	Yes	No
Carter	Daily Telegraph	Yes	Yes	Yes	Yes	Yes	Yes	No
Carter	Mercury	Yes	Yes	Yes	Yes	Yes	Yes	No
Carter	Sunday Times	No	No	No	No	No	No	Yes
Carter	Sun	Yes	Yes	Yes	Yes	Yes	Yes	No
Murphy	Guardian	Yes	Yes	Yes	Yes	Yes	Yes	No
Murphy	Evening Star	Yes	Yes	Yes	Yes	Yes	Yes	No
Patel	Mercury	Yes	Yes	Yes	Yes	Yes	Yes	No
Patel	Sun	Yes	Yes	Yes	Yes	Yes	Yes	No

Test data set 4: Payments

CustomerID	PaymentAmount	PaymentDate
Robson	£19.80	13/05/99
Newbourne	£25.00	12/05/99
Murphy	£5.10	13/05/99

User testing

The user will test the system. This testing may reveal aspects of the system that do not work as the user would expect, or functions that have been omitted that need to be added.

All evidence of testing is given below in the section headed Test Results.

The Schedule of Activities is a required part of the project. It could go at the beginning of the Design section.

Schedule of Activities

Plan for implementation

Month ending	01/10/99	01/11/99	01/12/99	01/01/00	01/02/00	01/03/00	01/04/00
Interview user	■						
Write up Analysis		■					
Design tables		■					
Design menus		■					
Design input forms			■				
Design reports			■				
Design test plan			■				
Write up Design				■			
Implement prototype				■	■		
Show to user					■		
Adjust design if nec'y.						■	
Add adv. form features						■	
Write macros						■	
Implement menus						■	
Test system							■
Write user manual							■
Show to user							■
Make final adjustments							■
Write evaluation							■
Annotate/document							■

Implementation and Testing

Test results

Test 1:Test password.

(Only "news" accepted)

Test 2: Test Main Menu options.

(All submenus open correctly - see screenshots in User Guide.)

Test 3: Add all newspapers from data set 3.

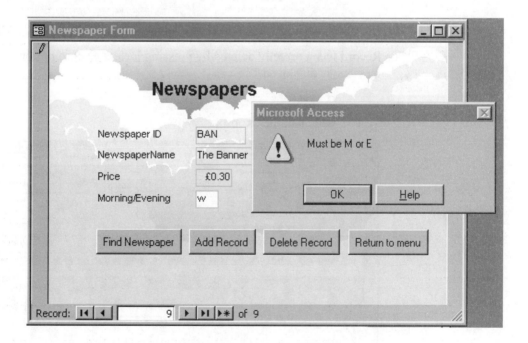

(Form opened but in Add mode, with no existing records visible. This has now been corrected by opening form in Edit mode. User presses **Add Record** button to go to new record.)

Test 4: Delete record for The Banner.

Form opened, user first finds correct record using Find Newspaper button.

Record then correctly deleted by pressing Delete Record button. (A warning message is displayed.)

Test 5: Add customer Robson.

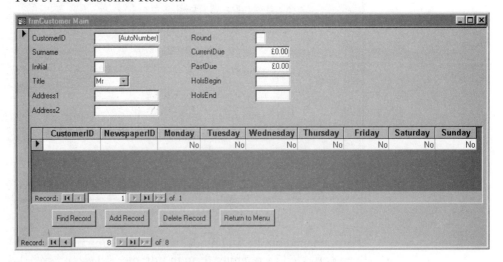

(Focus appeared in **CustomerID** field. This was corrected by setting its tab stop property to *No*. Some text box sizes needed changing. Now works correctly. Further customisation of the form will be carried out - see output for Test 7.)

Test 6: Test Edit/Delete by deleting Robson.

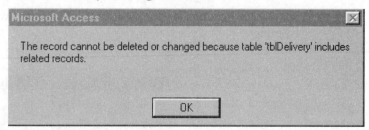

(The test did not work. The relationship between Customer and Delivery needs to be altered to include 'Cascade Deleted Records'. This problem was fixed and a message appears as shown below.)

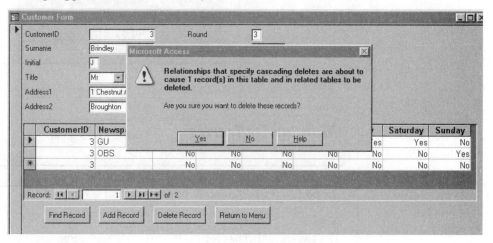

Test 7: Add the whole data set including Robson.

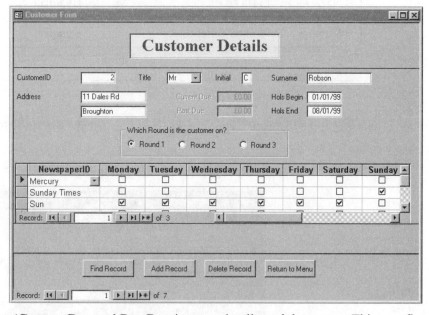

(**CurrentDue** and **PastDue** incorrectly allowed data entry. This was fixed by setting the **Enabled** property to *No*, and the **Tab Stop** property to *No*. The form caption and labels were customised and an option group used for **Round**.)

Test 8: Print Round sheet for Monday morning.

A dialogue box appears for the user to specify weekday and whether Morning or Evening:

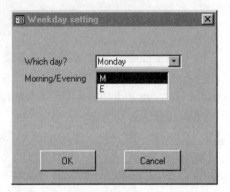

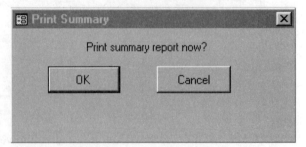

Monday Deliveries		Morning/Evening: **M**

Round	1	
Surname	*Address1*	*Newspaper*
Robson	11 Dales Rd	Sun
Nazarali	13 Dales Rd	Mercury
Nazarali	13 Dales Rd	Guardian
Murphy	15 Elgar Crescent	Guardian

(This test worked well; a few aspects of the report needed tidying up.)

Test 9: Print summary report for Monday morning.

(After the Round report is printed this dialogue box appears. If the user presses OK the following report is printed:

Monday Newspaper Summary Sheet

	Daily Telegraph	
Quantity	1	

	Evening Star	
Quantity	1	

	Guardian	
Quantity	4	

	Mercury	
Quantity	3	

	Sun	
Quantity	2	

(The user pointed out that there was supposed to be a separate summary report for each round. However he thought this report would also be needed as it would show how many newspapers needed to be ordered each day.)

(You should produce evidence and commentary for all tests in your test plan. The rest of the test results are not shown here for space reasons.)

Commentary on Implementation

- In the initial design, the user was asked the question 'Which round?' before a round sheet was printed. However the user did not think this was necessary as round sheets were needed every day for every round. The report is therefore grouped on round with a page break between rounds so that each paper boy/girl can take the sheet for their round. Sorting on address within Round means that the houses on each street are grouped together making it easy to find the deliveries for a particular address.

Don't be afraid to admit to errors in your implementation. Much better to show that you noticed them, than to ignore them.

- A separate summary sheet was originally planned for each Round, morning and evening. This requirement was overlooked and did not get discovered until Mr Green tested the system, when he noticed that the summary report showed all the papers required for all rounds both morning and evening. He thought this would be a useful report but the other reports need to be included in the system.

- The user has to specify which day of the week the round sheet is for. Originally the criteria was entered into the query, e.g. [Which day of the week?]. However this left the possibility that the user would misspell a day and the report would then not print correctly. In the revised design a dialogue box is used with list boxes for Day of Week and Morning/Evening. The items selected from the two lists are then used as criteria in the query and to select which report to print, which eliminates the possibility of error.

- Separate queries and reports are used for each day of the week. This could be changed with a slightly more sophisticated dialogue box and query. At the moment only Monday and Tuesday queries and reports are implemented, which is sufficient to show the method used.

- It was not possible to implement the password system at college but this was tested at home and worked satisfactorily. The database has to be opened in exclusive mode to set or unset the password.

- All reports are output in Print Preview mode for development purposes to save excessive printing. This setting will be changed in the operational package.

- Testing revealed many errors. For example functional testing revealed that I had forgotten to put the item **Return to main menu** on **the Invoicing and Payments** menu. Minor errors in forms, reports and macros showed up.

- The test data did not include any customers with no deliveries, or newspapers which were not delivered to any customers. Further testing would be required to ensure that such data does not cause any unexpected results.

Evaluation

Performance criteria

The Evaluation is a very important part of the project. It will show whether you have appreciated the user's requirements and your awareness of any weaknesses in your system.

The performance criteria have largely been met. Specifically:

1. It is very quick to enter the details of a new customer and their delivery requirements, using a Form and Subform. Checkboxes for weekdays are easy to fill in and a list box for newspaper names makes it easy to enter which newspapers are required. The option group for Round number ensures that a valid entry is made.

2. Any number of newspapers can be entered into the subform.

3. Using the manual system of recording holidays in a book means that the customer can tell the shop about 2 or 3 holidays if they wish to. These can then be recorded a week or so before they occur. The Round sheet and Summary sheet take into account which customers are on holiday.

4. The Round sheet is sequenced by address. This is not satisfactory because it needs to be printed in the sequence that newspapers are delivered on the Round. The house number could have been put in a separate field from the street so the report could be sorted on Street and house number/name, or an extra field could be added to show where each address is located on a particular Round.

5. To add a newspaper the user selects Add Newspaper for the Newspaper menu and then clicks the Add Newspaper. A customised Find button makes it very fast to find a particular newspaper if say a price change needs to be recorded.

6. Payment amounts cannot be altered once they have been posted as the user has no access to the payments on the Archive file. In the original design the Payment form had properties set in such a way that no record could be edited or deleted once it was entered, but Mr Green wanted this changed as he felt it would be too complicated to enter a corrective payment if an error was spotted

during a data entry session. If a payment is entered twice, for example, it will not be accepted as the key is a combination of CustomerID and date.

7. The Audit trail is provided by the Archive file (**tblPaymentArchive**). All payments are added to this file when payments are posted to the customer file, and the Payments file is then emptied ready for the next batch of payments. Normally payments will be done once a week but they can be done as often as convenient.

8. The system of printing receipts as soon as the invoices are printed is tried and tested at hundreds of newsagents using computerised systems. It is very simple, and if the customer pays a different amount from the one on the invoice, both copies of the receipt are altered by hand so that the correct payment is entered into the system.

9. Customer payments are entered from the copy of the receipt and this is a very fast process taking only a few seconds once the relevant option has been selected from the menu.

10. Mr Green had no trouble opening the database and using all the menu options. He did not like the messages that Access automatically generates when Append, Update and Delete queries are performed and one enhancement that could be made is to suppress these messages.

Enhancements

The Summary report is very basic, being produced from a wizard, and needs to be smartened up.

No system is perfect so try and give a realistic assessment of improvements that could be made. The suggestions made here range from trivial to fairly major system design changes.

In the current system it is left up to the user not to delete a customer who still has outstanding payments. A routine could be added to ensure that it is not possible to delete a customer with outstanding payments. However this might cause problems with customers who leave town owing small amounts which are written off as bad debts. Mr Green felt that it was better to leave this aspect as it stands.

Occasionally during a newspaper strike a newspaper cannot be delivered or an alternative is provided, making the invoice incorrect. However Mr Green felt that this happened so rarely it was not worth changing the system to cater for non-deliveries.

The integration with the existing Accounts system is a further problem to be tackled at a future date. Payments received from customers need to be transferred to the main accounts system. A summary of weekly payments was included in the original requirements list but this has been omitted from the final project. When I originally started the project I did not realise how much time it would take to complete all the tasks discussed with Mr Green, and as time progressed I decided to limit the scope by omitting this report.

A letter from the user is included below.

(Or not, in this case – but you should make every effort to get user feedback, both verbal and written.)

User Manual

Introduction

This software is designed to help keep track of customers, newspaper deliveries, invoicing and payments. It has been designed to run on a PC running Windows 95 and needs Access 97 to be installed. It needs about 1Mb of disk space to store the application and at least as much again to store data.

Starting the system

Load Access and from the menu select File, Open. The application is called **Newsproject.mdb** and is held in a directory named **News**.

Security and passwords

You will be asked to enter the password. The password is currently *news* but you should change this as soon as possible, by opening the database in **Exclusive** mode (this is an option you can check when you select **Newsproject.mdb** as the file to load.) Then select **Tools, Security, Set Database Password**.

The main menu

When you have entered the password you will see the main menu appear, as shown below.

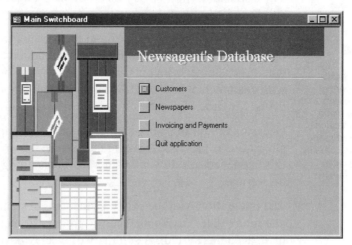

If you are short of time, do what I have done here – go through one section thoroughly and state which sections are omitted. You will lose few if any marks. Try to show screen shots of all important aspects either in the test output or in the User Manual, but not necessarily in both.)

The Customer menu

(Options on the Customer menu – omitted here for reasons of space.

The Newspaper menu

(Options on the Newspaper menu – omitted here for reasons of space.)

The Invoicing and Payments menu

Selecting this option will bring up the following menu:

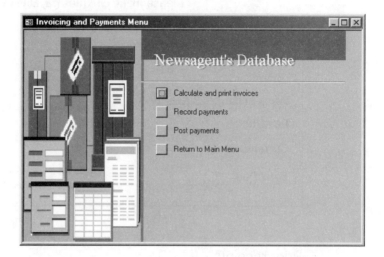

Calculate and print invoices

This option calculates each customer's weekly invoice by adding any Past Due amount to the cost of this week's newspapers.

You will see several messages similar to the following as the processing goes through various stages. Simply press **Yes** in each message box.

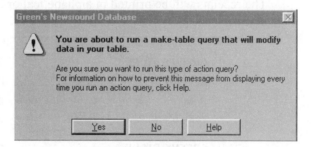

The final message reminds you to load the perforated stationery:

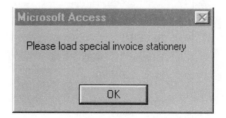

Invoices will then be printed 4 to a page as shown below. They will be printed Round by Round, sequenced by address within Round for convenient hand delivery with the day's newspapers.

Please make cheques payable to Green's Store. Thank you.

Robson   **Green's Store**
11 Dales Rd   **66 Pepper Rd**
Broughton   **Broughton**

Week ending: 03 April 1999

PastDue   £17.00

CurrentDue   £2.80

Total Due   £19.80

Print receipts

Once you have printed all the invoices, you should print the receipts. Two copies of each receipt will be printed side by side on special perforated stationery. When an invoice is paid, the shop assistant will give the customer the right hand copy and write the date paid on the left hand copy. It will then be easy to enter all payments using the receipts which have had the right hand copy torn out. Put a tick on each receipt as it is entered to ensure that you do not enter the same payment twice.

The receipts will be printed in alphabetical order on customer name, as shown below:

GREEN'S STORE			**GREEN'S STORE**		
RECEIPT			**RECEIPT**		
Brindley	A/C	3	Brindley	A/C	3
W/E 03/04/99		£15.70	W/E 03/04/99		£15.70
GREEN'S STORE			**GREEN'S STORE**		
RECEIPT			**RECEIPT**		
Carter	A/C	6	Carter	A/C	6
W/E 03/04/99		£16.00	W/E 03/04/99		£16.00
GREEN'S STORE			**GREEN'S STORE**		
RECEIPT			**RECEIPT**		
Murphy	A/C	8	Murphy	A/C	8
W/E 03/04/99		£5.10	W/E 03/04/99		£5.10
GREEN'S STORE			**GREEN'S STORE**		
RECEIPT			**RECEIPT**		

Record payments

Select this option to record payments from the receipt documents as described above. The Payments form will open and you can enter payments as shown below:

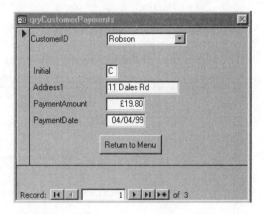

Post payments

Before you print the next week's invoices, you must post these payments so that the payment made is deducted from each customer's Total Due amount. Once again you will see several messages as the processing steps are completed, and the final message will appear as shown below.

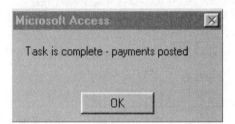

Click **OK** to complete the posting operation.

Quit application

This option on the main menu closes the application without closing Access. All the work you have done is saved automatically.

Backups

You should take a daily backup of the database on to a floppy disk, which should be stored in a secure location with a weekly backup stored off-site. Backups will be done using Windows Explorer.

Technical manual

This section is designed for a competent Access developer to maintain or enhance the system. It could also include installation instructions.

Macros

Processing invoices (mcrInvoices)

The screenshot of the macro **mcrInvoices** gives a general overview.

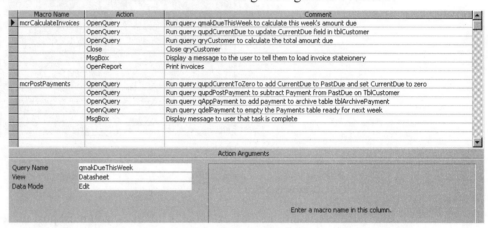

The details of the macro action arguments are shown below. (Printed using **Tools, Analyse, Documenter**.)

C:\AccessProjects\News\NewsProject.mdb
Macro: mcrInvoices

*I am not in favour of including output such as this generated by **Tools, Analyse, Documenter**. It is very difficult to follow and a waste of paper. The description of each macro in the Design section is much more helpful. However, VB code which you have written should be included, well annotated.*

Properties

Date Created:	30/03/99 17:33:21	Last Updated:	03/04/99

Actions

Name	Condition	Action	Argument	Value
mcrCalculateInvoices				
		OpenQuery	Query Name: qmakDueThisWeek	
			View:	Datasheet
			Data Mode:	Edit
Run query qmakDueThisWeek to calculate this week's amount due				
		OpenQuery	Query Name:	qupdCurrentDue
			View:	Datasheet
			Data Mode:	Edit
Run query qupdCurrentDue to update CurrentDue field in tblCustomer				
		OpenQuery	Query Name:	qryCustomer
			View:	Datasheet
			Data Mode:	Edit
Run query qryCustomer to calculate the total amount due				
		Close	Object Type:	Query
			Object Name:	qryCustomer
			Save:	Prompt
Close qryCustomer				
		MsgBox		

		Message: Please load special invoice stationery	
		Beep:	Yes
		Type:	None
		Title:	

Display a message to the user to tell them to load invoice stationery

	OpenReport	Report Name:	rptInvoices
		View:	Print Preview
		Filter Name:	
		Where Condition:	

Print invoices

mcrPostPayments

	OpenQuery	Query Name:	
		qupdCurrentToZero	
		View:	Datasheet
		Data Mode:	Edit

Run query qupdCurrentToZero to add CurrentDue to PastDue and set CurrentDue to zero

	OpenQuery	Query Name:	qupdPostPayment
		View:	Datasheet
		Data Mode:	Edit

Run query qupdPostPayment to subtract Payment from PastDue on TblCustomer

	OpenQuery	Query Name:	qappPayment

Macro: mcrInvoices

		View:	Datasheet
		Data Mode:	Edit

Run query qAppPayment to add payment to archive table tblArchivePayment

	OpenQuery	Query Name:	qdelPayment
		View:	Datasheet
		Data Mode:	Edit

Run query qdelPayment to empty the Payments table ready for next week

	MsgBox	Message: Task is complete - payments posted	
		Beep:	Yes
		Type:	None
		Title:	

Processing Round Sheets (mcrRoundSheets)

Queries

The most complex query is **qryMondayDelivs** (and similar ones for the other days of the week. These find all customers who are not currently on holiday and use a field from the dialogue box **fdlgTimeOfDay** to determine whether this is a morning or evening round.

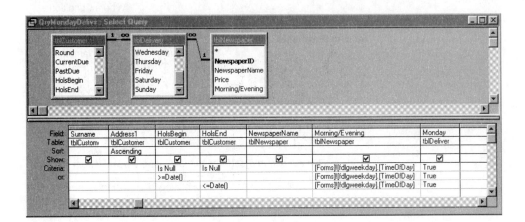

Reports and Forms are as shown in the design and user documentation.

(6,300 words)

(This Project report is not long, and is not complete in all aspects but even as it stands it is in the Grade A range for a Major Project within the NEAB Mark Scheme given in Appendix B. It is quality and not quantity which counts – try to be concise. Do not repeat yourself and do not waffle!)

Appendix B

AQA Project Guidelines
2001-2002

Assessment Criteria

Assessment of Project Work

It is necessary to provide a structure for the assessment of project work so that all teachers are, in general, following a common procedure. Such a procedure will assist with the standardisation of assessment from centre to centre. Each project is therefore to be assessed in accordance with the criteria set out below. In assessing candidates, centres must ensure that comparable standards are observed between different teaching groups. Each centre must produce a single order of merit for the centre as a whole.

Criteria for the assessment of Unit 3

The following categories are to be used in the assessment of the project.

Specification	13 marks
Implementation	20 marks
User Testing	12 marks
Evaluation	6 marks
User Documentation	9 marks
	60 marks

11-13   A detailed requirements specification has been produced for the identified problem, which matches the needs of the stated end-user(s).

The input, processing and output needs, which match the requirements specification, are clearly stated.

Effective designs have been completed which would enable an independent third party implementation of the solution.

An appropriate test strategy has been determined. An effective test and full testing plan has been devised. The testing plan includes the test data and expected outcomes and directly relates to the requirements specification.

8-10   A detailed requirements specification has been produced for the identified problem, which matches the needs of the stated end-user(s).

The input, processing and output needs, which match the requirements specification, are stated.

Designs have been completed but lack detail so as not to allow an independent third part implementation of the solution or, are inefficient in relation to the problem stated.

A test strategy has been determined and testing plan have been devised but are limited in scope or do not relate to the requirements specification stated.

4-7   A requirements specification has been produced for the identified problem but does not fully match the needs of the stated end-user(s) or lacks detail and clarity.

The input, processing and output needs are stated but do not fully match the requirements' specification or are not sufficiently clear.

Design work has been attempted but is incomplete and does not reflect an efficient solution to the problem stated.

A test strategy has been determined but is either incomplete or does not relate to the requirements specification stated. The testing plan is either vague or missing.

1-3   The requirements specification is vague or missing.

The input, processing and output needs are only vaguely considered or are absent.

There is little or no design effort.

The test strategy and testing plan are vague or missing.

0   The candidate has produced no work.

Implementation (20 marks)

16-20   An effective solution has been developed which is operable in the proposed environment by the intended end-user.

Appropriate data capture and validation procedures, data organisation methods, output contents and formats and user interface(s) have been used.

Generic and package specific skills have been fully employed in an effective and appropriate manner.

The selection of the chosen hardware and software facilities has been fully justified in relation to the solution developed.

11-15   A solution has been developed which is operable in the proposed environment by the intended end-user but has some inefficiences.

There is evidence of the use of some appropriate data capture and validation procedures, data organisation methods, output contents and formats and user interface(s).

Generic and package specific skills have been fully employed but not always in an effective and appropriate manner.

The selection of some of the chosen hardware and software facilities has been justified in relation to the solution developed.

6-10   A partial solution has been developed, but those aspects completed are useable by the intended end-user.

There is some evidence of the use of some data capture and validation procedures, data organisation methods, output contents and formats and user interface(s).

Generic and package specific skills have been employed but not always in an effective and appropriate manner.

The selection of some of the chosen hardware and software facilities has been only vaguely justified in relation to the solution developed.

1-5   A solution has been developed which is very limited and is not practically operable in the proposed environment by the intended end-user.

       Few, if any, data capture and validation procedures, data organisation methods, output contents and formats and user interface(s) have been used.

       The generic and package specific skills used are simplistic and/or were not always applied appropriately.

       The selection of the chosen hardware and software facilities are not justified in relation to the solution developed.

0   The candidate has not implemented the system.

Testing (12 marks)

9-12   The test strategy and test plan previously devised have now been followed in a systematic manner using typical, erroneous and extreme (boundary) data.

       The results of testing are fully documented with outputs cross-referenced to the original plan.

       Corrective action taken due to test results will be clearly documented.

5-8   The test strategy and plan devised have been followed in a systematic manner but using only normal data.

       The results of testing are partially documented with some evidence of outputs cross-referenced to the original plan.

       There is some evidence of corrective action taken due to test results.

1-4   The test strategy and plan devised have been followed in a limited manner using only normal data.

       There is little or no documentation of the results of testing.

       There is little or no indication of corrective action required due to test results.

0   There is no evidence of testing.

Evaluation (6 marks)

4-6   The effectiveness of the solution in meeting the detailed requirements specification has been fully assessed with the candidate showing full awareness of the criteria for a successful information technology solution.

       The limitations of the solution have been clearly identified.

1-3   The effectiveness of the solution in meeting the original requirements specifications has only been partly assessed with the candidate showing only partial awareness of the criteria for a successful information technology solution.

       The limitations of the solution are vague or missing.

0   There is no evidence of evaluation.

User Documentation (9 marks)

7-9   There is extensive user documentation for the solution which covers all relevant aspects including normal operation and common problems and is appropriate to the needs of the end-user.

4-6   A user guide is present which describes the functionality of the solution and is appropriate to the needs of the end-user.

1-3   A limited user guide is present which describes only the basic functionality of the solution.

0   There is no evidence of user documentation.

Criteria for the assessment of Unit 6

It is expected that the teacher will be involved in various stages in the development of the candidate's solution. However, in the award of marks, the teacher should attempt to assess solely the candidate's contribution. In applying the criteria account should be taken of the amount of assistance given. The criteria give scope for discriminating between candidates who have tackled more demanding problems as against those who have undertaken less demanding ones. The following categories are to be used in the assessment of the project. The criteria for marking these categories are listed below. The project is marked out of a total of 90.

Analysis	18 marks
Design	16 marks
Implementation	15 marks
Testing	15 marks
User Guide	8 marks
Evaluation	10 marks
Report	8 marks
Total	90 marks

Analysis (18 marks)

15 – 18   The candidate has identified an appropriate problem in conjunction with their end-user and independently of the teacher.

A clear, statement covering both the context and the nature of the problem was provided.

The candidate has clearly identified and delimited a substantial and realistic problem, and has recognised the requirements of the intended user(s) and the capabilities and limitations of the resources available.

All of the requirements are specified and clearly documented.

The candidate has fully identified the information flow and data dynamics of the problem.

The analysis indicates an appreciation of the full potential of the appropriate hardware and software facilities available and also, if appropriate, their limitations.

The candidate has identified the user's current IT skill level and training needs.

Qualitative and quantitative evaluation criteria have been identified in details. Analysis has been completed without undue assistance.

10 – 14   The candidate has identified an appropriate problem with reference to their end-user and independently of the teacher.

A clear outline statement covering both the context and the nature of the problem was provided.

The candidate has identified a substantial problem and has recognised many of the requirements of the intended users and many of the capabilities and limitations of the resources available.

The documentation is intelligible but is lacking in some respects.

The analysis indicates which software will be used but it may not be obvious how the software will be used.

The candidate has partly identified the information flow and data dynamics of the problem.

Reasonable evaluation criteria have been identified.

Some assistance has been required to reach this stage.

Alternatively, the candidate has identified a relatively straightforward problem and has proceeded unaided, covering most or all of the points required for 15-18 marks.

6 – 9   The candidate has required some guidance from the teacher to identify an appropriate problem with an end-user.

A simple outline statement was provided.

The candidate has selected a substantial problem and attempted to identify many of the requirements of the intended users and many of the capabilities and limitations of the resources available but has required assistance in analysing the problem.

The candidate has identified only a limited subset of the information flow and data dynamics of the problem.

The documentation is available but is incomplete.

Alternatively, the candidate has identified a fairly simple problem and has recognised most of the requirements of the intended users and most of the capabilities and limitations of the resources available.

The candidate has required assistance in analysing the problem.

The documentation is complete in most respects.

3 – 5   The candidate required considerable guidance from the teacher to identify an appropriate problem with an end-user.

A superficial outline statement was provided.

The candidate has identified a fairly simple problem and has recognised some of the requirements of the intended users and some of the capabilities and limitations of the resources available.

Few, if any, indications of what must be done to carry out the task are present.

There is little indication of how the software will be used.

The candidate has not identified the information flow and data dynamics of the problem.

Documentation is weak and incomplete.

The candidate has required much assistance in analysing the problem.

1 – 2   The candidate has identified a simple problem or been given a straightforward problem.

There is only minimal recognition of either the requirements of the intended users or capabilities and limitations of the resources available.

The documentation is poor and substantial assistance has been required.

0   No analysis is present.

Generation of possible solutions and solution design

The design phase includes the bringing together of the results of the analysis and the gathering and ordering of information related to the background of the problem into the generation of a range of possible solutions which meet them. This may be alternative types of package or alternative solutions within a package.

The solution design should be specified so that a competent person can implement it. There should be a clear specification of how each of the sub-tasks identified in the analysis is to be solved.

The detailed design (16 marks)

13 – 16　A relevant range of the appropriate approaches to a solution have been considered in detail. Compelling reasons for final choice of solution are given which have been fully justified and the likely effectiveness has been fully considered.

A completely detailed solution has been specified such that a competent third party could carry it out. The proposed solution is clearly broken down into sub-tasks with the necessary indications of how these are to be solved. All of the requirements are specified and clearly documented.

A well defined schedule and work plan have been included showing in detail how the task is to be carried out. This shows what is required in a comprehensible manner – it can include layout sheets, record structures, spreadsheet plans, design for data-capture sheets, etc. as appropriate.

An effective and full testing plan has been devised, with a comprehensive selection of test data and reasons for the choice of the data clearly specified.

This stage has been done without assistance.

9 - 12　A relevant range of appropriate approaches to a solution have been considered. Reasons for final choice of solution are given which have been justified and the likely effectiveness has been reasonably considered.

A solution has been specified such that a competent third party could carry it out but with some difficulty. The proposed solution is broken down into sub-tasks with some indication of how these are to be solved. Some of the requirements are specified and clearly documented.

A schedule and work plan have been included showing how the tasks are to be carried out. This shows what is required in a reasonable manner – it can include layout sheets, record structures, spreadsheet plans, design for data-capture sheets, etc. as appropriate.

A testing plan has been devised, with some test clearly specified.

This stage has been done without undue assistance.

6 – 8　A limited range of approaches which may have required some assistance. The reasons given for the final choice are weak and the likely effectiveness has not been discussed in detail.

Sufficient detail has been given so that the candidate, but not another person, can replicate the solution at a later date. An attempt has been made to break down the solution into sub-tasks with some indications of how these are to be solved. The documentation is clear but lacking in some respects.

A schedule and work plan are present but limited.

A testing plan is present.

This has been done without undue assistance.

3 – 5   Only one approach considered which may have required considerable assistance. Only vague reasons given for the final choice and the likely effectiveness has not been discussed.

Sufficient detail has been given so that the candidate, but not another person, can replicate the solution at a later date but with some difficulty. An attempt has been made to break down the solution into sub-tasks but with insufficient indications of how these are to be solved. The documentation is lacking in many respects.

A schedule and work plan should be present but are poorly thought out.

A testing plan is present but is poor.

Substantial assistance may have been required.

1 – 2   Little or no consideration has been given to approaches to the solution. No or invalid reasons given for final choice of solution.

A superficial outline of the solution has been chosen so that the candidate is unable to replicate the solution at a later date. Little attempt has been made to break down the problem into sub-tasks. The schedule and work plan are vague or missing. The testing plan is vague or missing. The documentation is poor and substantial assistance may have been required.

0   No detail of chosen solution given.

Implementation (15 marks)

11 – 15   The candidate has fully implemented the detailed design unaided, in an efficient manner with no obvious defects. All of the appropriate facilities of the software and hardware available were fully exploited. The documentation is clear and thorough.

6 – 10   The candidate has implemented the essential elements of the design, reasonably effectively and largely unaided. The implementation has exploited some of the relevant features of the software and hardware available. The documentation lacks detail or may be missing completely.

Alternatively, the candidate has fully implemented a simple design.

1 – 5   The design has only been partially implemented. The implementation has exploited few of the relevant features of the software and hardware available. The documentation lacks detail or may be missing completely.

0   There is no implementation.

Testing (15 marks)

11 – 15   The candidate has shown insight in demonstrating effective test data to cover most or all eventualities. There is a clear evidence of full end-user involvement in testing. The system works with a full range of test data (typical, extreme, erroneous); the test outputs are annotated fully.

6 – 10   The candidate has demonstrated a range of appropriate test data perhaps with some assistance. There is some evidence of end-user involvement during testing. The system works with a limited range of test data; the tests outputs are annotated to a limited extent.

1 – 5   There is little evidence of testing. There is only limited involvement of the end-user in testing. It does not meet the design specification.

0   There is no evidence of testing.

User Guide (8 marks)

6 – 8   A comprehensive, well illustrated user guide is produced that deals with all aspects of the system (Installation, backup procedures, general use and trouble shooting).

4 – 5   An illustrated user guide is produced that deals with general use of the system but only vaguely considers the other areas required for 6 – 8 marks.

1 – 3   A user guide is produced that deals with general use of the system.

0   No user guide is present.

Evaluation of the project (10 marks)

9 – 10   The candidate has considered clearly a full range of qualitative and quantitative criteria for evaluating the solution. The candidate has fully evaluated his/her solution intelligently against the requirements of the user(s). Evidence of end-user involvement during this stage is provided.

6 – 8   The candidate has discussed a range of relevant criteria for evaluating the solution. The candidate has evaluated his/her solution against the requirements of the user(s) in most respects. Some, but not all, performance indicators have been identified. Any modifications to meet possible major limitations and/or enhancements have been specified maybe with assistance.

3 – 5   The system has only been partially evaluated against the original specification and the requirements of the user(s). This may be because the original specification was poor. Few, if any, performance indicators have been identified. Discussion concerning the limitations or enhancements to the system are largely absent or have required some prompting.

1 – 2   Little attempt at evaluation has been made. No performance indicators have been identified. Discussion concerning the limitations or enhancements to the system are absent or limited and have required considerable prompting.

0   No attempt at evaluation has been made.

Preparation of the report (8 marks)

7 – 8   A well-written, fully illustrated and organised report is produced. It describes the project accurately and concisely.

5 – 6   A well-written report is produced but it lacks good organisation. Alternatively a well-organised report is produced but it is of limited quality.

3 – 4   The report is of generally poor quality but shows some evidence of organisation. There are a number of deficiencies and omissions.

1 – 2   The report is poorly organised and presented with few or no diagrams. There are a considerable number of omissions.

0   No report is present.

Evidence to support the award of marks

Coursework must be presented in a clear and helpful way for the moderator. It must be annotated to identify, as precisely as possible, where in the work the relevant assessment criteria have been satisfied so that the reasons why marks have been awarded are clear. An indication must also be given at the appropriate point in the work, or in accompanying information, of any further guidance given by the teacher (or other person) which has significant assessment implications.

Teachers should keep records of their assessments during the course, in a form which facilitates the complete and accurate submission of the final assessments at the end of the course.

When the assessments are complete, the final marks awarded under each of the assessment criteria must be entered on the Candidate Record Form, with supporting information given in the spaces provided. A specimen Candidate Record Form appears as Appendix B; the exact design may be modified before the operational version is issued.

The Candidate Record Form must be attached to the candidate's work.

Index

1NF 3
2NF 4
3NF 5
Aligning objects 100
Analysis 149, 168
AND queries 43
Appending imported records.................. 129
Ask the user a question 92
Assignment statement 137
Attribute.. 2, 3
Autoexec macro 119
AutoForm... 27
   columnar 27
   tabular 30
AutoNumber 12, 13
   data type 7
AutoReport
   columnar 65
   tabular 67
Blanks, as criteria................................... 41
Booking systems 145
Boolean data type..................................... 7
Border style property............................... 73
Calculated fields..................................... 47
Caption, changing................................... 48
Cascade delete related records 22, 37
Cascade update related fields 22
Chart Wizard.. 79
Check box... 34
ChtMondayDeliveries 80
Combo box................................... 105, 111
Command button...................................... 86
Comment in VBA 138
Composite key 4, 16
Compound key 16
Continue a long VBA statement 139
Control
   on a form 104
Copying a table 54
Count function....................................... 52
Criteria
   setting in a query 40
Currency data type 7
Data entry form 27
Data flow diagrams 151
Data types 7
Database
   creating a new 10
   design 3, 156
   window 11
Datasheet view 16, 27
Date functions 42, 69
Date/Time data type 7
Debugging code 141

Degrees of relationship 2
Delete a record 37
Design 156, 168
   macros 160
   modules 160
Development 161
DFD .... *See* Data flow diagram
Dialogue box 43, 92
   using to capture criteria................... 96
Dim statement.................................... 137
DoCmd 138
Documentation
   technical 169
   user 169
Entit*y* 2
Entity-relationship diagram............... 2, 157
Evaluation 161, 169
Event properties 82
Excel
   analysing data in 129
   importing data from 125
Exporting data 130
FdlgReport.. 94
Field
   calculated in query 47
   deleting... 15
   hiding in a query 40
   inserting 15
   inserting in a report 97
   moving 15
   properties...................................... 12
Field name rules 13
Fields.. 13
   arranging and sizing 30
   rearranging on a form 101
Find a record 36
First Normal Form 3
Flat file 2
FmnuCustomer....................................... 91
Focus.. 139
Form
   adjusting size................................ 35
   arranging and sizing fields 30
   changing background 31
   control 104
   creating from query 44, 49, 110
   footer 86
   properties...................................... 91
   unbound 92
   with subform 32
Form view 27
Freeze columns 26
FrmCustomerDues 50
FrmPayments 112

FrmProducts 134
FrmTransactions 134
Functions, in criteria 42
Gantt chart... 159
Grouping 75
Header and footer, in a document 165
Hide columns 26
If..Then in a macro 91
If..Then..Else 140
Implementation 168
Importing records into Access 126
Inappropriate projects 147
Index fields 13
Input-Process-Output 144
Installation 161
Interviews.. 150
Join types 45
League tables 147
Link table 5
List box 105
Looking for blanks 41
Lookup fields
    sorting 23
Macro 81
    Autoexec 119
    complete list of actions 98
    conditions in 91
    design 160
    running 84
Macro group 82
Mail-merge 122
Many-to-many... 2
Mark scheme 162
Maximise 81
McrAddCustomer 82
McrCancel 95
McrEditCustomer 83
McrInvoices... 85
McrMaximise 81
McrOK 94
McrOverdue 92
McrReports 95
McrViewReport 94
Memo data type... 7
Menu
    creating 88
    designing 113, 158
Merge with MS Word 122
MmnuCustomer.. 83
Module 131
    design 160
Moving
    columns 26
    objects 100
Naming conventions 8
Normalisation... 3

Null 41
Number data type 7
Object.. 8
    aligning and spacing................................ 100
    drop-down list 31
    moving 100
    referring to in expressions......................... 139
    selecting 69, 99
Object Browser 138
Office Assistant.. 17
Office Links 122
One-to-many 2
One-to-one 2
Option group 102
OR queries... 43
Order entry systems 146
Outline for project..................................... 162
Page break, inserting in a report...................... 77
Page selector 70
Password
    setting 120
    unsetting 121
Performance criteria.................................... 155
Picture on a form....................................... 107
Plan for implementation 159
Posting customer payments............................... 61
Primary key 2
    altering 16
    composite 4
    defining 13, 16
Problem definition 148
Process customer payments 56
Project, outline 162
Projects
    inappropriate 147
Prompt user 43
Properties
    Event 82
    field 12
    form.. 82
Prototyping... 161
Pseudocode 160
QappPayment... 64
QdelPayment... 64
QmakDueThisWeek....................................... 59
QryCustomer..................................... 47, 49
QryCustomerPayments 110
QryDelivery... 46
QryDueThisWeek.. 58
QryMondayDelivs....................................... 75
QryMondaySummary 53
QryRound.. 44
QryRound1... 41
Query
    Append.. 63
    criteria 96

Delete 64
Make-Table 58
running 40
Select 38
Summary 57
Totals 51
types of 38
Update 54
Wizard 46
QupdCurrentDue 60
QupdCurrentToZero 62
QupdHolsOver 55
QupdPostPayment 63
Rearranging fields 101
Referential integrity 22
Relational database 2, 145
Relationship 2
defining 21
deleting 23
Many-to-many 2
One-to-many 22
Reordering topics 164
Report
basing on a query 74
customising 75
edit format 67
grouping 76
sorting 76
Wizard 71
Resizing a form area 100
RptCustomer 73
RptInvoices 78
RptMondayDelivs 77
RptNewspaper 68
Same value, as previous record 17
Sample project 149
Saving a query 44
Second Normal Form 4
Section width 70
Security 120, 160
Select Case 140
Select Object box 69
Selecting objects 99
Selection statements in VBA 140
Snackbar.mdb 131
Sort order, on a report 76
Sorting records 32
in a query 40
Special Effects tool 108
Startup options 120
Stock control systems 146
Sub and **End Sub** 137
Subform 32

Sum function 57
Summary options 72
Switchboard
creating 114
editing 118
viewing 116
Syntax 84
Systems Life Cycle 148
Tab order, changing 103, 104
Table 2
copying 54
design 7
design window 12
editing structure 15
link 157
Table of Contents 167
Tabs 11
TblArchivePayment 61
TblDelivery 19, 22, 25
TblNewspaper 7, 18
TblPayment 60
TblProducts 132
TblTransactions 132
Technical documentation 169
Terms of Reference 148
Test strategy 160
Testing 168
Text data type 7
Third Normal Form 5
Toolbars, displaying 28
Toolbox 29
Toolbox, displaying 77
Updating using a query 59
User documentation 169
User interface 156
User to enter criteria 43
Validation
rule 14
text 14
Visual Basic for Applications (VBA) 131
Visual Basic procedure, planning 136
Wildcard 42, 88
Wizard
Answer 17
AutoForm 28
Chart 79
Command button 86
Form 32
Lookup 13
Option group 102
Query 46
Report 71
Zoom key 57